SHORTLIST

Manchester

WHAT'S NEW | WHAT'S ON | WHAT'S BEST

www.timeout.com/manchester

Contents

Don't Miss

Itineraries

Manchester by Area

Essentials

Published by Time Out Guides Ltd
Universal House
251 Tottenham Court Road
London W1T 7AB
Tel: + 44 (0)20 7813 3000
Fax: + 44 (0)20 7813 6001
Email: guides@timeout.com
www.timeout.com

Managing Director Peter Fiennes
Editorial Director Ruth Jarvis
Business Manager Daniel Allen
Editorial Manager Holly Pick
Assistant Management Accountant Ija Krasnikova

Time Out Guides is a wholly owned subsidiary of Time Out Group Ltd.

© Time Out Group Ltd
Chairman & Founder Tony Elliott
Chief Executive Officer David King
Group Financial Director Paul Rakkar
Group General Manager/Director Nichola Coulthard
Time Out Communications Ltd MD David Pepper
Time Out International Ltd MD Cathy Runciman
Time Out Magazine Ltd Publisher/Managing Director Mark Elliott
Group Commercial Director Graeme Tottle
Group IT Director Simon Chappell

Time Out and the Time Out logo are trademarks of Time Out Group Ltd.

This edition first published in Great Britain in 2011 by Ebury Publishing
A Random House Group Company
Company information can be found on www.randomhouse.co.uk
Random House UK Limited Reg. No. 954009
10 9 8 7 6 5 4 3 2

Distributed in the US and Latin America by Publishers Group West (1-510-809-3700)
Distributed in Canada by Publishers Group Canada (1-800-747-8147)

For further distribution details, see www.timeout.com

ISBN: 978-1-84670-225-9

A CIP catalogue record for this book is available from the British Library.

Printed and bound in Germany by Appl.

The Random House Group Limited supports The Forest Stewardship Council (FSC®), the
leading international forest certification organisation. Our books carrying the FSC label are
printed on FSC® certified paper. FSC is the only forest certification scheme endorsed by the
leading environmental organisations, including Greenpeace. Our paper procurement policy can
be found at www.randomhouse.co.uk/environment

Time Out carbon-offsets all its flights with Trees for Cities (www.treesforcities.org).

Manchester Shortlist

The **Time Out Manchester Shortlist** is one of a new series of guides that draws on Time Out's background as a magazine publisher to keep you current with what's going on in town. As well as Manchester's key sights and the best of its eating, drinking and leisure options, the guide picks out the most exciting venues to have recently opened and gives a full calendar of annual events. It also includes features on the important news, trends and openings, all compiled by locally based editors and writers. Whether you're visiting for the first time, or you're a regular, you'll find that the *Time Out Manchester Shortlist* contains all you need to know, in a portable and easy-to-use format.

The guide divides central Manchester into six areas, each of which contains listings for Sights & Museums, Eating & Drinking, Shopping, Nightlife and Arts & Leisure, with maps pinpointing all their locations. At the front of the book are chapters rounding up these scenes city-wide, and giving a shortlist of our overall picks in a variety of categories. We also include chapters on attractions beyond the centre and itineraries for days out, plus essentials such as transport information and hotels.

Our listings give phone numbers as dialled in Manchester. To dial them from elsewhere in the UK, preface them with **0161**. To call from outside the UK, use your country's exit code, followed by 44 (the international code for the UK), 161 (without the initial zero) and the number given.

We have noted price categories by using one to four pound signs (**£-££££**), representing budget, moderate, expensive and luxury. Major credit cards are accepted unless otherwise stated. We also indicated when a venue is **NEW** .

All our listings are double-checked, but places do sometimes close or change their hours or prices, so it's a good idea to call a venue before visiting. While every effort has been made to ensure accuracy, the publishers cannot accept responsibility for any errors that this guide may contain.

Venues are marked on the maps using symbols numbered according to their order within the chapter and colour-coded according to the type of venue they represent:

❶ Sights & Museums
❶ Eating & Drinking
❶ Shopping
❶ Nightlife
❶ Arts & Leisure

Map key

Major sight or landmark	▨
Railway station	▨
Park	▢
Hospital/university	▢
Pedestrian Area	▢
Dual carriageway	▤
Main road	═
Airport	✈
Church	✚
Tram station	Ⓜ
Tram line	▬
Area	SALFORD

Time Out **Manchester** Shortlist

EDITORIAL
Consultant Editor Susie Stubbs
Deputy Editor John Shandy Watson
Section Editors Sights & Museums Susie
Stubbs; Eating & Drinking Matthew Hull
& Dan Feeney; Shopping Matthew Hull;
Nightlife Sian Cummins; Arts & Leisure
Susie Stubbs; Hotels Matthew Hull
Listings Editor William Crow
Travel Intern Amaya Dent (Fancy dress;
Dark days, bright nights)
Proofreader Marion Moisy

DESIGN
Art Director Scott Moore
Art Editor Pinelope Kourmouzoglou
Senior Designer Kei Ishimaru
Group Commercial Designer Jodi Sher

Picture Editor Jael Marschner
Acting Deputy Picture Editor Liz Leahy
Picture Desk Assistant/Researcher
Ben Rowe

ADVERTISING
New Business & Commercial Director
Mark Phillips
**Magazine & UK Guides Commercial
Director** St.John Betteridge
Advertising Sales (Manchester) Richard
Delooze at Media Sales Network
Production Controller Chris Pastfield
Copy Controller Alison Bourke

MARKETING
**Sales & Marketing Director, North America
& Latin America** Lisa Levinson
Senior Publishing Brand Manager
Luthfa Begum
Group Commercial Art Director
Anthony Huggins
Marketing Co-ordinator Alana Benton

PRODUCTION
Group Production Manager
Brendan McKeown
Production Controller Katie Mulhern

PHOTOGRAPHY
Photography by Ben Rowe, except pages 7, 15, 22, 29,32, 34, 70, 73, 84, 89, 96, 104,
115, 117, 127, 147 Nathan Cox; pages 8/9, 44, 90, 131, 143, 144, 150, 160 Simon
Buckley; page 36 (top) Edward Brownrigg; page 36 (bottom left) Tristram Kenton; page
36 (bottom right) Joel Chester Fildes; page 38 Piotr Anderszewski; pages 50, 65, 128,
130, 169 Shutterstock; page 149 (top) Ian Tilton; page 149 (bottom) Joel Pammenter;
pages 68, 152, 167 Alamy; pages 171, 179 The Rocco Forte Collection.

The following images were provided by the featured establishments/artists: pages 21,
39, 40, 56, 123, 163, 164, 172, 177, 181,182.

Cover photograph: Craig Easton.

MAPS
Maps by: JS Graphics (john@jsgraphics.co.uk). Maps are based on material supplied by
Lovell Johns Ltd, except maps on pages 118-119 and 141, which are supplied by Netmaps.

Thanks to Marketing Manchester.

About **Time Out**

Founded in 1968, Time Out has expanded from humble London beginnings into the
leading resource for those wanting to know what's happening in the world's greatest
cities. As well as our influential what's-on weeklies in London, New York and Chicago,
we publish nearly 30 other listings magazines in cities as varied as Beijing
and Mumbai. The magazines established Time Out's trademark style: sharp writing,
informed reviewing and bang up-to-date inside knowledge of every scene.
  Time Out made the natural leap into travel guides in the 1980s with the City Guide
series, which now extends to over 50 destinations around the world. Written and
researched by expert local writers and generously illustrated with original photography,
the full-size guides cover a larger area than our Shortlist guides and include many more
venue reviews, along with additional background features and a full set of maps.
  Throughout this rapid growth, the company has remained proudly independent, still
owned by Tony Elliott four decades after he started Time Out London as a single fold-out
sheet of A5 paper. This independence extends to the editorial content of all
our publications, this Shortlist included. No establishment has been featured because
it has advertised, and no payment has influenced any of our reviews. And, for our critics,
there's definitely no such thing as a free lunch: all restaurants and bars are visited
and reviewed anonymously, and Time Out always picks up the bill.
For more about the company, see www.timeout.com.

Don't Miss

Sights & Museums

The blending of history and modern development in Manchester is a constant and very visible process. Driven by the 1996 IRA bomb and the staging of 2002's Commonwealth Games, the last couple of decades have seen as furious a programme of rebuilding as the city has experienced since the cotton mills and their attendant slums sprang up in 19th-century 'Cottonopolis'. Although a UK-wide recession has put a damper on development, economic woes are unlikely to stall things for long: this is a city that takes the rough with the smooth – and usually comes out fighting.

Perhaps one of the reasons for this is that the anchor of history holds steady here. Manchester is no stranger to upheaval, having witnessed and absorbed abrupt incursions of interlopers from Roman legions to Bonnie Prince Charlie's Jacobite rebels. In fact, quite often, the city has been the one leading the rebellion, this being the place that saw the birth of everything from the Suffragette movement and Robert Owen's socialism to Marx and Engels' *Communist Manifesto*.

To put it another way, Manchester is a city that walks with a swagger. Even during the dark days of post-industrial gloom it possessed a remarkable self-belief – an attitude that undoubtedly saw it emerge, at the turn of the millennium, as one of the UK's strongest cities. Some of the credit, if that's the appropriate word, must go to the 1996 explosion. Although regeneration had been ticking

8 Time Out Shortlist | Manchester

Heaton Park p145

SHORTLIST

Best architecture
- Imperial War Museum North (p141)
- John Rylands Library (p61)

Best restoration projects
- Manchester Monastery (p153)
- People's History Museum (p67)

Best for people-watching
- Cornerhouse (p125)
- Exchange Square (p61)

Best-kept secrets
- Elizabeth Gaskell House (p151)
- Greater Manchester Police Museum (p91)
- St Mary's (p67)
- Victoria Baths (p153)

Most impressive history
- Chetham's Library (p57)
- Manchester Cathedral (p64)
- Town Hall (p67)

Most beautiful stained glass
- Manchester Cathedral (p64)
- Manchester Jewish Museum (p145)

Best for kids
- Manchester Museum (p120)
- MOSI, Museum of Science & Industry (p129)

Most emblematic
- Salford Lad's Club (p136)
- Strangeways (p146)

Most impressive views
- Imperial War Museum North tower (p141)

Most impressive art
- Manchester Art Gallery (p64)
- Whitworth Art Gallery (p120)

along for some years, the largest bomb to be detonated in mainland Britain did ultimately provide the impetus for a renaissance that has left areas of the centre unrecognisable to anyone who last saw them a decade earlier. This allows the city to present itself as a living, vibrant and developing location, but has itself come at a cost, as much of the character of the old city is being threatened by pricey new development.

Still, the enviable sweep of history remains. Manchester's museums have benefited from the financial quantum leap in the wake of the bomb, with old favourites such as the Manchester Art Gallery (p64), MOSI (p129) and the People's History Museum (p67) all on the receiving end of multi-million pound refits. And entirely new attractions, such as the Lowry (p142), Imperial War Museum North (p141) and Sportcity (p143), have arrived in very modern architectural forms, wrenching the city into the 21st century.

MANCHESTER
INTERNATIONAL
FESTIVAL

18 extraordinary days of world premieres.

www.mif.co.uk

John Rylands Library p61

New public spaces

The arrival of self-explanatory
New Cathedral Street nicely connects
old and new Manchester, and opens
up the old sightline between the
cathedral and St Ann's church (now
bordered by glossy shops). In the
background, Beetham Tower (p128)
looms. The new public spaces of
Cathedral Gardens (p57), Exchange
Square (p61) and Spinningfields (see
box p76) have added much-needed
fresh air, but decent green space still
comes at a premium. A drive to turn
the centre into a residential area
has led to inevitable clashes, and
although the Northern Quarter was
voted the UK's best neighbourhood
(in the 2010 Urbanism Awards),
the city centre's 'community'
remains a fairly notional concept:
the lack of green space, healthcare
and schools conspires to make
loft-style living the preserve of
the young and unencumbered.

Unsung treasures

A conurbation of this size can
support only so much fresh activity,
and the dramatic burst of new
attractions that coincided with the
millennium has inevitably calmed
down. With the only attraction in
the pipeline a cinema and theatre
complex (to house Cornerhouse
and the Library Theatre Company
come 2014), locals are now making
the most of what they've got.

And what the city has got,
in terms of historic attractions,
is pretty impressive. The
refurbished John Rylands Library
(p61), a staggering neo-Gothic
monument on Deansgate, is equalled
by the high drama of Pugin's
Manchester Monastery (p153).
The city's libraries raise their own
flag for architectural endeavour,
from the medieval Chetham's (p57)
to the quiet refuge of the Portico.
Niche museums have flourished:
the Gallery of Costume (p151)
reopened in 2010 after a £1.3 million
overhaul; while museums dedicated
to transport, police and the Jewish
community may be small but are
nevertheless fascinating.

It does seem slightly incongruous,
then, that a city blessed with so
many historic treasures has only
just got round to shouting about
them. Perhaps, with their eyes

The Lowry

Pier 8
Salford Quays
M50 3AZ
www.thelowry.com

Gallery Opening Times:
Sun-Fri 11am-5pm;
Sat 10am-5pm
Entry is free, but please
make a donation.

THE LOWRY
ART & ENTERTAINMENT

The Lowry boasts an award-winning programme where you can find the best in drama, dance, opera, ballet, comedy, music and family shows. There's participatory activity for all ages, and the Galleries showcase the work of LS Lowry alongside that of artists of local, national and international renown. This unique building also contains a restaurant, coffee shop and theatre bars, all set against stunning backdrops.

so firmly fixed on regeneration, it simply didn't occur to city leaders to talk up Manchester's past. Or perhaps the city's history is so firmly embedded in the collective psyche that Mancunians rarely felt the need to trumpet what it is that makes their home so unique. It's certainly a city that, to the outsider, can be perplexing: architecturally disparate, unlovely in parts, Manchester's charms are often buried beneath a layer of shoulder-shrugging effrontery.

Neighbourhoods

Much of the centre is heavily commercial; the Northern Quarter is strenuously fashionable, while Chinatown is great for eating out.

The medieval quarter, from St Ann's Square to the cathedral, is home to the city's most pleasing architecture. Castlefield is where epochs collide most impressively, from the Roman settlement where Manchester began, to the canals that are the enduring fingerprints of the Industrial Revolution.

Salford Quays has been transformed. Just a decade ago it was a museum-less concept waiting to spark. It is now home to Imperial War Museum North and the Lowry, enlivened by the new development of Media City UK. North Manchester is mainly residential, but offers much impressive parkland – including Heaton Park (p145), the jewel in the city's green crown, containing Grade I-listed Heaton Hall, and other, less-heralded gems such as Boggart Hole Clough – while beyond affluent South Manchester the path heads towards Cheshire and fertile National Trust territory.

Manchester often requires a little effort on the part of the visitor to make the most of its sometimes hidden charms; consequently,

it offers an element of discovery in the simplest journey. The compact centre makes walking an attractive option. A much-underrated activity in Manchester, as in many UK cities, is strolling and observing the upper levels of buildings; once your gaze rises above the dreary chain-store fronts, unexpected architectural delights are often revealed. Try the old warehouses around Balloon Street, or the grandeur of King Street. Guided walks from the Visitor Centre (p108) can add context and historical facts.

Otherwise, the established attractions are uniformly good. Even those that divide opinion, such as the National Football Museum, are fascinating buildings, and a large part of the city's sightseeing can be done for free. The good folk of Manchester are unlikely to hand anything to you on a plate, but, should you be prepared to make the first move, it is a city whose rich history and more recent renaissance makes it one of Britain's most rewarding, if not quite conventional, urban centres.

MOSI, Museum of Science & Industry p129

Koffee Pot p93

Eating & Drinking

For a long time, Manchester didn't really do food. It always knew it could do music, football and politics – and if you gave it half a chance it would tell you – but food was different. Critics from the capital decried that restaurants were years, if not light years, behind those in the South; Manchester was nothing more than a mass of takeaways and chain eateries. Then, following the IRA bomb in 1996 and the city's subsequent facelift, Manchester began to get the sorts of restaurants it had hitherto only dreamed about, and it wasn't long before it started mouthing off about it. Manchester, as journalist and professional northerner Stuart Maconie once said, is a city that fancies itself rotten – so why not let it wine you, dine you and show off why it's such a good catch over a meal?

Eating

As befitting a city that's home to a mishmash of cultures, Manchester straddles a culinary crossroads pitched somewhere between North and West England and South and East Asia. In part spurred by a shift in consciousness around sustainable eating, there has been a spike in the popularity of Modern British cuisine, with restaurants such as Gabriel's Kitchen (p154), Albert's Shed (p133) and the aptly named The Modern (p72) using regionally sourced ingredients in reinterpretations of classic dishes. Corned beef hash, Bury black pudding and fish stew are the order of the day.

The re-emergence of British cooking is complemented by one of the most varied selections of international restaurants in

the country, from Japanese places such as the thrilling Sapporo Teppanyaki (p134), where dinner becomes a gastronomic showcase, to Indian restaurants such as the multi-award-winning EastZEast (p108). Ironically, the best examples of South and East Asian food aren't to be found among the gaudy neons of Chinatown or the Curry Mile but are instead located in Salford, Castlefield or Piccadilly.

With so many styles of cooking within such close proximity, cross-pollination was inevitable, and it's not unusual for Mancunian menus to feature a fusion of local and international flavours. At the Michael Caines Restaurant at Abode (p108), partridge is served with cumin purée and lentils, while at Chaophraya (p69) you can order *panang nua yang*, a delicious if slightly genre-bending dish that combines beefsteak, Yorkshire pudding, red chilli and kaffir lime leaves.

There seems to be an assumption that Mancunian foodies must have a twice-cooked, goose-fat chip on their shoulder because the city doesn't possess a Michelin-starred restaurant, but this is actually far from true. Perhaps it's a case of having been there and done that, with the French (p71) at the historic Midland Hotel once the recipient of Britain's first Michelin star, but diners seem quite unruffled by the city's lack of such an accolade now. Excellent fine dining establishments such as Obsidian (p72) and Choice Bar & Restaurant (p133) continue to provide top-quality dishes meant for eating and enjoying rather than Michelin-style box-ticking. And a short bus or tram ride will take you to the talked-about restaurants that pepper Manchester's suburbs – Isinglass (p154) in Urmston, Aumbry (p146) in Prestwich and Damson (p166) in Stockport – all of which produce world-class food

SHORTLIST

Best new
- Aumbry (p146)
- Mark Addy (p137)
- An Outlet (p111)
- San Carlo Cicchetti (p75)
- Zouk Tea Bar & Grill (p122)

Dine in style
- Choice (p133)
- Damson (p166)
- French (p71)
- Michael Caines Restaurant at Abode (p108)

Tea time
- Koffee Pot (p93)
- North Tea Power (p94)
- Teacup (p95)
- Slattery (p146)

To the pub!
- Briton's Protection (p69)
- Horse & Jockey (p154)
- Marble Beer House (p157)
- Peveril of the Peak (p121)

Best bar none
- Cloud 23 (p133)
- Odd (p94)
- Pure Space (p121)
- Taurus (p111)

On the go
- Abdul's (p120)
- Barburrito (p108)
- Katsouris Deli (p72)
- Shlurp (p75)

Hangover hunger
- Abergeldie Café (p91)
- Kro2 (p121)
- This & That (p95)
- Trof (p158)

For a rainy day
- Gabriel's Kitchen (p154)
- Isinglass (p154)
- Lass O'Gowrie (p121)
- Soup Kitchen (p94)

DON'T MISS

at a fraction of the price you might expect to pay in London or Paris.

Then there are those dining heroes who are a little too rock 'n' roll to get a look-in with the Michelin judging panel. At Lounge Ten (p72) you can enjoy a sumptuous feast and racy entertainment in decadent silk-draped surroundings worthy of a bacchanalian orgy, while at the Mark Addy (p137), head chef Robert Owen-Brown has created a buzz by throwing together unfashionable and uncommon ingredients with the kind of electrifying swagger that you'd associate with the city's most famous musical progeny. Or, to put it in the words of the late Tony Wilson, 'This is Manchester: we do things differently here.'

Although the city centre is crammed with the usual array of charmless chain coffee houses, a short wander away from Market Street reveals a revolutionary tea party, with chai and cake, and even a pint of real ale and packet of pork scratchings, usurping the ubiquitous latte and biscotti as the accompaniments to a catch-up with friends. From super-twee Teacup (p95) to connoisseur's choice North Tea Power (p94) and hipster hangout the Koffee Pot (p93), the Northern Quarter is hooked on the leafy stuff. Further afield, Slattery (p146) in Whitefield is worthy of a pilgrimage for those in search of a great cuppa and a slice of something sweet.

Like all British cities, Manchester has its fair share of grim fast-food outlets, although 'fast' doesn't have to mean 'bad' – if you know where to look. Abdul's (p120), which has branches along the length of the Oxford Road corridor, prepares tender, delicately spiced kebabs; Shlurp (p75) makes its own delicious soups; while local success-story Barburrito (p108) will wrap you up a Mexican tortilla filled with freshly prepared meat, rice and salsa.

Horse & Jockey p154

Drinking

'I was looking for some action,' once sang Oasis front-monkey Liam Gallagher, 'but all I found was cigarettes and alcohol.' Thanks to the 2007 smoking ban, cigarettes may have gone out of the window, or at least on to a canopied patio, but alcohol is certainly still the preferred lubricant for 'action' in Manchester.

The Northern Quarter is the heart of the city-centre bar scene, and you'll find bikes chained up outside its numerous quirky watering holes. Odd (p94), Night & Day Café (p102) and Dry Bar (p93), the latter formerly owned by members of New Order, are places long favoured among local creative types for their fine selections of rare and obscure beers, and their playlists filled with rare and obscure sounds. The Northern Quarter is not just for the cool kids, though, and if your tastes are more mojito than microbrew then you could do worse than the low lights, dark wood and leather booths of Simple (p94) or Black Dog Ballroom (p100), both on Tib Street.

If you're having cocktails in Manchester, though, you owe it to yourself to visit the 'sky bar' at the Hilton, Cloud 23 (p133). Choose from a menu that includes drinks inspired by the music of local legends. Some (Hand in Glove: gin with sugar, lime and pink grapefruit) are a bit more successful than others (Sally Cinnamon: brandy, cinnamon and apple), but it's secondary to what you'll be looking at – an incredible, unequalled view of the city.

In addition to its raft of bars and cocktail dispensaries, Manchester and its environs are home to plenty of smoke-worn traditional pubs. The Briton's Protection (p69), on the edge of Deansgate, has the widest selection of whiskies for miles around, and an authentic snug to nurse your glass in. The Peveril of the Peak (p121), largely unchanged since World War II, is a tiled wedge on the corner of Great Bridgewater Street with a warm atmosphere and an antique table-football game. In Salford, the mammoth Crescent (p136) might not be too pretty but it is home to no less than four beer festivals a year, while in trendy Chorlton the Marble Beer House (p157) and Horse & Jockey (p154) are both CAMRA-listed pubs providing an excellent array of local draft ales in comfortable surroundings.

Michael Caines Restaurant at Abode p108

Afflecks p97

WHAT'S BEST
Shopping

It would be unreasonable to expect any city to emerge from the lingering UK-wide recession unscathed, but so far Manchester has escaped with minor cuts and bruises, brushing itself off in readiness for a new chapter in its retail history.

The high end

King Street (see box p76), once dubbed the 'Bond Street of the North', was one of the credit crunch's first casualties in Manchester. The Posh 'n' Becks effect of the early millennium – which allowed consumers, for a dazzling moment, to aspire to the lifestyle of footballers and their WAGs – saw King Street flourish, its flagstones pounded by designer soles as shoppers flocked to its high-end stores. Unsurprisingly, when the recession hit, footfall on the renowned street slowed and many shops were forced to close. While King Street wasn't exactly knee-deep in tumbleweed, the number of empty shop windows starkly reinforced the fact that the times were now, definitely, a-changing. Thankfully, King Street is making a comeback, with a new and eclectic mix of tenants moving in, such as local music hero Liam Gallagher's own-brand Pretty Green (p82).

As the economic outlook has begun to improve, however, the big-name designer brands have moved back in – only this time not to King Street.

Instead, the centre of the high-end retail action has shifted to Spinningfields (see box p76).

This business district, a new-build haven on the banks of the River Irwell that is home to all manner of corporate and banking HQs, is centred around a lively new public space, Hardman Square. It's flanked at one end by the striking presence of the Civil Justice Centre, the largest (and surely most architecturally exciting) civil court to be built in Britain in over 100 years. At its opposite boundary, running down from Deansgate, shopping street The Avenue serves the suited and booted of Spinningfields, hosting flagship stores from the likes of Mulberry (p81), DKNY, Flannels (p78) and Armani.

Of course, Spinningfields isn't the only place where you can splash your cash: Selfridges (p82), Harvey Nichols (p81) and House of Fraser (p81) all offer an ingenious mix of clothing, household goods, technology and food designed to relieve you of your readies.

Independent streak

As well as the well-heeled and wealthy, Manchester is home to one of the biggest student communities in Europe. They may not be rich, but their collective force creates a market for all things hip and quirky, and it's to the Northern Quarter that they flock for all the one-of-a-kind finds they desire.

This former run-down garment district is studded with independent boutiques and retro stores such as Pop (p99), Retro Rehab (p100) and Oklahoma (p99). Indie institution Afflecks (p97) continues to sell a huge choice of 'pre-loved' clothing, kitsch gifts and posters destined to cover the walls of student halls.

As is so often the case with trendy areas, more exclusive names are beginning to move in, but the Northern Quarter is still the domain of affordable niche retailers.

S H O R T L I S T

Best new
- A Few Fine Things (p97)
- Flannels (p78)
- Urban Outfitters (p83)

Best department stores
- Harvey Nichols (p81)
- Selfridges (p82)

Best for culture vultures
- Craft & Design Centre (p97)
- Magma (p98)
- Piccadilly Records (p99)

Best for street style
- General Store (p78)
- McQueen (p161)

Heaven for foodies
- Selfridges food hall (p82)
- Unicorn Grocery (p161)

Most innovative
- Rockers (p100)
- Seen (p82)

Best for kids
- Habitat (p78)
- Pixie (p161)

Great fun
- Fred Aldous (p97)
- Oklahoma (p99)
- Pop (p99)

Most coveted by WAGs
- Agent Provocateur (p77)
- Vivienne Westwood (p83)

Best for gifts
- Afflecks (p97)
- C Aston (p77)
- Hotel Chocolat (p81)
- Wowie Zowie! (p161)

Best bargains
- Office Sale Shop (p82)
- Retro Rehab (p100)
- TK Maxx (p83)

Something for all

Market Street, Manchester's mainstream shopping hub, continues to be packed, especially at weekends. High-street brands such as H&M, Debenhams and TK Maxx (p83), and edgier neighbours such as All Saints and Urban Outfitters (p83), line up against the looming Arndale Centre, itself home to an enormous Next and Topshop (p83). Rebuilt after the IRA bomb, the Arndale still has its 1970s tiled tower but now features a glittering extension, making it the country's biggest inner-city shopping mall.

The Marks & Spencer store nearby is connected to the Arndale by a handy footbridge; opposite, there's a neat row of shops such as Paperchase and Size, all perfumed by the pungent bath bombs peddled by Lush. The nearby Triangle shopping centre (p83), looking a little empty of late, is the address of Green & Benz, Bravissimo, East and Jigsaw. For a less intense shopping experience, visit the small boutiques, upmarket shops and jewellers in the elegant trio of the Barton, St Ann's and Royal Exchange arcades.

The intimate layout of the city centre means that nowhere is truly exclusive. Shoppers can happily hop between areas: skint but savvy youngsters make a day of it at Selfridges, while WAG wannabes are as comfortable browsing the graffitied rabbit-warren of the Northern Quarter in a hunt for vintage pieces as they are at the cosmetic counters of Harvey Nichols.

Beyond the centre

For those who prefer to stay away from the chaos of the city centre, the suburbs do a very good job of keeping up. Bohemian Chorlton is popular with local residents, but also attracts outsiders looking for a leisurely afternoon stroll. Chorlton's Beech Road has a quirky (if small) selection of exclusive clothing shops and galleries, while nearby Manchester Road offers gift shops, delis galore and the vegan Unicorn Grocery (p161).

Also in South Manchester, both Didsbury Village and West Didsbury's Burton Road are home to bookshops, fashion retailers and imaginative delis. The outlying towns of Stockport, Bury and Bolton, meanwhile, appeal with high-street shopping and excellent markets.

In Salford Quays, the Lowry Outlet Mall (p142) serves residents of the nearby modern apartments. In the doldrums for a number of years, the mall has recently been boosted by the addition of a Gap outlet, while Whistles, Nike and Marks & Spencer all offer discounts of up to 70 per cent. It's likely that the mall will continue to improve as its new neighbour, Media City, brings an influx of fresh shoppers.

Out of town, too, and perennially popular, is the massive Trafford Centre (p161). Faux palm trees and Romanesque sculptures might not be to everybody's taste, but there's a lot to be said for under-cover shopping, extended opening hours and free parking.

Whether because of its strong industrial heritage or a simple love of shopping, Manchester was never going to let a little thing like a recession get it down. Locals are justifiably proud of one of the widest arrays of shops outside the capital, and many others flock to the city from elsewhere in the North West and beyond. From high street to independent, and from second-hand to glossy designer goods, Manchester does shopping very well.

Craft & Design Centre p97

Band on the Wall p100

Nightlife

Manchester's legendary nightlife has eclecticism at its heart, and the city has resisted boiling down the best elements of its after-hours scene to a generic cover-all template. So while Manchester is proud of its musical history, it refuses to stifle innovation with nostalgia. A mosaic of nightlife options coexist here, making it an exhilarating city to step out in.

The city's manageable size makes it easy to hop between districts, yet each retains a unique identity, from the creative vibrancy of the once-industrial Northern Quarter to the leafy, bar-loving southern suburbs. Manchester, it seems, is a city that doesn't tolerate homogeny, and many of its most dynamic nightlife ventures proclaim that they have sprung up as antidotes to the status quo. Whether it's established

or brand-new bands, clubbing or comedy that floats your boat, or if you have no agenda but to try things out, Manchester's nightlife has something for you.

Clubs

Two decades after 'Madchester' and the baggy revolution that made the city the club capital of Europe, Manchester's most famous musical pedigree is still alive and kicking, thanks to the appearance of new Factory Records ventures such as FAC251: The Factory (p124), as well as an armada of nostalgia nights. All well and good, especially when these scions of Madchester are as forward-thinking as FAC251, but Manchester is no one-trick pony.

A rapidly growing electro scene, spearheaded by Mint Lounge (p102) and Attic (p122), is well worth investigating. For underground techno, house and a dizzying list of other styles, check out Sankeys (p148), reopened, reinvented and duly rewarded with the honour of *DJ Magazine*'s number-one club in the world title. Harmless but mediocre indie nights are everywhere, but thankfully easy to spot (and avoid) from their rampant drinks promotions and queues of bop-hungry students. Lovers of quality indie and rock 'n' roll should venture instead to another reopened and redesigned club, South (p86), which promises to burst the city centre's image-conscious bubble with a roster of floor-stomping nights, including Clint Boon's 'Ultimate' Saturday-night gig. Across town, the Star & Garter (p114) invites you to wipe your vintage pumps on the way out, with its musically credible and yet amicably poseur-ish weekend club nights.

Manchester's Northern Quarter has more nightlife to choose from than any other city district. Most bars keep late hours and are independently run; a refreshing antidote to the identikit chain bars of which even Manchester has its share. The quirky aural entertainments on offer here provide an apt warm-up for yet another reopened former favourite enjoying rude health, Band on the Wall (p100). In addition to the live music that has been its staple since its previous incarnation, Band on the Wall plays host to a number of club nights, including the perennially popular Keep it Unreal with Mr Scruff.

If scruffy chic isn't your thing, and you want instead to air your designer labels, the exclusive Circle Club (p85) offers a stylish and occasionally celebrity-studded experience. Elsewhere, a dressy pre-club drink may be found

SHORTLIST

Best for gigs
- Deaf Institute (p124)
- Manchester Apollo (p162)
- Night & Day Café (p102)
- Ruby Lounge (p105)

Underground sounds
- Mint Lounge (p102)
- Sankeys (p148)

Best for laughs
- Comedy Store (p134)
- Frog & Bucket (p102)
- Iguana Bar (p162)

Best reopened venues
- Band on the Wall (p100)
- Sankeys (p148)
- South (p86)

Best-kept secrets
- Cask (p134)
- Corridor (p136)
- Purple Pussycat (p86)

Best for gay clubbers
- Cruz 101 (p113)
- Essential (p113)

Most eclectic line-ups
- Deaf Institute (p124)
- FAC251: The Factory (p124)

Best for all-night dancing
- Cruz 101 (p113)
- Queer (p114)
- Sankeys (p148)
- Warehouse Project (p116)

Best for playing dress-up
- Star & Garter (p114)
- Tiger Lounge (p87)

Most glamorous
- Circle Club (p85)

Best out of town
- Electrik (p162)
- Fuel Café Bar (p162)

NOHO

Stevenson Square,
Manchester, M1 1FB
info@noho-bar.com
0161 236 5381

Bar available for hire • Table
reservations • Music (DJ's
8pm Thurs-Sat) • Free Entry

By day you wouldn't know it exists, by night the large shutters go up and it comes to life.

The Grade II listed building has stunning floor to ceiling windows, original parquet flooring and has kept its height for an 'open feel'. NoHo is an independent bar set in a truly one-of-a-kind space, with experienced bartenders that offer a seasonal cocktail menu. Low-lit chesterfields, connect four and other classic games, with films shown off the huge 'drive in movie' style wall art. Resident DJ's offer a mixture of grooves and beats, turning it into a late night boogie den. NoHo is ideal for birthdays, anniversaries, engagement parties and of course, corporate events. NoHo can accommodate up to 180 guests.

www.noho-bar.com

Open: Sun-Thurs 5pm-1am, Fri/Sat 5pm-3am (Mon closed, available for hire)
• No food • Nearest Train Station: Piccadilly • Metrolink: Piccadilly Gardens •

among the several modern bars that punctuate Deansgate Locks, but the wannabes can often outnumber the it-crowd whose shoulders they head there to rub, with predictably tacky results.

Music

Two decades after the city-defining 'Madchester', Manchester's home-grown music scene has finally shifted to a more genre-defying mix of influences. While some local acts on the rise scorn the 'Manchester band' tag for fear of pigeonholing, others acknowledge that it need not mean consignment to the Factory Records' cast-off bin. Manchester-bred stadium-fillers such as Elbow and Doves bring sounds from the city to international ears, but to experience the true scope of the 'Manchester sound' there's no better place than Manchester itself, and no better place to start than the wealth of unsigned acts playing in smaller venues such as Fuel Café Bar (p162).

Further up the career scale, the city-centre champion of the independents, Ruby Lounge (p105), hosts local and touring bands who have yet to fill a venue the size of Manchester Apollo (p162). For stellar acts, there's the MEN Arena (p86), scaling the live experience up (and down) to a distant view of the likes of Rihanna or Westlife.

Size of venue and fame of band are not always synonymous, however; scene stalwart Night & Day Café (p102) occasionally supplements its usual unsigned bands with pro acts such as the Von Bondies, which sell out faster than you can say 'I'm with the band.' The Deaf Institute (p124), meanwhile, has been known to offer unsigned or open-mic performers a stage recently trodden by acts of the calibre of Kate Nash or Kitty, Daisy and Lewis. The Institute, the third

venue in local chain-bar venture Trof, is arguably Manchester's most beautiful music venue, and this Grade II-listed building lets acts loose in a music hall complete with domed roof and elegant bird-covered wallpaper. For a different, yet equally Mancunian, music experience, head to Matt & Phred's Jazz Club (p102) in the Northern Quarter – but book ahead as weekends get busy.

Music festivals

The Castlefield music festival Dpercussion is sadly no more, but the city is awash with niche festivals. These tend to feature a mix of indoor and outdoor venues – in May, the Hungry Pigeon festival presents hundreds of live acts across the Northern Quarter, while FutureEverything showcases the latest digital and electro offerings in venues as diverse as Bridgewater Hall (p105) and Madlab.

Matt & Phred's Jazz Club p102

Autumn's In The City remains one of the city's best live music gigs, and its recent move to the Northern Quarter has kept things fresh: this is the place to spot music's Next Big Thing, as well as to poke fun at the antics of the A&Rs who flock to the industry convention that accompanies it. Salford newcomers Un-convention and Sounds from the Other City both give their Manchester counterparts a lo-fi run for their money.

Festivals usually offer wristbands that allow multiple entries for a smallish outlay (leaving you with ample change for your beer money), although the more popular sell out well in advance. The festivals scene is fairly fluid: existing events wither away and new ones appear with confusing regularity. It's best to keep an eye on bar posters or online to ensure you don't miss the newest.

Gay & lesbian

Manchester's Gay Village – the area around Canal Street immortalised in TV series *Queer as Folk* – is now so established that one-time defiant innovators such as Manto (p114) are now tourist draws in their own right. Previous fears of over-development within the Village have, thankfully, proved unfounded, although that may be more down to the recession putting the brakes on new builds than inspired planning. Whatever the reason, this famous stretch of the Rochdale Canal is packed with drinkers every weekend, and at the first glimmer of good weather. Although some revellers are undeniably the tourists and hen parties it had been feared might discourage regulars, the sense of community here remains palpable, and there really is something for everyone. Cavernous venues Via (p116) and Essential (p113) both provide something special for

clubbers, as well as alfresco drinking during the day. And while karaoke options are plentiful, there is room for credible clubbing experiences – such as the funky house night at Cruz 101 (p113) – niche bars such as Vanilla (p116), and even the odd boutique hotel.

Comedy

Manchester is enjoying an energetic resurgence in comedy thanks to three central locations: the flagship Comedy Store (p134), old favourite the Frog & Bucket (p102) and relative newcomer Opus (p86). All three offer a complete night out – acts at the Comedy Store can be enjoyed over dinner, the Frog & Bucket invites cheesy post-show dancing, while Opus's comedy and club venues share premises – and there's plenty of nightlife nearby. If your Comedy Store budget stretches to a ticket but not a meal, try Cask (p134) on nearby Liverpool Road; a cosy bar that allows you to bring in food from the chip shop next door.

Fancy yourself as a stand-up comic? Mondays at the Frog & Bucket play host to Beat the Frog, with respect and other prizes for any amateur act who can perform five minutes of original comedy before the frog banishes them from the stage. Entrance as an audience member or competitor (book your slot in advance) is free, and since the Frog & Bucket kicked-started the careers of laughter legends such as Peter Kay and Dave Gorman, you never know what it might lead to. A further dedicated comedy night can be found a bus ride away from the city centre in Chorlton's Iguana Bar (p162). Its 'Mirth on Mondays' night has been running for eight years and is so confident of its own longevity that it offers lifetime membership with discount privileges.

DON'T MISS

Bridgewater Hall p125

WHAT'S BEST
Arts & Leisure

Manchester is emerging from more than a decade's worth of cultural construction. The magnificent Bridgewater Hall (p125) was among the first of the new-builds, followed by Salford's Lowry centre (p142) and a number of new or renovated museums.

But building and rebuilding is only half the story. Alongside the shiny new arts complexes, the city has shored up its cultural confidence, and nowhere is this more evident than in Manchester's festivals scene. Autumn has now become the unofficial start of the festival season, although there are now so many events that activity is pretty much year-round. Leading the pack is the ambitious biennial Manchester International Festival (p37), followed up by food and drink, comedy, science and literature events. Music festivals now abound in Manchester, with In The City, Un-convention and Sounds from the Other City all regular fixtures.

Meanwhile, venues have also upped the ante, with many now offering so much under one roof that it's easy to lose whole days sampling their individual cultural wares – venues such as Cornerhouse (p125), with its bookshop, bar, café, galleries and cinemas.

But it's the unmistakable infusion of Mancunian flavour that makes downtime here so good. Whether it's the laid-back vibe of Studio Salford at the King's Arms (p137), Islington Mill (p139) staging some of the city's most exciting art and music events, or the myriad festivals that spring up in the Northern Quarter every summer, you'll never forget where you are. The industrial heritage settings – the neoclassical grandeur of the Portico (p88), the glass-roofed atrium of the Craft & Design Centre (p97) – are unique. If it sometimes feels you can't move for exposed brick and restored ironwork, that's no bad thing, for, while the city may have its feet firmly planted in historical soil, its face is defiantly turned to a bright future.

Film

There's great enthusiasm for film in Manchester, with festivals including the UK's largest student film festival, Exposures, as well as the Family Friendly Film Festival. The UK's first and only such kid-friendly event, it's a rare chance to expand the young uns' experience of film – through workshops, interesting venues and a film choice that hits higher than the usual cartoon fare.

When it comes to venues, forget the bland anonymity of the multiplex: Cornerhouse (p125) is king. Its screens show the widest selection of arthouse, independent and foreign language films in town, while visits from international directors (Danny Boyle is its patron) add an additional dimension for cinephiles. In fact, Cornerhouse is so popular, often bursting at the seams at evenings and weekends, that it is scheduled to move into a new, purpose-built arts complex in 2014.

Theatre

No youngster itself, theatre stalwart the Royal Exchange (p88) is the home of new playwriting talent in the city, its annual Bruntwood Playwriting Competition revealing a dedication to new work that's being replicated elsewhere, most notably at Contact Theatre (p125) and summer's 24:7 Theatre Festival.

Other theatrical venues of note include Bolton's Octagon (p148)

DON'T MISS

SHORTLIST

Most anticipated event
- Manchester International Festival (p37)

Best new festival
- Un-convention (p41)

Best film festivals
- Family Friendly Film Festival (p37)
- Exposures (p41)

Grand dame of classical music
- The Hallé (p125)

Best for cutting-edge dance & theatre
- Contact Theatre (p125)

Champion of new playwriting
- Royal Exchange (p88)

Best eclectic arts centre
- Islington Mill (p139)

Best cinema
- Cornerhouse (p125)

Loveliest hidden gems
- Chetham's Library & School of Music (p57)
- Portico Library (p88)
- Victoria Baths (p153)

Best participatory sports
- Chill Factore (see box p163)
- Great Manchester Run (p37)

Biggest rivals
- Manchester City (p148)
- Manchester United (p165)

Best spiritual retreat
- Manchester Buddhist Centre (p105)

Lushest park
- Fletcher Moss Gardens (p151)

and the Lowry (p142) which, while it rarely commissions work, acts as a receiving house for some of the UK's biggest touring shows. Made homeless by the renovations to Central Library, the renowned Library Theatre Company has found a temporary home at the Lowry. In 2014, it moves to a new home, sharing space within the Cornerhouse development.

Literature

Readers and writers in the city have rarely had it so good. Novelist Colm Tóibín and the Poet Laureate, Carol Ann Duffy, regularly hold public debates and events (courtesy of the two universities at which they are employed; see box p123), while the city's Literature Festival continues to grow, boosted by developments such as the new International Anthony Burgess Foundation (p127), the £10,000 Manchester Writing Prize and the refurbished Elizabeth Gaskell House (p151). Edgier action comes courtesy of the Manchester Blog Awards and spoken-word events at Contact Theatre. All of which adds up to a rich, if sometimes a little underground, writing scene.

Dance

Manchester's best classical dance performances come courtesy of the Lowry, Palace Theatre (p127) and Opera House (p87). The latter two,

Studio Salford at the King's Arms p137

sister venues run by the same organisation, put on reliable touring shows from the English National Ballet. The Lowry, meanwhile, excels at contemporary dance, bringing Carlos Acosta back to Manchester in 2011, plus works by the Birmingham Royal Ballet and contemporary international touring companies. For more experimental work, head to Contact Theatre or Greenroom (p127), whose intimate spaces mean you can get up close to the newest moves in contemporary and urban dance.

Classical music

Under Mark Elder, the Hallé orchestra, which chalked up 150 years in 2008, is enjoying the kind of critical and popular success unseen since its 1960s Sir John Barbirolli heyday. The Bridgewater Hall (p125), performing home of the Hallé, celebrated a triumphant first decade in 2006, its success no doubt helped by the friendly rivalry between Mark Elder and the equally charismatic head of the BBC Philharmonic, Gianandrea Noseda. Noseda's artistic direction is formidable: when he led the Phil through its first complete cycle of the Beethoven symphonies in 30 years, the performances were uploaded on to the BBC's website. Some 1.4 million quick-fire downloads later, the Phil realised it had someone rather special fronting its orchestra. The Phil moves into Media City in 2011.

The public profile of the Royal Northern College of Music (RNCM; p127) improved when it opened a new wing on Oxford Road in 2007, while the University of Manchester's Quatuor Danel quartet – arguably one of the best quartets in Europe – regularly plays at the Martin Harris Centre. Manchester International Festival is also having a positive impact on classical music, with Manchester Camerata's joint performance with Elbow in 2009 one of the festival's highlights – a genuinely moving event that reflected the entire musical spectrum currently at play in the city.

Sport & leisure

This city of sporting prowess seamlessly produces world-class athletes and stages international events. The two football clubs, City (p148) and United (p165), ignite passionate debate wherever you go, and the city boasts four rugby league clubs, one of rugby union's top teams (Sale Sharks) and Lancashire Cricket Club, based (for now, at least) at Old Trafford.

But there's also room for specialist events. Manchester Velodrome (p148) houses a 3,500-seat track for what might be considered a minority sport (track cycling), and yet the venue's winter season races regularly pull in 3,000 punters a pop. Its 'Revolution' events – spectator-friendly, with a 'night at the races' feel – are often packed, while Sportcity has hosted everything from the National Badminton Championships to the Paralympic World Cup. Sometimes the city even merges its two major passions, sport and music: the Velodrome (complete with an appearance by the British Cycling Team) played host to a spectacular Kraftwerk gig in 2009, as part of Manchester International Festival (p37).

Another draw here is the ease with which visitors can indulge in healthy pursuits. If trekking through the urban landscape leaves you yearning for space and fresh air, then head north for Heaton Park (p145) or south for the 1,000-acre Tatton Park (p153), one of the jewels in the National Trust's crown.

DON'T MISS

Calendar

Manchester International Festival

The following are the pick of the annual events that happen in Manchester. Further information can be found nearer the time from flyers and seasonal guides available from tourist information centres (p189), or www.visitmanchester.com.

January

Mid Jan
National Winter Ales Festival
www.alefestival.org.uk/winterales
A selection of over 200 brews, with a good range of winter warmers.

Jan/Feb
Chinese New Year
Chinatown
www.manchester.gov.uk
Fireworks and the Golden Dragon Parade enliven the city's Chinatown.

February

Early Feb
National Squash Championships
Sportcity, p143
www.nationalsquashchamps.co.uk
England's finest battle it out for the national title.

March

Early-mid Mar
Manchester Irish Festival
Various locations
www.manchesteririshfestival.co.uk
A two-week festival culminating in one of the UK's largest St Patrick's Day parades.

Mid Mar
¡Viva! Spanish & Latin American Film Festival
Cornerhouse, p125
www.vivafilmfestival.co.uk
Ten days of Hispanic film screenings, with a healthy selection of premières and previews.

May

Mid May **FutureEverything**
Various locations
www.futureeverything.org
Electronic, experimental music and arts, with international and local artists participating.

Mid May
BUPA Great Manchester Run
City Centre
www.greatrun.org
See box p41.

Mid May-Sept **Screenfields**
Spinningfields
www.spinningfieldsonline.com
Free outdoor film screenings, with deckchairs and picnics available.

Mid May **Spring Market**
St Ann's Square, City Centre
www.manchestermarkets.com
Specialist food, drink, plants and gifts.

Late May
Eurocultured Street Festival
New Wakefield Street, City Centre
www.eurocultured.com
A mix of urban dance, street art, DJs and live music.

June

Ongoing Screenfields (see May).

Late June-mid July (2011, 2013)
Manchester International Festival
Various locations
www.mif.co.uk
See box p38.

Late June
Manchester Day Parade
Deansgate, City Centre
www.themanchesterdayparade.co.uk
An exuberant street celebration of Mancunian pride.

July

Ongoing Screenfields (see May); Manchester International Festival (see June).

Mid July
Family Friendly Film Festival
Various locations
www.familyfriendly.org.uk
A fortnight of U-rated films and workshops.

Mid-late July **24:7 Theatre Festival**
Various locations
www.247theatrefestival.co.uk
New and original theatre performed in venues across the city.

Late July **RHS Flower Show at Tatton Park**
Tatton Park
www.rhs.org.uk/tatton
Horticultural heaven, over ten days.

Late July
Manchester Jazz Festival
Various locations
www.manchesterjazz.com
Popular festival featuring around 50 bands in indoor and outdoor venues, over two weeks.

August

Ongoing Screenfields (see May).

Mid-late Aug
Manchester Pride
Gay Village
www.manchesterpride.com
Ten days of floats, parades and parties.

See it here first

The all-new Manchester International Festival.

Manchester International Festival

For years, Manchester's global contribution to culture was largely based on three things: politics, football and music. That changed in 2007 when the city launched the ambitious – and often audacious – Manchester International Festival (p37), a biennial arts bonanza that in its first year led Miranda Sawyer to describe Manchester as 'the beating cultural heart of Britain'.

Fast-forward four years and the festival shows no signs of slowing down. The 2011 line-up includes a new play by Victoria Wood, and the Hallé's Mark Elder presiding over a 'staged examination' of Wagner's four-opera Ring Cycle. A few familiar faces are set to return too. Damon Albarn, the Blur and Gorillaz musician who lit the fuse beneath the inaugural festival with his circus- and opera-inspired *Monkey: Journey to the West*, presents a new work, as does the legendary performance artist Marina Abramovic. In 2009, Abramovic stripped the Whitworth Art Gallery bare before delivering an unforgettable four-hour incursion into performance art. This time, the performance is loosely based on her own life;

it stars Willem Dafoe and 'heavenly' original music by Antony Hegarty.

With each edition premiering around 20 new works, Manchester International Festival's only real downside comes courtesy of its main selling point: it claims to be the only festival in the world that consists solely of new work – so you'll see no old favourites here. Because of this, 'you can never predict what's going to happen,' says festival director Alex Poots, though with two successful festivals under his belt, it's safe to assume that the 2011 affair will again demonstrate its by-now trademark mix of high art, entertainment and Mancunian flair. As an example – and perhaps one of the best events at the 2009 festival – was when Mercury Prize-winners Elbow teamed up with the Hallé. The subsequent gig at Bridgewater Hall left many in the audience on their feet, shouting for more. It's this combination of the unexpected, the joyously Mancunian and the beautifully delivered that makes Manchester International Festival one of the city's must-dos in 2011 and beyond.
■ www.mif.co.uk

September

Ongoing Screenfields (see May).

Late Sept-1 Jan
Warehouse Project
Store Street Car Park
(beneath Piccadilly Station)
www.thewarehouseproject.com
Three months of underground raves
with the biggest names in dance and
electronica, culminating in a New
Year's Day closing party. See box p116.

October

Ongoing Warehouse Project
(see Sept).

Oct-Nov (2011, 2014)
Asia Triennial Manchester
Various locations
www.asiatriennialmanchester.com
City-wide exhibitions and events that
showcase South Asian art.

Early Oct
Dashehra Diwali Mela
Platt Fields Park, Fallowfield
www.indianassociation.org.uk
Bhangra, Bollywood, dance, food and
fireworks.

Early-mid Oct **Manchester
Food & Drink Festival**
Various locations
www.foodanddrinkfestival.com

Manchester Pride p37

Manchester Comedy Festival

Ten days of gourmet activity, with food markets, celebrated chefs and restaurant events.

Mid-late Oct
Manchester Literature Festival
Various locations
www.mlfestival.co.uk
Ten days of literary delights.

Mid Oct **In The City**
Various locations
www.inthecity.co.uk
Mix with the pros as they try to spot music's next big thing.

Mid Oct **Manchester Fest Market**
St Ann's Square, City Centre
www.manchestermarkets.com
A dozen days of local, sustainable and speciality foods.

Mid Oct
Manchester Science Festival
Various locations
www.manchestersciencefestival.com
Over 200 events, from walks and demos to comedy and stargazing.

Mid Oct **Great Northern Contemporary Craft Fair**
Spinningfields
www.greatnorthernevents.co.uk
Annual exhibition of gifts, jewellery, fabrics and furniture from the UK's brightest designer-makers.

Late Oct
Manchester Comedy Festival
Various locations
www.manchestercomedyfestival.com
Two weeks of up-and-coming stand-ups, as well as big-hitters.

Late Oct **Manchester Blog Awards**
www.manchesterblogawards.com
Long-established showcase of the city's
online writing talent.

Late Oct **Buy Art Fair**
Spinningfields
www.buyartfair.co.uk
Commercial contemporary art fair that
attracts big-name and emerging artists
and features more than 80 galleries.

Late Oct **Grimm Up North**
Various locations
www.grimmfest.com
A smörgåsbord of horror, gore and
sci-fi films and related spooky events.

November

Ongoing Warehouse Project
(see Sept); Asia Triennial
Manchester (see Oct).

Mid Nov
Christmas Lights Switch On
Albert Square, City Centre
www.manchester.gov.uk

Mid Nov **Un-convention**
Various locations
www.unconventionhub.org
Salford music industry festival that's
as appreciated by music-lovers as it is
by music-makers.

Mid Nov-late Dec
Manchester Christmas Markets
Albert Square and St Ann's Square
www.manchestermarkets.com
Stocking-fillers, glühwein and festive
food at the North West's biggest, oldest
and best Christmas markets.

Late Nov/early Dec **Exposures**
Cornerhouse, p125
www.exposuresfilmfestival.co.uk
Four days of screenings by the UK's
very best student filmmakers.

December

Ongoing Warehouse Project
(see Sept); Manchester Christmas
Markets (see Nov).

On your marks…

Get set for the Great
Manchester Run.

Set up in 2003 and televised
live on the BBC, this 38,000-
strong race, held in May (listings
p37), has quickly become one
of the most popular events in
the British running calendar.

Organised by the brains behind
the Great North Run, Manchester
was the natural choice to host
a new 10k: the city renowned
for football also excels in cricket,
cycling, rugby – and running.
And with a route typically taking
in Manchester United's ground,
fleet-of-foot football fans get the
best of both worlds.

The run attracts some of the
world's best athletes, with Haile
Gebreselasse breaking records
here since 2005. Even for the
less energetic, the setting makes
for a good day out. Both runners
and spectators can enjoy the
views at Salford Quays, with the
route skirting the Imperial War
Museum North. Strategically
placed bands, classical musicians
and DJs add to the atmosphere,
while those wanting to make
a weekend of it can watch their
kids participate in the Junior
Run at Sportcity on the Saturday,
before making for the finish line
themselves on the Sunday.

The only downside is the
inevitable road chaos. If you're
planning on racing, ditch the car
and take the tram, train or bus.
And to make sure you get a place
at the starting line, sign up for
email reminders at www.greatrun.
org as early as possible before
the race – entry is by ballot,
with places allocated in January.

FASHION BEAUTY FOOD

HARVEY NICHOLS

EXCHANGE SQUARE MANCHESTER 0161 828 8888

www.harveynichols.com

Itineraries

Free Trade Hall

Manchester:
A Secret History

Is it a characteristic defiance, a certain insecurity or just sloppiness that leads to Manchester being so coy about its astonishing past? The city has been midwife to the Industrial Revolution, to the Football League and to communism. The first TUC congress was held here, Ernest Rutherford split the atom and Alan Turing oversaw the beginnings of the computer age in the city. And yet these gems are largely overlooked. A little craning of the neck and a certain amount of initiative is needed, but in a city centre as compact as Manchester's, the past can be explored with minimal effort. It should take an hour to complete this walk, which goes from one side of the city centre to the other, and across 2,000 years of history.

Start on **Miller Street**, in the shadow of the **Co-operative Insurance Tower**, at the junction with Rochdale Road. It may take a heroic feat of imagination to picture it now, but this is where modern Manchester – indeed, it could be argued, the modern world – was born in 1780, when Richard Arkwright built his first cotton mill, thus kick-starting the Industrial Revolution.

Perhaps somewhat symbolic of the unsentimental greed of the capitalist revolution that it inspired, the site lies unrecorded, buried for years beneath a car park, but it was latterly drawn attention to when Channel 4's *Time Team* programme excavated the site in 2005.

Over to the north, the rising towers of what is now called the Green Quarter loom above the old slum district of Red Bank. Friedrich Engels – himself the beneficiary of his family's cotton wealth – paid several visits to this area (as well as to Little Ireland, behind Oxford Road station) to document

Co-operative Insurance Tower

the appalling living conditions. His observations led to the writing of his *Conditions of the Working Classes in England* in 1844.

Walk downhill from here and turn left on to Corporation Street. Soon you will see Victoria Station on the right, with **Balloon Street** on the left. If you're curious about that street's name, then a small blue plaque above your head records that the pioneering aeronaut James Sadler made the city's first balloon ascent near here in 1785. The derelict block on the right – City Buildings – was the site of the home of Ann Lee, who would go on to establish the utopian Shaker movement in late 18th-century America. In her day, the road was called Toad Lane; today it is **Todd Lane**, but this row of buildings facing the National Football Museum is now not even dignified with a road sign.

Continue along Corporation Street underneath the striking glass **Arndale Bridge**, and notice the **red pillar box** on the right. This is the postbox that was somehow left standing when the IRA bomb exploded a few feet away in 1996.

Take the next left turn now, where the garish experience of **Market Street** will drive away all thought of history for five gaudy minutes (less, if you run). Just past the Market Street Metrolink stop, you will reach the corner of **Piccadilly Gardens** (p107). Look up to your right. Now home to a Santander bank, this building was the Royal Hotel in 1888, and an innocuous plaque records that the Football League was formed here in April of that year. It seems appropriate that the city should have gone on to such a distinguished footballing history.

Walk down **Mosley Street** now, past Manchester Art Gallery and across **Princess Street**. Immediately to your right is the site of John Dalton's laboratory, where Dalton helped to establish the principles of modern atomic theory. Carry on to the end of **St Peter's Square** – the central cenotaph garden marks the site of the demolished St Peter's Church – and turn right a short way along Peter Street to reach what is now the **Radisson Edwardian** (p176), one of the city's plusher hotels. This was formerly the **Free Trade Hall**, one of the numerous reminders of the city's radical past that has been transformed into a distinctly more capitalist present. Around this site, back in 1819, a public protest for parliamentary reform degenerated into bloodshed – the infamous Peterloo Massacre – when sabre-wielding troops galloped into a crowd of around 60,000, killing 11 and injuring 400 (the blue plaque now on the wall rather charitably refers to this as being the crowd's 'subsequent dispersal').

Various musical anecdotes can be relayed about the Free Trade Hall. From 1858 to 1996, the spot was home to the Hallé orchestra, Britain's longest-established symphony orchestra, which is now situated five minutes away in the Bridgewater Hall (p125). Bob Dylan received his infamous 'Judas' heckle here shortly after going electric in 1966, while in the upstairs Lesser Free Trade Hall, in 1976, the Sex Pistols played two momentous gigs. The show's promoters, Howard Devoto and Pete Shelley, would go on to form Buzzcocks, while also in attendance were future members of Joy Division, Simply Red, the Fall, the Smiths and Anthony H Wilson.

Turn back the way you came and take one of the next two right turns, either of which will lead you to the recently renamed **Manchester Central Convention Complex** (p64; previously called G-Mex), which was formerly the Victorian-era Central railway station. Bear right and follow **Lower Mosley Street**, with the Bridgewater Hall on your left, then cross the road at the traffic lights and note the housing development on your left at the next crossroads. Another example of Manchester's viciously unsentimental attitude towards its heritage, the site of the **Haçienda** – in its day perhaps the most famous club in the world – now resides beneath the block of flats that today bears its name. To be fair, when open, the club would go out of its way not to advertise its presence; at the height of the 1990s Madchester rave scene it was identified merely by a small brass plaque.

From here, go right down **Whitworth Street West** towards Deansgate for the short walk to Castlefield. The best route is to turn right at the Deansgate traffic lights, walk beneath the railway bridge and go left down **Liverpool Road**. Note the signs to your left pointing out the remains of Roman Manchester. Here lie the disappointingly scarce remnants of the four **Roman forts** built between the first and fifth centuries; most of the remains were destroyed during the Industrial Revolution, as the Rochdale canal and the still-standing railway viaducts were ploughed unsentimentally through. The **Beetham Tower** (p128) looms close over the site now, an imposing reminder of the distance travelled in the two millennia since.

Beetham Tower

Manchester Cathedral

Manchester in...

...one hour

As 60 minutes isn't very long, we'll give you a choice. One option is to indulge yourself in **Exchange Square**: the city's retail-cum-cultural epicentre is a fantastic public space designed in the wake of the 1996 IRA bombing. Here, you'll find the **Triangle**, a shopping mall located in the former Corn Exchange, as well as **Selfridges**. In the distance looms the hulk of the **Arndale Shopping Centre** and the **Printworks** entertainment complex. Give the defiantly quirky **Paramount Book Exchange** on Shudehill (No.25, 384 9509) a try if you have time.

Alternatively, if you leave Exchange Square via Shambles Square, you'll pass two of the city's oldest public houses – the **Old Wellington Inn** and **Sinclair's Oyster Bar** (p74). Incredibly, this is the third home for both places: they were moved here in 1971 to make way for redevelopment, and then shifted again during the post-bomb rebuild. Manchester's often overlooked 600-year-old **Cathedral** (p64) is next door on Cateaton Street; beyond it is **Chetham's Library & School of Music** (p57). The library's ancient texts should hold the interest of any bibliophiles for a little while. Enjoy a browse in the reading room, a former haunt of a certain K Marx. The School of Music puts on free lunchtime concerts. If, after all that, you've still a few minutes to spare, hot-foot it up Corporation Street and on to Cross Street, where you can fall into **Mr Thomas's Chop House** (No.52, 832 2245, www.tomschophouse.com) for the famous corned beef hash cake and another crafty pint.

...an afternoon

It's always edifying to combine a cuppa with some culture, so start proceedings in the café of the **John**

Printworks

Wellington Inn

Rylands Library (p61) at the end of Deansgate, where, over a brew, you can peer up at the building's unrestrained neo-Gothic architecture.

Deansgate itself is a major stretch of listed Mancunian real estate, central to the city's emergence as a railway and canal capital, which links the north and south. There are dozens of drinking dens dotted along this key artery: if you're in need of further refreshment, try the **Knott** (p133), a bar that offers tasty ales and hearty food.

Halfway up the old thoroughfare sits **St Ann's Square**, an elegant civic space created in the 18th century. The square and its surrounding streets and passages were designated a Conservation Area by Manchester City Council in the 1970s. If you're not grabbed by the neoclassical **St Ann's Church** (p67), which sometimes stages music recitals, you may

be more inspired by the big-brand stores here, such as Habitat and Gap. Wander up and down the Barton Arcade and visit the former **Kendal's** department store. Now a **House of Fraser** (p81), the shop is still referred to locally by its old name. **King Street**, parallel to St Ann Street, offers higher-end boutiques, with the likes of Whistles, Joseph and Vivienne Westwood.

As afternoon turns to evening, a couple of nearby cultural options slide into focus: the **Opera House** (p87) and the **Royal Exchange** theatre (p88). Before a performance at either, head into **Harvey Nichols** (p81) for a long cocktail, as the sun (if you're lucky) begins to dip.

...24 hours

Mornings in Manchester are usually relatively calm: even Market Street and the Arndale Centre are quiet

Manchester Cathedral

St Ann's Passage

before lunch. However, there's more interesting shopping and street life elsewhere: have a roam around the **Northern Quarter's** offbeat fashion outlets, the shops of **Afflecks**, and the commercial and artistic studios of the **Craft & Design Centre**, formerly the Smithfield Fish Market.

As you wander back into the city centre, a couple of cultural spaces beckon. The striking **Bridgewater Hall** (p125) stages lunchtime concerts a couple of times a week, and dishes up sandwiches and snacks daily in its Touchstones Café Bar. There's also a café at **Cornerhouse** (p125), home to a gallery and cinema. If you're here on a Sunday, try the Breakfast Club deal – a full English with a classic film screening.

To balance the modern with the ancient, trip along to Deansgate and visit the excellent **People's History Museum** (p67), which dispenses a history lesson as seen through Mancunian eyes. Even if you're not hungry yet, it's worth crossing the River Irwell, a short walk from the museum, and nibbling and sipping at the Lowry Hotel's afternoon tea: the **River Restaurant** (p139) offers gliding waiters, exquisite cakes and champagne to wash it all down.

If you're quick, there'll be enough time for a little fresh air and green grass. Head for **Fletcher Moss Gardens** (p151) in Didsbury, before an early-evening pint at one of the nearby countrified inns and an aesthetically pleasing vegetarian meal at Simon Rimmer's **Greens** restaurant (p154). There'll be no need for a late-night taxi, at least not if you're sleeping at the **Didsbury House Hotel** (p183), a vivacious little Victorian boutique conversion.

Civil Justice Centre p52

Industrial Past, Cultural Future

From its early beginnings as a Roman fort to today's reinvented post-industrial city, Manchester is the sort of place that doesn't stand still for long. This walk begins at one end of **Deansgate** and, via a circuitous route that requires around two hours (and features a few watering holes), takes in one of the city's oldest settlements alongside one of its newest, in an apt demonstration of the ever-changing nature of this city.

Start your walk at **Beetham Tower** (p128). The brashest symbol of Manchester's modernity, and the city's tallest building, it provides a handy landmark by which to navigate. The tower packs in top-end apartments, a Hilton hotel and a 23rd-floor cocktail bar; it's also not a bad place to sample a high-rise high tea (noon-4pm daily, £15), should the mood take you.

Feeling refreshed, head down **Liverpool Road**, where, between the White Lion pub and the Ox (p134), you'll find a small park. Cut across it into Castlefield and you'll immediately step back in time: here, you'll find the replica of a **Roman fort**. The original was built in AD 79 and named 'Mamucium', Latin for 'breast-shaped hill' (it was also known as 'Mancunium'); it's where modern Manchester first began. Mamucium was abandoned in AD 410; its stone remains led to locals christening the area the 'Castle-in-the-field'.

Today, Castlefield's peaceful cobbled streets and gentle canals belie its once frenetic nature: the Bridgewater and Rochdale canals, as well as a railway (more on that later), made this a clanking, dirty hub of Industrial Revolution commerce. The area inevitably fell

Dukes 92

into decline during the grim, post-industrial years but, thankfully, in 1972, it was designated the UK's first 'urban heritage park'. Its cleaned-up canals and cobbles now make it one of the best places to head for when the sun shines. If you have time, stop off at the ever-popular **Dukes 92** (p133), a canalside pub that peddles decent pints and hearty grub in the best alfresco setting the city has to offer.

When you've finished off that pint, head back towards Liverpool Road via the **Castlefield Arena**. Although often quiet, the arena has been the site of many a momentous occasion, from the public news of the city's failed bid to host the 2000 Olympics (a few years later, the city got its commiseration prize in the form of the 2002 Commonwealth Games) to a broadcast of Elbow's performance with the renowned Hallé Orchestra during the 2009 Manchester International Festival. The tickets for that Bridgewater Hall gig sold out within hours of going on sale; a live (and packed) broadcast was swiftly set up at the

arena to assuage the disappointed. In a rather lovely twist, fans got more than they could have hoped for when Elbow front-man Guy Garvey turned up at the arena during the intermission, belted out an impromptu song, and then hot-footed it back to the Bridgewater Hall to finish his set. The arena is often used during the summer for music, art and sports events.

Head along **Potato Wharf** to get back on to Liverpool Road. Opposite and to your left is a sandstone-coloured Georgian terrace, the rather unassuming site of the world's oldest passenger railway station. It was here, in 1870, that 700 passengers gathered to witness the first Manchester to Liverpool run, which promised to cut the travel time between the two cities to an almost inconceivable (for that time) hour-long journey. The inaugural run didn't go quite according to plan, with political protests and even a tragic death (of William Huskisson, President of the Board of Trade, who fell into the path of the oncoming train), but, despite this, the railway did what the Liverpool and Manchester Railway Company had hoped: it changed British industrial transport forever. The station is now part of **MOSI** (p129); train-spotters can hop on board a steam train here and travel along a short stretch of the original tracks.

Turn right and head back up Liverpool Road, and then left on to **Lower Byrom Street**, passing the main entrance of MOSI, recently spruced up after a £9 million refit. Continue down Lower Byrom Street and, on the left, you'll spot the back of the **Granada TV studios**. With *Coronation Street* celebrating its 50th anniversary in 2010, and the studios responsible for such small-screen gold as *World in Action* and *Brideshead Revisited*, the impact of this site on British television can't be overestimated. Typically for a city always on the move, this particular piece of TV history is about to be lost forever: ITV Granada shifts its base to Media City, over in Salford Quays, in 2011.

Cross the road and head up a set of stone steps into the often overlooked **St John's Gardens**, one of the few green spaces in the city centre. Built in 1769, the church that once stood here was demolished in 1931; beneath your feet lie the remains of 22,000 people. Emerge on to **St John Street**, stopping to admire its rows of Georgian terraces, and head straight on, back on to Deansgate.

On this spot, you are standing directly above the mid-point of the city's forgotten waterway, the **Salford Junction Canal**. Once connecting the Rochdale Canal and the River Irwell, the waterway closed in the 1930s and was mostly filled – although this, and the warren of underground tunnels that lie beneath the city's streets, are now occasionally open for guided walks. (Check the website www.manchesterconfidential.co.uk for details of upcoming tours.)

From Deansgate, turn left down **Quay Street**, passing the Grade II-listed **Opera House** (p87) on your right. Continue down Quay Street, turning right before the Irwell Bridge to walk along the **River Irwell**.

On the opposite bank you'll see the **Mark Addy** (p137), one of Salford's better pubs; its traditional British menu and real ales are particularly recommended. A converted landing station, the pub is named after a 19th-century Salford hero who is reckoned to have saved around 50 people from drowning in the highly polluted waters of the River Irwell. Addy, a landlord whose pub was close to the river, was awarded numerous commendations for his actions (including the Albert Medal, now housed in the Salford Museum & Art Gallery; p136) but may have paid the ultimate price for his heroism: it's thought he contracted tuberculosis after jumping into a particularly fetid stretch of water to rescue a young boy.

At the bridge, walk up the steps to return to street level. Turn right on to **Bridge Street** to find a pair of Manchester's most intriguing new buildings. On the corner is the **People's History Museum** (p67), freshly reopened after a £12.5 million refurbishment. Its new Corten steel entrance wing, immediately to your right, links to the glorious Grade II-listed Pump House inside.

Rising up beyond the museum is the **Civil Justice Centre**. Known locally as the 'filing cabinet' because of its unusual cantilevered design, its western face features the largest suspended glass wall in Europe, which allows you to see the inner workings of the courts – the intention being that it would reflect the transparency of the British legal system.

Follow this glass wall and then turn left into **Spinningfields**, Manchester's new business district. **Hardman Square**, the small open area at its centre, plays host to all manner of enjoyable events each year, from the summer-long Screenfields (p37) outdoor film programme and the Great Northern Contemporary Craft Fair (October; p40) to the city centre's only festive ice rink. There are a number of chain eateries surrounding the square, including **Giraffe** (839 0009, www.giraffe.net) and **Carluccio's** (p69), which ably, if unexcitingly, cater to both office workers and visitors.

Leave Hardman Square and turn right on to **The Avenue**, the city's new high-end shopping street, whose residents include DKNY, Oliver Sweeney, Phillip Stoner and LK Bennett. The Avenue is topped off, at its Deansgate end, by the flagship Armani store, whose angular, contemporary lines juxtapose somewhat sharply with its nearest neighbour, the neo-Gothic **John Rylands Library** (p61). The clash between architectural styles is softened somewhat by the library's new-ish glass extension; a visual link between old and new.

Back on Deansgate, turn left and head towards **House of Fraser** (p81) on the corner of Deansgate and King Street West. No ordinary department store, the 175-year-old, six-storey building was, for almost 70 years, better known as Kendal's. Harrods bought the store in 1919 and promptly renamed it, but after protests it reverted to the original moniker. Sadly, when House of Fraser took over the store in 2005, the name was consigned to history – although locals still affectionately (or perhaps just stubbornly) call it Kendal's. The towering art deco building has been used variously as an air raid shelter and venue for Miss Great Britain, while its make-up counters have appeared on TV programmes from *Corrie* to *Ashes to Ashes*.

Today, Kendal's provides you with two ways to end your walk: in the chichi surroundings of **Tom's Champagne Bar** (third floor) or in the new **San Carlo Cichetti Restaurant** (ground floor; p75), whose Italian tapas dishes mirror the excellent meals churned out by its bigger brother **San Carlo** (p75) across the road.

Kendal's is an appropriate place to finish this walk, as it reflects, in miniature, the constant reinvention of Manchester – a reinvention that almost always comes with a self-conscious nod to the past.

Mark Addy

A world of experience on your doorstep

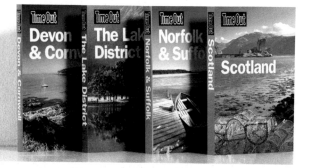

Manchester by Area

John Rylands Library p61

City Centre

The 1996 IRA bomb is often credited with kick-starting the regeneration of Manchester's City Centre. Work had in fact been under way for some years, but the blast that ripped the heart out of the city did provide an unprecedented opportunity to remodel it. The Corn Exchange became the **Triangle** arcade, the **Royal Exchange** got a £30-million facelift, and the much-maligned **Arndale Centre** was overhauled and extended. New public squares were unveiled: **Exchange Square**'s concentric benches now provide a stopping point for shoppers; while **Cathedral Gardens** will soon house the **National Football Museum**.

A glass twist of a footbridge connects **Selfridges** to the Arndale, and just below it sits the postbox that became a symbol of the city's determination to recover from the IRA blast. Despite being within a few feet of the explosion, the postbox somehow survived intact. It stood proud when all around was shattered, and it's a poignant place now to post your postcards.

Manchester's renaissance continues today, albeit at a slower pace. **Spinningfields** is a new district built along the banks of the River Irwell. Home to numerous corporate HQs, it also houses the all-new **People's History Museum**, not to mention several flagship stores along high-end shopping boulevard, The Avenue.

Slotted between Victoria Station and the Triangle, a corner of medieval Manchester lives on. The 15th-century **Chetham's Library** sits above the confluence of the rivers Irk and Irwell. Not far away squats **Manchester Cathedral**, close by Hanging Ditch. Local folklore has it that the ditch refers to the practice of tying a noose around the neck of miscreants and kicking them off the bridge. In truth, it marks the course of the River Irk, where 12th-century fullers (cloth cleaners) would hang their cloth to dry.

Chetham's played a pivotal role during the Industrial Revolution. Manchester became the world's largest centre of manufacturing (nicknamed 'Cottonopolis'), and was rammed with impoverished mill workers. Friedrich Engels and Karl Marx regularly met at Chetham's to discuss what they saw. Between them, they penned two central socialist texts: *The Condition of the Working Classes in England* and the *Communist Manifesto*.

Further toward the south, Alfred Waterhouse's **Town Hall** is a reminder of Manchester's industrial ambition and is one of its most important buildings. Ford Madox Ford's wall murals are particularly notable, but even the corridors, with mosaic floors and vaulted ceilings, are remarkable.

Chetham's isn't the only atmospheric library here. The **John Rylands Library** is a neo-Gothic masterpiece, while the **Portico** leans to the neoclassical. Further down the road is the **Central Library**. This relative newcomer (1934) was once the largest public library in the UK.

Sights & museums

Abraham Lincoln Statue

Lincoln Square, Brazenose Street, M2. Metrolink St Peter's Square, or City Centre buses, or Deansgate or Oxford Road rail. **Map** p58 C4 ❶

An imposing if slightly incongruous presence amid the nearby office blocks, this statue was given to the city in 1919 in recognition of the support that Lincoln received from the citizens of Manchester in his campaign against slavery. It was moved into the City Centre in 1986, from its original location in Platt Fields Park.

Cathedral Gardens

M4. Metrolink Victoria, or City Centre buses, or Victoria rail. **Map** p59 D2 ❷

A windswept patch of open space wedged between the National Football Museum, Chetham's Library, Victoria Station and the Triangle. Its grass slopes (often worn down to bare earth) and layered water features are colonised every Saturday by hordes of teenage alt-rock tribes and pockets of clattering skateboarders, putting the space to vibrant if unpredicted use.

Central Library

St Peter's Square, M2 5PD (234 1900, www.manchester.gov.uk). Metrolink St Peter's Square, or City Centre buses, or Oxford Road rail. **Map** p59 D4 ❸

The Central Library's classical-revival style disguises the fact that it was built only in 1934, since when it has become one of the city's most recognisable landmarks. Its graceful exterior arc makes a photogenic match with the neighbouring sweep of the Town Hall extension. Inside, the circular library is dominated by a domed reading room, whose echoing acoustics make it almost impossible to study in silence. Note that the library qill be closed for renovation until 2013.

Chetham's Library & School of Music

Long Millgate, M3 1SB (834 7961, www.chethams.org.uk). Metrolink Victoria, or City Centre buses, or Victoria rail. **Open** 9am-12.30pm, 1.30-4.30pm Mon-Fri. **Admission** free. **Map** p59 D2 ❹

Chetham's is a stunning piece of the 15th century that has survived more or less intact to the present day, the former college's library and surrounding cloisters exuding an almost tangible sense of history. Within its impressive walls, Karl Marx and adopted Mancunian Friedrich Engels met to research the birth of Communist theory. Reading bays with lockable iron gates (a novel security measure introduced in 1740)

City Centre

0   400 m
0   400 yds
© Copyright Time Out Group 2011

SALFORD pp135-142

CASTLEFIELD & DEANSGATE LOCKS pp128-134

Salford Cathedral

People's History Museum

Civil Justice Centre

Manchester Crown Court

Magistrates & Coroners Court

John Rylan Library

SPINNINGFIELDS

Opera House

Free Trade Hall

MOSI (Museum of Science & Industry)

St Johns Gardens

Great Northern Square

Air & Space Gallery

Manchester Central Convention Complex

Legend:
- ① Sights & museums
- ① Eating & drinking
- ① Shopping
- ① Nightlife
- ① Arts & leisure

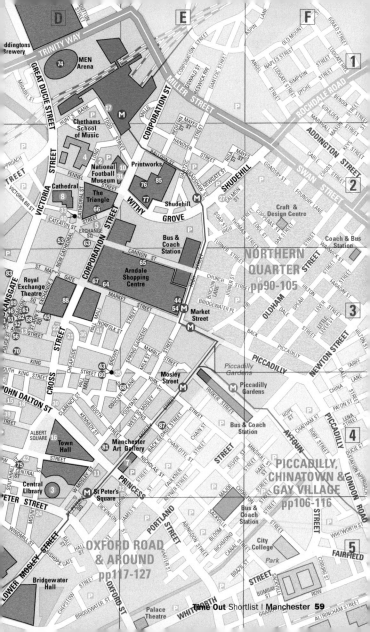

John Rylands Library

are a feature. This is a functioning library (and the oldest in the English-speaking world), so always ring ahead to check all rooms are available to visit. Weekly guided tours take in further buildings – booking well in advance is recommended. The adjoining school of music is the largest of its kind in the UK and puts on 100 public performances a year, plus free lunchtime concerts most weekdays.

Exchange Square

M4. Metrolink Victoria, or City Centre buses, or Victoria rail. **Map** p59 D2 ⑤
Another of the new spaces afforded by the bomb, Exchange Square has rows of amphitheatre seating (with decorative metal bars to spoil the fun of more adventurous skateboarders) arranged, like living-room furniture around a television, to face the Triangle's big screen. A playful water feature is occasionally given the washing-up liquid treatment by mischievous youths. Surrounded as the square is by shopping centres (the Arndale, Selfridges, the Triangle), and enlivened by occasional public events, there's no danger of anyone using it to get a rest, but it's an inventive communal space.

John Rylands Library

150 Deansgate, M3 3EH (306 0555, www.manchester.ac.uk/ library). Metrolink St Peter's Square, or City Centre buses, or Deansgate rail. **Open** noon-5pm Mon, Sun; 10am-5pm Tue-Sat. **Admission** free. **Map** p58 C4 ⑥
Despite giving the impression of near-medieval antiquity, this glorious building is in fact just over a century old, having first opened in 1900. Among its astonishing treasures is the world's oldest surviving fragment of the New Testament. Hands-on activities, touch-screen digital displays and a changing programme of exhibitions all bring artefacts to life, while the guided tours are highly recommended. See box, right.

Literary treasures

A neo-Gothic cathedral to learning that speaks volumes about Manchester's grand industrial past, the **John Rylands Library** was built in 1900 in memory of one of the city's many cotton magnates. It's a building that proves the theory that, during the Industrial Revolution at least, money really was no object. The interior is a heady mix of stonework, stained glass and ornate bookcases, all clustered around a cavernous reading room, while the unusual red sandstone exterior has long made the library a striking fixture on Deansgate.

The original building wasn't without its problems, though: a leaky roof, wheelchair-unfriendly steps and an intimidating entrance conspired to keep visitors away. A £16.8 million redevelopment in 2007 saw both the restoration of the building's original features and the inclusion of a new visitor wing. Linking the library, visually at least, to the new-builds of Spinningfields opposite, this glass-fronted entry houses a small shop and café, and provides full disabled access to the rest of the building. Best of all is the improved access to the collection – which is, after all, the real draw. Spanning five millennia and including the St John Fragment, the world's oldest known surviving New Testament text, and a selection of William Caxton's books from the 15th-century revolution in printing, 'breathtaking' doesn't begin to cover it.
■ Listings, see left.

MANCHESTER BY AREA

NATIONAL
FOOTBALL
MUSEUM
DRAMA
HISTORY
SKILL
ART
FAITH
STYLE
PASSION
FOOTBALL

OPENING SOON

The National Football Museum is coming to Manchester
Urbis Building, Cathedral Gardens, Manchester M4 3BG
www.nationalfootballmuseum.com

Manchester City Council is providing transitional funding for the redevelopment
of the National Football Museum.

Image courtesy of Homes of Football.

People's History Museum

People's History Museum

In 2010, after a £12.5 million development that included the construction of a new wing and the overhaul of the Grade II-listed Pump House, the People's History Museum reopened, its stated aim to tell the story of the 200-year march towards British democracy. So far, so worthy, right? Not a bit of it. This is a museum that handles political reform lightly, bringing historical fact to life via a range of unusual exhibits, from a Clarion Club café hidden inside a cupboard to a table where you make up flat-pack boxes – and then work out how little you'd be paid if you were a 19th-century homeworker eking out a living this way.

The museum building itself is a showstopper. Made of Corten steel, its striking rusted façade provides a contrast to its shinier glass-and-steel neighbours. And form follows function: the museum's windowless upper floors are wrapped in steel to provide the climate-controlled home for a collection that includes the world's largest assemblage of political protest banners.

The ground floor is, however, glass-fronted, enticing passers-by inside and providing the building's hub (this is where you'll find the riverfront café, for example). The Museum has doubled in size, allowing more of its collection to be on display, while temporary and permanent exhibitions trace a path through two centuries of political campaigning, from the Suffragettes to the Trade Unions.

Manchester is rightly proud of the museum – this is a city that has seen more than its fair share of political reform, and the story of British politics is often a Mancunian one (the city is the birthplace of socialism, universal suffrage and the global co-operative movement; it's also where Marx and Engels drafted the *Communist Manifesto*). Discover just how far Britain has travelled in 200 years, or at the very least sample the wartime-inspired menu and (possibly) the city's largest selection of home-made cakes in its café – either way, democracy never tasted so good.

■ Listings p67.

MANCHESTER BY AREA

Manchester Art Gallery

Mosley Street, M2 3JL (235 8888, www.manchestergalleries.org). Metrolink Mosley Street, or City Centre buses, or Piccadilly rail. **Open** 10am-5pm Tue-Sun. **Admission** free. **Map** p59 E4 ❼

The gallery is home to some stunning Pre-Raphaelite art; highlights from the three floors of its permanent collection include Rossetti's *Astarte Syriaca*, notable pieces by Modigliani and Turner, and a superb collection of Impressionist paintings of early 20th-century Manchester by the underrated Adolphe Valette, Lowry's early art teacher. There is also a programme of international exhibitions. The building itself, designed by Charles Barry in 1824, had a £35 million extension and refit in 2002, letting in more light, and opening a new wing and interactive children's gallery. A good café, restaurant and shop round out the mix.

Manchester Cathedral

Cathedral Yard, M3 1SX (833 2220, www.manchestercathedral.org). Metrolink Victoria, or City Centre buses, or Victoria rail. **Open** 9am-5.30pm daily. Times vary Easter, Aug, Christmas. **Admission** free. **Map** p59 D2 ❽

A church building of some description has existed on this site since the first millennium, and the present cathedral has adapted to damage inflicted variously during the Civil War, from a direct hit from German bombers in 1941 and by the IRA bomb of 1996. Of particular note is the beautiful wooden roof, the Anglo-Saxon Angel Stone (possibly a survival from an earlier church on the site) and the stained-glass Fire Window, which evocatively bleeds flame-coloured light into the Regimental Chapel.

Manchester Central Convention Complex

Off Lower Mosley Street, M2 3GX (834 2700, www.manchestercentral. co.uk). Metrolink Deansgate-Castlefield, or City Centre buses, or Deansgate rail. **Map** p59 D5 ❾

This site was the city's third main station (Central Station) in the late 19th century, which closed shortly after the railway line became obsolete in 1969. In 1986, the building was resurrected as G-Mex (Greater Manchester Exhibition centre) hosting sports and trade events. It was also used as a concert venue – the Smiths and Oasis played here – before the MEN Arena usurped that role. Now with an attached conference centre (previously a separate entity), the place was rebranded and opened as Manchester Central in 2007. It regularly hosts major international events and political conferences.

National Football Museum

NEW *Cathedral Gardens, M4 3BG (www.nationalfootballmuseum.com). Metrolink Victoria, or City Centre buses, or Victoria rail.* **Open** see website for details. **Admission** see website for details. **Map** p59 E2 ❿

Although the National Football Museum's move to Manchester (from Preston) has not been without controversy, it seems fitting that Manchester, a city known the world over for its footballing prowess, will soon be its home. Due to open in late 2011, the museum holds both the FIFA and FA collections, including the hallowed ball used in that World Cup final (1966, if you must ask), while changing exhibitions will add interest to permanent displays. The museum itself is housed inside Urbis, once Manchester's ill-fated 'museum of the city', a striking glass building that is being given an £8 million overhaul in readiness for its latest incarnation as the home of British football.

Peace Garden

St Peter's Square, M2. Metrolink St Peter's Square, or City Centre buses, or Oxford Road rail. **Map** p59 D4 ⓫

Manchester became the world's first nuclear-free city, in 1980, at the height of world nuclear paranoia. Today, the world may be no safer and the garden isn't especially peaceful, bordered as it

National Football Museum

is by a busy bus route and tramline. Still, centred around the *Messenger of Peace* statue and sheltered by the Town Hall, it offers occasional lunchtime refuge for office workers – and pigeons.

People's History Museum

NEW *Left Bank, Spinningfields, M3 3ER (838 9190, www.phm.org.uk). Metrolink St Peter's Square, or City Centre buses, or Salford Central rail.* **Open** 10am-5pm daily. **Admission** free. **Map** p58 B3 ⑫
Reopened in 2010 after a £12.5 million development, Manchester's only national museum is dedicated to telling a 200-year tale of British democracy. Dry and dusty it isn't: interactive exhibits bring political history to life, while a brand-new wing, fused to the Grade II-listed Pump House and complete with a sunny riverside café, lets light flood inside. See box p63.

St Ann's Church

St Ann Street, St Ann's Square, M2 7LF (834 0239, www.stannsmanchester.com). Metrolink St Peter's Square, or City Centre buses, or Victoria rail. **Open** 9.45am-4.45pm Mon-Sat; 8.30am-4.45pm Sun. **Admission** free. **Map** p59 D3 ⑬
Manchester Cathedral (p64) and this church (built in 1712) have long been the two focal points of surviving old Manchester; indeed, the tower of St Ann's is said to mark the geographical centre of the old city. Despite now being swallowed up by the various surrounding temples of commerce, it remains a likeable and visible presence, hosting services and free concert recitals.

St John's Gardens

Lower Byrom Street, M3. Metrolink Deansgate-Castlefield, or City Centre buses, or Deansgate rail. **Map** p58 B5 ⑭
This nicely laid-out green oasis on the site of the demolished St John's church makes for a pleasant place to relax after a Castlefield museum visit. A central memorial cross calmly notes that 'around lie the remains of more than 22,000 people'.

St Mary's (The Hidden Gem)

Mulberry Street, M2 6LN (834 3547, http://hiddengem.catholicfaith.co.uk). Metrolink St Peter's Square, or City Centre buses, or Deansgate or Oxford Road rail. **Open** 10am-4pm Mon-Sat. *Exposition* 10am-4pm Mon-Sat. *Mass* 12.30pm Mon-Fri; noon, 5.15pm Sat; 10.15am, noon Sun. **Admission** free. **Map** p59 D4 ⑮
The aptly named Hidden Gem – founded in 1794 and claimed to be the oldest post-Reformation Catholic church in the country – is approached either from the drably unimaginative Brazennose Street or, more enticingly, via a pair of decorated alleyways leading from John Dalton Street. Outside, an impressively sculpted stone arch haloes the entrance doorway, while inside, Royal Academician Norman Adams' beautiful *Stations of the Cross* series of paintings adorns the walls. It's a busy functioning church, so visitors should show discretion if just sightseeing. Check ahead for times of services.

Town Hall

Albert Square, M60 2LA (234 5000, www.manchester.gov.uk). Metrolink St Peter's Square, or City Centre buses, or Oxford Road rail. **Open** *Albert Square reception* 9am-5pm Mon-Fri. **Admission** free. **Map** p59 D4 ⑯
Alfred Waterhouse's building, completed in 1887, remains a proud symbol of the city. Its imposing halls, host to a range of statuary, city council staff and civic wedding ceremonies, are usually, but not always, open to the public – ring ahead to check. Visitors are normally free to visit the ground floor Sculpture Hall (which also hosts occasional art exhibitions) and, on the first floor, the Great Hall, which features a noted series of 12 Ford Madox Brown murals. Still home to numerous council offices, much of the rest of the building is closed to the public for security reasons, but guided tours are available by appointment from the Visitor Information Centre (p108).

Marketing Manchester

Everyone likes a bargain, but Manchester's markets are about more than six pairs of socks for a pound. In fact, the City Centre's markets have experienced a resurgence of late, bucking the lingering recession by offering the kind of personal service that anonymous high-street chains just can't match. The specialist markets held sporadically throughout the year are highly recommended – in particular, the **Fine Food Market** (October), the sprawling **Spring Markets** (May-June) and the ever-expanding **Christmas markets** (November-December) – you'll see stalls dotted throughout the City Centre during these periods.

If you do happen to venture into Manchester outside these times, chances are you'll come across one of its weekly markets. The recently refurbished **Arndale Market** (p77), which was once a grim repository of cheap tat, now offers speciality teas, organic breads, hot food and crafts – all under one (waterproof) roof. **Piccadilly Gardens**, meanwhile, plays host to a range of weekend markets, from the **Fashion Market** (Tib Street, 10am-5pm Sat), which

allows you to browse one-off jewellery, vintage clothes, bags and handmade clothing, to the **Flower Market** (Piccadilly Gardens, 10am-6pm Thur-Sat) and the fortnightly **Real Food Market** (Piccadilly Gardens, 1st & 4th weekend of the month, 10am-6pm Fri, Sat). If you like to know the name of the goat that produced the milk for your cheese, this is the place to shop.

For a traditional vibe, visit the small, bustling **Longsight Market** (Dickenson Road, Longsight, 9am-4.30pm Wed, Fri, 9am-5pm Sat) for cheery fashions, plus meat, veg and exotic spices, while for a slice of second-hand heaven, its dedicated **vintage market** (9am-4pm Tue) offers second-hand goods at flea-market prices.

If size is your priority, then **Bury Market** (Murray Road, Bury, 9am-5pm Wed, Fri, Sat) – the biggest market in the North West, and just a 20-minute drive from Manchester City Centre – should fit the bill. With a history stretching back 500 years, and arguably the best black pudding in the country, the market draws 250,000 shoppers here every week for good reason.

■ For more on the city's markets, visit www.manchestermarkets.com.

Victoria Station

*Todd Street, Station Approach, M3
1PB. Metrolink Victoria, or City Centre
buses, or Victoria rail.* **Map** p59 D1 ⊕
Signs of its former splendour remain –
the lovely tiled map of the Lancashire
and Yorkshire Railway on the entrance
walls, the wood-panelled ticket offices –
but lately Victoria Station has felt
distinctly shabby, its roof perpetually
cupped by a safety net to catch any
collapses. Thankfully, a £25 million
restoration scheme, including new roof
and refurb of the original façade and station mosaics, is to be carried out over the
next few years. Regional rail services
and the Metrolink run from here, and
the Manchester Evening News (MEN)
Arena is accessed from the main plaza.

Eating & drinking

Ape & Apple

*28-30 John Dalton Street, M2 6HQ
(839 9624). Metrolink St Peter's
Square, or City Centre buses, or Oxford
Road rail.* **Open** noon-11pm Mon-Thur;
noon-midnight Fri, Sat; noon-9pm Sun.
Pub. Map p59 D4 ⊕
A pub of solid Victorian stock, this is
the City Centre bastion for local brew-
ers Holts, who still manage to produce
an excellent bitter for around £2 a
pint. There's a large bar menu, separate dining room upstairs and quaint
beer garden out back. Refurbished in
mid-2006, the pub is a bit on the bright
side, but it shouldn't be long before that
rich patina of a true pub returns.

Briton's Protection

*50 Great Bridgewater Street, M1
5LE (236 5895). Metrolink Deansgate-
Castlefield, or City Centre buses,
or Deansgate rail.* **Open** 11am-11pm
Mon-Thur; 11am-midnight Fri; noon-
midnight Sat; noon-10.30pm Sun. **Pub.
Map** p58 C5 ⊕
Like moths to a flame, drinkers are
drawn to the Briton's Protection by the
red neon sign over the door. The roomy
interior is pub perfection: brass fixtures

and fittings, and paintings commemorating the 1819 Peterloo Massacre.
(See if you can spot the two football
managers who feature in the paintings.) At lunchtime, punters are mostly
business people; later on, Bridgewater
Hall concertgoers sneaking in a pre-
show quickie. Brews from Jennings
and Robinson's are the staples, but the
real attractions are the 150-plus
whiskies and bourbons.

Carluccio's

*3 Hardman Square, M3 3AQ (839
0623, www.carluccios.com). Metrolink
St Peter's Square, or City Centre buses,
or Salford Central rail.* **Open** 8am-11pm
Mon-Fri; 9am-11pm Sat; 9am-10.30pm
Sun. **££. Italian. Map** p58 B4 ⊕
The Spinningfields branch of the
authentic Italian lover's chain of choice,
caters largely to lunch-breakers from
the nearby complex of corporate
offices. At weekends and on evenings,
though, particularly during warmer
months, the restaurant is a haven for
families thanks to a child-friendly
menu, outdoor seating and the best
lemonade in Manchester. Special mention should go to the takeaway picnic
baskets that they put together to keep
moviegoers sated during the annual
'Screenfields' season of outdoor film
showings nearby.

Chaophraya

*19 Chapel Walks, M2 1HN
(832 8342, www.chaophraya.co.uk).
Metrolink St Peter's Square, or City
Centre buses, or Victoria rail.* **Open**
noon-4.30pm, 5-11.30pm daily. **£££.
Thai. Map** p59 D3 ⊕
Chaophraya might be decorated with
the standard array of orchids, Buddha
statuettes and bamboo that charac-
terises Thai eateries, but the food is
anything but usual. From tried and
tested favourites such as *gang kiew wan*
(green curry) to uncommon fare such as
sorng pee norng (sea bass in tamarind
and chilli sauce) the menu is packed
with genuine flavour. Herbivores can

Sam's Chop House p74

rejoice, too, as *The Times* recently named Chaophraya the best vegetarian restaurant in the UK.

Corbieres

2 Half Moon Street, M2 7PB (834 3381). Metrolink St Peter's Square, or City Centre buses, or Victoria rail. **Open** 11.30am-11pm Mon-Thur; 11.30am-midnight Fri, Sat; noon-10.30pm Sun. **Bar**. **Map** p59 D3 ㉒

Corbieres is one of those perplexing places that you go into for one drink and end up leaving five hours later, slightly the worse for wear and wondering where the time went. It is one of those places where time really does stand still, which may be due to its subterranean position. It also claims to have the best jukebox in Manchester, something that the groups of dancing drinkers that regularly fill the place near to closing time will testify to.

Evuna

277-279 Deansgate, M3 4EW (819 2752, www.evuna.com). Metrolink Deansgate-Castlefield, or City Centre buses, or Deansgate rail. **Open** 11am-11pm Mon-Sat; 1-9pm Sun. **££**. **Spanish**. **Map** p58 C5 ㉓

Spanish restaurant Evuna is a must for oenophiles: it doubles as a wine merchant, selling some cracking Spanish bottles (and cases), and even has its own wine club. A particular highlight is the Coma Vella, a belting red that went down a treat with the sea bass baked in rock salt. You're also encouraged to share dishes, making this a fantastic place for groups.

French

Midland Hotel, Peter Street, M60 2DS (236 3333, www.qhotels.co.uk). Metrolink St Peter's Square, or City Centre buses, or Oxford Road rail. **Open** 7-10pm Tue-Sat. **£££**. **French**. **Map** p59 D5 ㉔

Over the years, this restaurant has built a reputation deserving of its definitive Gallic moniker. Indeed, a fair few years ago, it was the recipient of not just

Manchester's but also the country's first Michelin star; although that honour has since been consigned to the history books, the food still shines. It may not be a buzz restaurant these days, but little can rival French's chateaubriand or its richly refined surroundings.

Gaucho Grill

2a St Mary's Street, M3 2LB (833 4333, www.gauchorestaurants.co.uk). Metrolink Market Street, or City Centre buses, or Victoria rail. **Open** noon-10.30pm Mon-Thur, Sun; noon-11.30pm Fri, Sat. **£££**. **South American**. **Map** p58 C3 ㉕

Gaucho Grill or Grill on the Alley? Let the Steak Wars commence. Argentinian cuisine doesn't often top 'must-try' lists but Gaucho suggests it's worth attention. Starters range from salads to an array of ceviches, and the Argentinian beef steaks are served with one of seven sauces and a full choice of side dishes. With a well-chosen wine list that focuses on South America, and a lunchtime tasting menu, Gaucho is a real treat.

Grill on the Alley

5 Ridgefield, M2 6EG (833 3465, www.blackhouse.uk.com). Metrolink St Peter's Square, or Salford Central rail. **Open** noon-11pm daily. **£££**. **Grill**. **Map** p58 C4 ㉖

Mancunians don't often get a chance to barbecue, so the Grill is a welcome arrival with its food cooked over open flame to seal in moisture. You can choose from the lobsters that float placidly in their tank or from the display of fresh fish – there's even a chance to sample the notorious beer-fed and massaged Kobe beef. Complete the feast with a split, a delicious fruity milkshake.

Hare & Hounds

46 Shudehill, M4 4AA (832 4737). Metrolink Shudehill, or City Centre buses, or Victoria rail. **Open** 11am-11pm Mon-Sat; noon-10.30pm Sun. **Pub**. **Map** p59 E2 ㉗

This Grade II-listed building first opened as licensed premises in 1778; between the wooden panels, tiles and bar service bells, it's obvious that not much has changed since. Old-fashioned singalongs will sometimes take place around the piano, while the upstairs room looks like it has remained the same since it played host to the socialist debates of last century. And, of course, we'd be remiss not to mention the pub's home-produced pickled eggs.

Katsouris Deli

113 Deansgate, M3 2BQ (819 1260). Metrolink St Peter's Square, or City Centre buses, or Salford Central rail. **Open** *7am-4.30pm Mon-Fri; 9am-5.30pm Sat; 9am-4pm Sun.* **£.** **Deli-café.** **Map** p58 C4 ㉘

Katsouris has descended from Bury Market to bring City Centre punters the sandwiches they deserve. The salad bar offers healthy options, but it's the cakes and roast-meat sandwiches that really appeal. The chicken piri piri sandwich is an entire world of flavour for under £3.

Koreana

40a King Street West, M3 2WY (832 4330, www.koreana.co.uk). Metrolink St Peter's Square, or City Centre buses, or Salford Central or Victoria rail. **Open** *noon-2.30pm, 6.30-10.30pm Mon-Thur; noon-2.30pm, 6.30-11pm Fri; 5.30-11pm Sat.* **££.** **Korean.** **Map** p58 C3 ㉙

Operating since 1985, and much loved by critics and customers, Koreana still manages to have the feel of an undiscovered gem. Korean food has spicier flavours than Cantonese cuisine, and traditionally starters, soups and mains are served simultaneously. Koreana has a great special where for £15 per head you can feast on pork, squid and even a kimchi hotpot, consisting of fermented vegetables and chilli peppers.

Lounge Ten

10 Tib Lane, M2 4JB (834 1331, www.lounge10manchester.co.uk). Metrolink St Peter's Square, or City

Centre buses, or Victoria rail. **Open** *noon-10.30pm Mon-Thur; noon-11.30pm Fri, Sat.* **£££.** **Modern International.** **Map** p59 D4 ㉚

Lounge Ten exudes the decadent glamour and debauched sophistication of a turn-of-the-century Parisian cabaret club, yet still remains unmistakably Mancunian. The former home of the infamous Friday Supper Clubs, there's nowhere else you can feast on a tender breast (duck or turkey, naturally), a glass of champagne and live jazz in surroundings befitting a Roman orgy.

Modern

National Football Museum, Levels 5 & 6, Cathedral Gardens, M4 3BG (605 8282, www.themodernmcr.co.uk). Metrolink Victoria, or City Centre buses, or Victoria rail. **Open** *noon-3pm, 5-10pm Mon-Sat; noon-3pm Sun.* **£££.** **Modern British.** **Map** p59 D2 ㉛

The Modern combines a cracking menu with unparalleled views, so it's little wonder that the eaterie walked away with the Restaurant of the Year award at the 2009 Manchester Food and Drink Festival. Try the salt beef potato cake from the regionally sourced – and reasonably priced – Tastes of Manchester menu before sampling the lethal but delicious Hemingway daiquiri from the extensive cocktail list. And, with the National Football Museum opening downstairs in 2011, the upper level bar will soon provide the perfect place to stop off for a half-time beer and gourmet sausage roll.

Obsidian

Arora International Hotel, 18-24 Princess Street, M1 4LY (238 4348, www.obsidianmanchester.co.uk). Metrolink St Peter's Square, or City Centre buses, or Oxford Road rail. **Open** *noon-2pm, 5-10pm Mon-Sat; noon-6pm Sun.* **£££.** **Fine dining.** **Map** p59 D4/E4 ㉜

This restaurant and bar are located within the chic Arora International hotel (p173), but Obsidian is just as popular

Lounge Ten

with the Manc crowd as it is with expense-accounting visitors to the city. Bar staff boast an ability to mix bespoke cocktails and, while the surroundings are plush, they are not off-puttingly so. Dishes with a strong seasonal emphasis, such as Cheshire rib-eye steak and roast chicken with Jersey royals, are both recognisable and flavoursome, while a regularly refreshed cheeseboard features eight varieties of local, British and continental cheeses.

Old Wellington Inn/ Sinclair's Oyster Bar

4/2 Cathedral Gates, M3 1SW (834 0430). Metrolink Victoria, or City Centre buses, or Victoria rail. **Open** 11am-11pm Mon-Sat; noon-10.30pm Sun. **Pub. Map** p59 D2 ㉝

It's impossible to separate these two icons of the Mancunian spirit, joined as they are at the hip. Having survived all that was thrown at them by the Luftwaffe, they were then threatened by the wrecking ball in the late 1970s before inspired engineering intervened to allow both pubs to be raised several feet and various concrete monstrosities to be built around them. Ironically, it was this concrete that saved the pubs from another bomb, this time courtesy of the IRA in 1996. In the aftermath, the pubs were dismantled and moved some 300 metres to their current position, an upheaval that has only served to enhance their charmingly wonky appearances.

The Wellington is a free house dating back to the early 1500s, while Sinclair's is a couple of hundred years younger. Now owned by Samuel Smiths, it has an excellent downstairs seafood bar, although one lacking in oysters, despite the name. The pubs share an immense outdoor drinking area.

Opus One

Free Trade Hall (Radisson Edwardian Hotel), Peter Street, M2 5GP (835 8904, www.radissonedwardian.com). Metrolink St Peter's Square, or City Centre buses, or Oxford Road rail. **Open** 6-10.30pm Mon-Sat. **£££. Modern International. Map** p59 D5 ㉞

Opus One presents a unique opportunity to sip cocktails under the same roof where the Suffragettes first unfurled their 'votes for women' banner and Dylan was branded a folkie Judas. The luxurious decor, as well as the fabulous, and fabulously arranged, food has made the restaurant popular among Manchester's nouveau riche. With few dishes breaking the £20 barrier, though, a career in professional football is not a prerequisite for enjoying dinner here.

Room

81 King Street, M2 4ST (839 2005, www.roomrestaurants.com). Metrolink Market Street or Mosley Street, or City Centre buses, or Piccadilly rail. **Open** *Restaurant* noon-10pm Mon-Sat. *Bar* noon-11pm Mon-Wed; noon-midnight Thur; noon-2am Fri, Sat. **££. Retro. Map** p59 D3/E3 ㉟

Taking its inspiration from the infamous dishes of the '70s, Room's mission is to put the kitsch back into the kitchen. That might sound awful but fortunately Room takes classics, such as Lancashire hotpot and toad-in-the-hole, and brings them kicking and screaming into the 21st century, proving that the old(ish) ones are (sometimes) the best ones.

Sam's Chop House

Chapel Walks, M2 1HN (834 3210, www.samschophouse.co.uk). Metrolink St Peter's Square, or City Centre buses, or Victoria rail. **Open** noon-3pm, 5.30-9.30pm Mon-Sat; noon-8pm Sun. **££. British. Map** p59 D3 ㊱

If you fancy traditional British cooking, then Sam's is the place to go. It might be a beautiful old pub, but you don't go there for the Victorian tiles. Menu highlights include brown onion soup, dumplings, roast beef, corned beef hash, and steak and kidney pudding. Don't forget to leave room for dessert: the steamed lemon sponge with custard will make you weak at the knees.

San Carlo

King Street West, M3 2WY (834 6226, www.sancarlo.co.uk). Metrolink St Peter's Square, or City Centre buses, or Salford Central rail. **Open** noon-11pm daily. **££. Italian. Map** p58 C3 ③⑦

Big, busy and perennially popular, San Carlo has been dishing up traditional Italian fare for almost two decades. Although it may be part of a chain, the Manchester branch doesn't compromise on either quality or flair. Sure, pizza and pasta feature on the menu, but the real draws here are simple, well-executed dishes such as a sublime fish platter, pan-fried chicken and *tonno alla siciliana* (tuna medallions in olive oil, white wine and butter). A tapas-style outlet recently opened across the road (see below) but, despite creating its own competition, San Carlo remains one of the city's best bets for a good dish out.

San Carlo Cicchetti

[NEW] *Ground Floor, House of Fraser, 60 Deansgate, M60 3AU (839 2233, www.sancarlocicchetti.co.uk). Metrolink Market Street or St Peter's Square, or City Centre buses, or Victoria rail.* **Open** 8am-11pm Mon-Fri; 9am-11pm Sat, Sun. **££. Italian. Map** p58 C3 ③⑧

Partly trading on the success of its big brother across the road, this tiny Italian restaurant is tucked unobtrusively into the corner of a 175-year-old department store. Discreet waiter service and marble-topped tables contrast nicely with an informal tapas bar that runs one length of the L-shaped eaterie; both serve small Italian dishes such as lobster ravioli, breaded baby mozzarella and traditional crostini. Open for breakfast, lunch and dinner, and frequented by well-heeled shoppers, this is a gem of a place, perfect for a post-shop coffee or dinner *à deux*.

Shlurp

2 Brazennose Street, M2 5BP (839 5199, www.shlurp.co.uk). Metrolink St Peter's Square, or City Centre buses, *or Deansgate or Oxford Road rail.* **Open** 7.30am-3pm Mon-Fri. **£. Soup. Map** p59 D4 ③⑨

If you tell your bank manager that you're starting a business and that the unique selling point of said business is soup, then they'll probably tell you that the soup had better be good. Fortunately for Shlurp, their soups are very, very good indeed. The Asian chicken is great for warming you up on a raw, wet Manchester day, and the smoked haddock and corn chowder soup has won an award from the Guild of Fine Food Retailers. Everything is prepared in-house using fresh ingredients, including the dressings and meats. You can also get early morning bagels and coffee.

Sinclair's Oyster Bar

2 Cathedral Gates, M3 1SW (0871 207 1737). Metrolink Victoria, or City Centre buses, or Victoria rail. **Open** 11am-11pm Mon-Sat; noon-10.30pm Sun. **Pub. Map** p59 D2 ④⓪

For review, see p74 Old Wellington Inn.

Stock

4 Norfolk Street, M2 1DW (839 6644, www.stockrestaurant.co.uk). Metrolink Market Street, or City Centre buses, or Victoria rail. **Open** noon-2.30pm, 5.30-10pm Mon-Sat. **£££. Italian. Map** p59 D3 ④①

Stock's name and its imposing atmosphere survive from the building's previous incarnation as Manchester's stock exchange. Hard as the venue is to match, the menu nonetheless rivals it for stature. The pan-fried calf's liver with pancetta and crushed potatoes is particularly wonderful, and there are some excellent Italian wines from which to choose.

Tampopo

16 Albert Square, M2 5PF (819 1966, www.tampopo.co.uk). Metrolink St Peter's Square, or City Centre buses, or Oxford Road rail. **Open** noon-11pm Mon-Sat; noon-10pm Sun. **££. Eastern. Map** p59 D4 ④②

MANCHESTER BY AREA

Shopping central

St Ann's Passage

The **Exchange Square area** was entirely rebuilt after the 1996 bomb, and now attracts some of the biggest names in fashion. Stores on **New Cathedral Street** include Hobbs, Reiss, LK Bennett and Ted Baker, book-ended by a vast Zara and an M&S.

The **Arndale**, part monstrosity of 1970s planning, part rebuilt 21st-century mall, houses almost every significant high-street chain in Britain; and if they're not here, they'll be on nearby **Market Street**. The glittering **Arndale Extension** opened in 2006, with a huge Next department store, a new market area and more popular high-street brands such as Lush cosmetics, Waterstone's and Topshop.

In **St Ann's Square** things start getting pricier. It's home to three shopping arcades, the small **St Ann's Passage**, the jewel-like **Victorian Barton Arcade** and the **Royal Exchange Arcade**. The square offers a fountain and concrete benches, and often hosts temporary seasonal markets. Shops include Kurt Geiger, French Connection and Links of London.

Once *the* destination for designer shoppers, **King Street** is making a post-recession comeback.

It's got a new lease of life thanks to the eclectic mixture of small chains and individual shops that have joined the high-street fashion stores that stayed. This broad range of retailers suits the jumble of architectural styles, mixing Tudor façades and Georgian townhouses.

Manchester's wealthy business district, **Spinningfields**, is bracketed by the avant-garde Civil Justice Centre (aka 'the filing cabinet'), and **The Avenue**, a pedestrianised street attracting well-heeled Mancunians with its parade of high-end shops. As these include Armani, Mulberry, LK Bennett and Flannels, it's clear that the precinct has usurped King Street as the city's luxury retail quarter.

Relatively few must-visit shops line the **Albert Square area** – it's largely business around here. But **Bridge Street** offers several designer menswear shops to kit out those who work in its environs.

One of the city's main arterial roads, the mile-long **Deansgate** runs from Castlefield to the Cathedral. Shopping is relatively sparse at the far ends, but its mid-point is characterised by luxury furniture stores and outdoor clothing specialists.

Despite its subterranean location, Tampopo has a very light and airy feel, and the shared benches and tables give the restaurant a real buzz when the place is full. Rather than restricting, Tampopo's menu incorporates tastes from Japan, Malaysia, Indonesia and other Eastern destinations to deliver a Most Wanted of the region's cooking.

Shopping

For an overview of shopping districts in the City Centre, see box opposite.

Agent Provocateur

Unit GA, Manchester Club, 81 King Street, M2 4ST (833 3735, www.agent provocateur.com). Metrolink St Peter's Square, or City Centre buses, or Victoria rail. **Open** 10am-6pm Mon-Sat.
Map p59 D3 ㊸
One word: gorgeous. (For men, the one word is 'phwoar'.) But there's nothing sleazy about AP's beautifully constructed lingerie. The shop's interior suits the ethos perfectly, with lush carpet, glass cases featuring jewelled riding crops and the familiar blush-pink and black colour scheme. The changing room is worth a visit for the candlelit four-poster, birdcages and chandeliers offering a brief glimpse of what your life could be like if you buy those pricey knickers.

Arndale Market

Arndale Centre, 49 High Street, M4 3AH (832 3552, www.arndale market.co.uk). Metrolink Market Street, or City Centre buses, or Victoria rail. **Open** 9am-6pm Mon-Sat; 11am-5pm Sun. **Map** p59 E3 ㊹
See box p68.

C Aston

Unit 8, Royal Exchange Arcade, M2 7EA (832 7895). Metrolink Market Street, or City Centre buses, or Victoria rail. 9am-5.30pm Mon-Sat. **Map** p59 D3 ㊺
There are very few good reasons not to give up smoking, but this shop is one of them. Its smell immediately transports you to Havana, and the place offers every esoteric kind of cigarette, including a vast range of flavoured tobaccos, pipes, and Habanas in painted boxes. Even if you smoke only once a year, you may be tempted by the glittering Zippo displays, the Swiss army knives, or the giant-size rolling papers. Now why ever would they be of interest?

Cocu & Chadwick

11 & 12 Barton Arcade, M3 2BB (832 8032, www.cocuandchadwick.com). Metrolink Market Street, or City Centre buses, or Victoria rail. **Open** 10.30am-6pm Mon-Sat; 11am-4pm Sun.
Map p59 D3 ㊻
Resembling an Edwardian boudoir, with its gilt chaise and sweeping silk curtains, Cocu & Chadwick is devoted to corsetry. And rightly so – their structured pieces in jewel colours will create waists from wet dough, make balloons out of bee-stings, and bestow the gift of confidence on all who wear these be-ribboned, satin masterpieces. The store's philosophy lends itself perfectly to wedding dresses – they also design elegant bespoke bridal wear.

Duo

20-22 King Street, M2 6AG (819 1229, www.duoboots.com) Metrolink Deansgate-Castlefield, or City Centre buses, or Victoria rail. **Open** 10am-6pm Mon-Sat; 11am-5pm Sun. **Map** p59 D3 ㊼
Originally a mail-order company, Duo has expanded to the high street, and Manchester is home to one of only four of its physical shops. If you can't afford made-to-measure footwear, this is the next best thing. Here, staff measure calves as well as feet to provide perfectly-fitted, well-crafted women's boots. With enormous ornate mirrors and flock wallpaper, Duo's King Street store feels like a boutique hotel. Put your feet up and relax while you're measured – and walk away with a pair of boots that traipse all over the high-street theory that one size fits all.

MANCHESTER BY AREA

Elite

35 King Street West, M3 2PW (832 3670, www.elitedressagency.co.uk). Metrolink St Peter's Square, or City Centre buses, or Salford Central or Victoria rail. **Open** 10am-5pm Mon-Sat; 11am-4pm Sun. **Map** p58 C3 ㊽

This place should still be a secret but now it's not, because the Elite Dress Agency has been clothing Manchester's best turned-out for years. It carries a rapidly changing stock of barely-worn designer clothes; aficionados can snap up DKNY, Prada and Miu Miu for a fraction of the original price, or seek out more obscure US or European pieces, alongside Jimmy Choos and last season's It-bags. Packed rails and regular sales mean it's almost impossible to leave empty-handed.

Face Stockholm

6 King Street, M2 6AQ (831 9808, www.facestockholm.com). Metrolink Deansgate-Castlefield, or City Centre buses, or Victoria rail. **Open** 10am-6pm Mon-Sat; 11am-4pm Sun. **Map** p58 C3 ㊾

Manchester is home to Face Stockholm's only UK store. If a fake tan isn't your thing and you prefer to avoid looking like a clown, you'll love the natural-beauty philosophy behind this company. The store is bright, welcoming and staffed by professional make-up artists trained in giving the perfect makeover. You might not be instantly transformed into a Swedish beauty, but you will be tempted to buy the quality products on offer: over 200 lip shades and 150 blushers and eyeshadows, all in sleek, chrome-coloured packaging.

Flannels

NEW *Unit G08/G09a, Manchester Magistrates Court Retail, The Avenue, Crown Square, Spinningfields, M3 3FL (832 5536, www.flannelsfashion.com). Metrolink Deansgate-Castlefield, or City Centre buses, or Salford Central rail.* **Open** 10am-6pm Mon-Sat; 11am-5pm Sun. **Map** p58 C4 ㊿

This Manchester-based independent chain, stocking the cream of each season's fashion crop, recently upped sticks and moved from St Ann's Square to the city's new designer destination, Spinningfields. Adored by footballers and their wives, Flannels leans towards high glamour – Versace, D&G, Gucci and Cavalli – though such tastefully restrained labels as Armani and YSL also feature heavily. Take your gold card, and an understanding partner. If you're feeling less flush, head to one of Flannels' two outlet stores, on Oldham Street in the Northern Quarter, and in Salford's Lowry Outlet Mall (p142).

General Store

7 Barton Arcade, M3 2BW (839 3864, www.generalstore-uk.com). Metrolink St Peter's Square, or City Centre buses, or Victoria rail. **Open** 10am-6pm Mon-Sat; 11am-5pm Sun. **Map** p59 D3 (51)

With its name in bold, red lights above the door, General Store is an unlikely find in the elegant Victorian setting of the Barton Arcade. Home to cutting-edge (and home-grown) labels Elvis Jesus and Ringspun, the store stocks the latest ranges for both men and women. Fans of urban clothing love the cool decor and racks filled with rock 'n' roll T-shirts, slashed dresses, combat trousers and the latest jeans.

Habitat

11-16 St Ann Street, M2 7LG (0844 499 1129, www.habitat.co.uk). Metrolink Market Street or St Peter's Square, or City Centre buses, or Victoria rail. **Open** 10am-7pm Mon-Fri; 9.30am-6pm Sat; 11am-5pm Sun. **Map** p59 D3 (52)

This bright, spacious store stocks all the well-made, cleverly designed furniture you'd expect from Habitat. Iconic ranges in children's toys, lighting and soft furnishings are all on sale, while the attractive St Ann Street location beats soulless retail parks hands down. If you're not in the market for a new wardrobe or sofa, pick up a quality mug, photo frame or vase. Local bargain hunters also head to

MANCHESTER BY AREA

Selfridges p82

In-demand designers

Renegade Marmalade

Matthew Williamson, Ossie Clark, Henry Holland, Ringspun, Gio Goi, Red or Dead, Joe Bloggs: they've all got roots in Manchester. As well as staking a claim to being the shopping capital of the North, Manchester has long had a sterling fashion pedigree. So while big hitters such as **Bench** and **Hooch** are stocked in the funkier Northern Quarter boutiques such as **Wood** (Oldham Street), quirky, and very successful, street labels such as **Ringspun** and **Elvis Jesus** can just as easily be found in the Manchester-owned **General Store** (p78).

Oasis frontman Liam Gallagher made a fashionable return to his hometown in 2010, via **Pretty Green** (p82). Gallagher's own label is no mere vanity project, either: it recently picked up a 'Menswear Brand of the Year' accolade at the Draper's Awards, its mix of sharp tailoring and mod-inspired style proving a commercial success. Musical influence also abounds at **Gio Goi**, a Manc street label worn by the likes of Plan B and Deadmau5; its designer tees, hoodies and coats are stocked in **Selfridges** (p82).

For edgy womenswear, local fashionistas in the know head to the city's smaller boutiques. Alongside 're-loved' pieces crafted from vintage fabrics at **Retro Rehab** (p100), or 1950s styling at **Rockers** (p100), those with a few quid in their clutch bag rate **Renegade Marmalade** (Thomas Street), a subterranean boutique that stocks international labels Pretty Disturbia and Critical Mass. **Afflecks**, meanwhile, a four-floor emporium bursting at the seams with weekend teens, is a good bet for newer (as well as cheaper) labels – Oldham Street's **No Angel** (p98) started out at Afflecks, and, along with clubwear favourites **Me & Yu** and T-shirt label **Don't Feed the Bears**, still keeps a stall here. Almost all of Manchester's boutiques are online, although one of the city's best-known womenswear labels, **Gorgeous Couture** (www.gorgeous couture.com), a clothing line adored by celebrities for its body-conscious glamour, has dispensed with the real-life shopfront entirely: its sleek range of made-to-measure and off-the-peg jersey dresses are available only online.

Habitat's sale store in Wythenshawe for designer goodies at knock-down prices – get there early of a weekend as the heavily discounted furniture in particular rarely sticks around for long.

Harvey Nichols

Exchange Square, M1 1AD (828 8888, www.harveynichols.com). Metrolink Victoria, or City Centre buses, or Victoria rail. **Open** 10am-8pm Mon-Fri; 9am-7pm Sat; 11am-6pm Sun (browsing from 10.30am). **Map** p59 D2 ⑤③

Harvey Nichols is a beacon of luxury that opened as part of the 2003 Exchange Square development. Its three floors display beauty products, shoes and beautifully crafted womenswear – the likes of Gucci, Alexander McQueen and Roberto Cavalli are all on offer, as well as exclusive fashion brands such as Lanvin and Christian Louboutin. There's a floor of choice menswear morsels and a jewel of a food market, leading to the Second Floor Restaurant. It's a one-stop shop for the well-heeled, and a sublime browsing experience for everyone else. There's also a Dermalogica counter, hair salon and an absolutely fabulous nail bar.

Hotel Chocolat

Northern Extension, New Cannon Street, Arndale Centre, M4 3AJ (0870 442 8282, www.hotelchocolat.co.uk). Metrolink Shudehill or Market Street, or City Centre buses, or Victoria rail. **Open** 9am-7pm Mon-Sat; 11am-5pm Sun. **Map** p59 E3 ⑤④

Chocolate. In beautiful, minimalist black packaging, sprinkled with such enticements as swirls of cream, dried raspberries and orange peel. It's a long way from the corner shop's sweetie counter – and so are the prices. But worth every calorie and penny for a very special treat or gift.

House of Fraser

60 Deansgate, M60 3AU (0870 160 7254, www.houseoffraser.com). Metrolink Market Street or St Peter's Square, or City Centre buses, or Victoria rail. **Open** 10am-8pm Mon-Fri; 9am-8pm Sat; 10.30am-5pm Sun. **Map** p58 C3 ⑤⑤

The venerable old auntie of department stores, clocking up 175 years of trading in 2010, House of Fraser (or Kendal's, as it's better known by locals) should be praised for moving with the times. The unfailingly stunning window displays of this listed art deco store signpost six floors of on-trend fashion, homewares and cosmetics, while recent developments include a champagne bar and an Italian-style tapas eaterie.

Mappin & Webb

12-14 St Ann Street, M2 7LF (832 2551, www.mappin-and-webb.co.uk). Metrolink Market Street or St Peter's Square, or City Centre buses, or Victoria rail. **Open** 10am-5.30pm Mon-Sat; 11am-5pm Sun. **Map** p59 D3 ⑤⑥

A proper – and proper pricey – jewellers, Mappin & Webb proves that diamonds really are a girl's best friend. And so are watches, earrings, pendants, engagement rings… Glittering glass cases, smooth staff and a hushed, plush atmosphere.

Mulberry

NEW *Unit G3 & G4, The Avenue, Spinningfields, M3 3FL (839 3333, www.mulberry.com). Metrolink Deansgate-Castlefield, or City Centre buses, or Salford Central rail.* **Open** 10am-6pm Mon-Wed; 10am-7pm Thur, Fri; 10am-6.30pm Sat; 11am-5pm Sun. **Map** p58 C4 ⑤⑦

Stocked with classic clothing, iconic accessories and quality luggage, the new Mulberry store is a destination for both men and women seeking classic British style. Inhale deeply and savour the scent of baby-soft leather, often dyed in zesty colors and shimmering metallics. Treat yourself to a gorgeous bag but make sure your bank balance can take it: must-have handbags are often named after the celebrities who inspired them and come with price tags to match.

Office Sale Shop

3 St Ann's Place, M2 7LP (834 3804, www.office.co.uk). Metrolink Market Street or St Peter's Square, or City Centre buses, or Victoria rail. **Open** 10am-6pm Mon-Wed, Fri, Sat; 10am-7pm Thur; 11am-5pm Sun. **Map** p59 D3 ⑤⑧

While most sale shops trade by the motto 'you get what you pay for', here, all stock is ex-Office shoe store and of generally good quality. The only difference between this and the main Office outlet is that shoes have been dramatically marked down due to being end-of-line, last season or marginally scuffed. The place is forever overflowing with canny shoe-lovers of both sexes, loading up on £15 platforms and bargain baseball boots.

Oliver Sweeney

NEW *Unit G21, The Avenue, Spinningfields, M3 3HF (834 0086, www.oliversweeney.com). Metrolink Deansgate-Castlefield, or City Centre buses, or Salford Central rail.* **Open** 9.30am-6pm Mon-Wed; 9am-7pm Thur-Sat; 11am-5pm Sun. **Map** p58 C4 ⑤⑨

This modern store, with its glazed façade and lime-green decor, looks futuristic, but the wares are traditional. Perfectly placed for Spinningfields' suited and booted, Oliver Sweeney stocks high quality men's shoes and accessories. Smart brogues, boots, belts and scarves are all displayed neatly, and there's a comfortable central seating area for trying things on.

Pretty Green

NEW *81 King Street, M2 4AH (0845 539 2109, www.prettygreen.com). Metrolink St Peter's Square, or City Centre buses, or Victoria rail.* **Open** 10am-7pm Mon-Sat; noon-6pm Sun. **Map** p59 D3 ⑥⓪

Liam Gallagher may be better known for his music, but the former Oasis singer recently revealed an unexpected aptitude for high-fashion menswear too. The musician set up label Pretty Green in 2009, and has already opened stores outside London. The Manchester outlet is dominated by Gallagher's presence, with outsize portrait photos plastered all over the walls. Vanity snaps aside, though, there's much here to recommend: mod-style shirts, sharply tailored jackets and racks of casual polo shirts epitomise a style that offers both class and attitude – perfect for a little Oasis-style swaggering.

Ran

8 St Ann's Arcade, M2 7HW (832 9650, www.ranshop.co.uk). Metrolink Market Street or St Peter's Square, or City Centre buses, or Victoria rail. **Open** 9.30am-6pm Mon-Sat; 11am-5pm Sun. **Map** p59 D3 ⑥①

This hard-to-find pair of shoe and clothing shops rewards perseverance. Small premises house an eclectic mix of shoes on one side of St Ann's Arcade, and clothes for men and women – from cutting-edge or rare labels such as F Troupe, Fila Vintage and Eighties Casuals – on the other. A friendly, personal service makes Ran worth the hunt.

Seen

6 St Ann's Arcade, St Ann's Square, M2 7HN (835 2324, www.seen.co.uk). Metrolink St Peter's Square, or City Centre buses, or Victoria rail. **Open** 10am-6pm Mon-Sat. **Map** p59 D3 ⑥②

Calling themselves 'the coolest opticians on the planet' is a brave claim for anyone to make, but Seen do, to their credit, stock a huge range of rare designer frames. The atmosphere is far less clinical than that of your average optician's shop. Bright decor and friendly, dedicated staff make Seen stand out more than the top letter on a sight chart.

Selfridges

1 Exchange Square, M3 1BD (0870 837 7377, www.selfridges.com). Metrolink Victoria, or City Centre buses, or Victoria rail. **Open** 10am-8pm Mon-Fri; 9am-8pm Sat; 10.30am-5pm Sun. **Map** p59 D2 ⑥③

It would be a crime not to guide the discerning visitor to Selfridges; five floors of loveliness, desirability and luxury. The basement food hall is worth a trip in itself, with several counters serving speciality food, plus a Yo! Sushi conveyor belt. For divine wine and top-notch dinner parties, this is the ultimate treat. Upstairs, you'll find cosmetics, menswear – with a mix of street and classic labels – luxury womenswear, shoes and the champagne bar/restaurant, while the top floor offers younger, funkier (read 'cheaper') high-street labels. Not to be missed.

TK Maxx

51-55 Market Street, M1 1WA (832 2337, www.tkmaxx.com). Metrolink Market Street, or City Centre buses, or Piccadilly rail. **Open** 9am-8pm Mon-Fri; 9am-7pm Sat; 11.30am-5.30pm Sun. **Map** p59 E3 ⓺⓸

For designer bargains, TK Maxx is unbeatable. Dedicate at least two hours to searching through the endless racks of last-season and surplus stock designer finds. There's menswear, womenswear, underwear, handbags, kidswear and a brilliant homewares section, where the high-quality stock changes regularly and Egyptian cotton sheets are ten a penny (nearly). The shoe department is an essential fashionista spot, with up to 80% off Lulu Guinness and Kurt Geiger.

Topshop

Arndale Centre, M4 3AQ (615 8660, www.topshop.com). Metrolink Market Street, or City Centre buses, or Victoria rail. **Open** 9am-6pm Mon-Fri; 9am-7pm Sat; 10am-6pm Sun. **Map** p59 E3 ⓺⓹

OK, nearly every town has a Topshop, but Manchester's branch of the high-street staple is particularly impressive. This huge store stocks the catwalk-inspired trends that make the brand famous, along with smaller concessions, affordable accessories and an enormous choice of shoes. Men aren't forgotten, with an in-store branch of Topman offering the freshest jeans and printed T-shirts. Arrive early in the morning to bag the most in-demand garments, or late in the evening to avoid the fashion-conscious crowds.

Triangle, Exchange Square

37 Exchange Square, M4 3TR (834 896, www.trianglemanchester.co.uk). Metrolink Shudehill or Market Street, or City Centre buses, or Victoria rail. **Open** 10am-6pm Mon-Wed, Fri; 10am-8pm Thur; 9am-6pm Sat; 11am-5pm Sun. **Map** p59 D2 ⓺⓺

This slick shopping centre sprang from the ashes of the Corn Exchange (another casualty of *that* bomb), and while the old building's unique character has now been obscured by gleaming white walls, chrome and glass stairs, the shops are impeccably chosen. Brands such as East and Jigsaw rub shoulders with funky retailers such as Bravissimo lingerie and Aspecto urban clothing. Although a little empty in parts (due to a swathe of recent closures), the Triangle is still worth a visit.

Urban Outfitters

NEW *41-43 Market Street, M1 1PW (817 6640, www.urbanoutfitters.co.uk). Metrolink Market Street, or City Centre buses, or Victoria rail.* **Open** 10am-7pm Mon-Wed, Fri, Sat; 10am-8pm Thur; noon-6pm Sun. **Map** p59 D3 ⓺⓻

This cavernous, glass-fronted store may be located on Manchester's main shopping row but its stock is far from high street. Students and hipsters flock inside for three floors of cool concessions, costume jewellery, vintage clothing and quirky homewares, all accompanied by a booming, on-trend soundtrack. Expect to feel decidedly out of place if you're aged over 25.

Vivienne Westwood

47 Spring Gardens, M2 2BG (835 2121, www.hervia.com). Metrolink St Peter's Square, or City Centre buses, or Victoria rail. **Open** 10am-6pm Mon-Sat; noon-5pm Sun. **Map** p59 E4 ⓺⓼

One Central Street p86

Viv is from nearby Glossop, so it's only right that she should have a dedicated boutique here. And it does her justice. Carved mahogany display cases reveal glittering Westwood orb jewellery, the latest collections are hung beside huge gilt mirrors and there's a chaise longue on which to try the latest shoe ranges. The pricey but stunning main collection is sold alongside the diffusion line T-shirts – and every self-respecting Manc fashionista owns a tartan Westwood bag.

Waterstone's

91 Deansgate, M3 2BW (837 3000, www.waterstones.com). Metrolink Market Street or St Peter's Square, or City Centre buses, or Victoria rail. **Open** 9am-8pm Mon-Sat; 10.30am-5pm Sun. **Map** p59 D3 **69**
Committed bibliophiles may sigh for the good old days of musty corridors, rickety library steps and personal recommendations; yet Waterstone's still dominates the high street. Its Deansgate store is a vast temple to the published word, and has a particularly good arts section. There's a quiet, table-service café, helpful staff, and three floors of shiny, ink-scented stock to get lost in. Its newer Arndale store has a great kids' section (with colouring-in tables, reading benches and toys).

White Company

21-23 King Street M2 6AW (839 1586, www.thewhitecompany.com). Metrolink St Peter's Square, or City Centre buses, or Victoria rail. **Open** 10am-6pm Mon-Sat; 11am-5pm Sun. **Map** p59 D3 **70**
Who would have thought that such a simple idea could end up manifesting itself so successfully? The concept is in the name – everything sold in this shop is white. Towels, sheets, nighties – every type of household linen, in fact – but all made and presented so stylishly that it's hard to imagine why anyone ever wanted avocado towels to match their bathroom suite. Tasteful pieces of furniture are also on sale.

Nightlife

Circle Club

Barton Arcade, M3 2BJ (288 8118, www.thecircleclub.com). Metrolink Market Street or St Peter's Square, or City Centre buses. **Open** (closing times depend on event) 10am-late Mon-Sat; 5pm-late Sun. **Map** p59 D3 **71**
Hidden round the back of St Ann's Square, the Circle is tough to find unless you know where to look: it's a perfect members' club location. The door policy is notoriously strict – you won't get in unless you've been invited. But if you make it past the velvet rope, get ready to enjoy a swish bar and a comfy lounge, plus dancing alongside the city's creative elite – and more than the occasional celeb.

42nd Street

2 Bootle Street, M2 5GU (831 7108, www.42ndstreetnightclub.co.uk). Metrolink Deansgate-Castlefield, or City Centre buses, or Deansgate rail. **Open** 10pm-2.30am Tue; 10pm-3am Wed-Sat. **Map** p58 C4 **72**
An unreconstructed indie club peddling the predictable soundtrack of Manchester tunes past and present, plus assorted Britpop and other guitar-based anthems. Friendly and popular with students, 42nd Street is busy most nights of the week.

Manchester 235

Great Northern, 2 Watson Street, M3 4DT (828 0300, www.manchester235.com). Metrolink Deansgate-Castlefield, or City Centre buses, or Deansgate rail. **Open** 2pm-6am daily. **Map** p58 C5 **73**
Inhabiting a slightly tired-looking leisure development, Manchester 235 is a luxury, Vegas-influenced restaurant/bar/casino/live music complex. It was the casino that made the headlines on the club's launch; now it's the edgy new music showcased here that has people talking. A good choice for a slick, smart and sophisticated night out.

MANCHESTER BY AREA

MEN Arena

Victoria Station, M3 1AR (950 5000, www.men-arena.com). Metrolink Victoria, or City Centre buses, or Victoria rail. **Open** times vary. **Map** p59 D1 **74**

The City Centre's largest concert venue (aka the Manchester Arena) is a stopping-off point for those commanding a big crowd: typically big pop acts (à la Aguilera), household-name comedians (Eddie Izzard) and (mostly) middle-of-the-road rock bands.

One Central Street

1 Central Street, M2 5WR (211 9000, www.onecentralclub.co.uk). Metrolink St Peter's Square, or City Centre buses, or Oxford Road rail. **Open** 10pm-5am Sat; other nights depend on events. **Map** p59 D4 **75**

A beautifully designed basement club/bar with a big sound system that attracts a mixed crowd of switched-on students and Mancs. Aside from the cocktails, the main draw is a glamorous rotation of Saturday nights from the likes of K-Klass, Miss Moneypenny's and Soul Avengerz. The great atmosphere rarely disappoints.

Opus

Printworks, Withy Grove, M4 2BS (834 2414, www.opusmanchester.com). Metrolink Shudehill, or City Centre buses, or Victoria rail. **Open** noon-3am Mon, Wed-Sat; noon-midnight Tue, Sun. **Map** p59 E2 **76**

With a bar, restaurant, comedy, live music and club facilities, this is one of the most well-rounded (and liveliest) venues in the mainstream Printworks development. Big-name Friday and Saturday night sessions have proved a hit, as have regular club nights, soundtracked to commercial dance, soul and funky house.

Pure

Printworks, Withy Grove, M4 2BS (819 7770, www.puremanchester.com). Metrolink Shudehill, or City Centre
buses, or Victoria rail.* **Open** 10.30pm-3am Fri; 10pm-4am Sat. **Map** p59 E2 **77**

A 2,500-capacity mega club from the people behind London's Heaven, Pure was piloted in the Printworks site in 2006 after the former tenants failed to make it work. They started by stripping out the clutter (a bowling alley, restaurants) and installing a £300,000 Funktion One sound system, and now have local radio DJs taking the helm at weekends. Exclusive PA slots have included Alexandra Burke, the Black Eyed Peas and Basshunter.

Purple Pussycat

19A Back Bridge St, M3 2PB (834 5111, purplepussycat.co.uk). Metrolink Deansgate-Castlefield, or City Centre buses, or Salford Central rail. **Open** 10pm-4am Mon-Sat. **Map** p58 C3 **78**

The name and the neon outside suggest something seedier than the cheeky electro- and funk-oriented disco within this club. The strip-joint theme continues inside, with dancing poles, a mirrored ceiling and urinals complete with red lips. A grimy kind of glamour is implied, but the dress code is casual, making the Purple Pussycat a good choice for a spontaneous afterhours boogie. Keep your eyes peeled – the Purple Pussycat is found only with due care, or by those lucky enough to stumble across it. A true antidote to the beaten track.

South

4a South King Street, M2 6DQ (www.tokyoindustries.com/south). Metrolink St Peter's Square, or City Centre buses. **Open** 11pm-3am Mon-Sat. **Map** p58 C3 **79**

South reopened in 2010, redesigned by Ben Kelly of Haçienda and FAC251 fame. The old space has been modernised – the new additions include a bespoke Funktion One sound system – without compromising the well-loved underground 'dive' feel. Clint Boon of Inspiral Carpets plays indie and rock 'n' roll tracks to a discerning crowd on

Saturdays. Wednesday's Colorkode house and techno, and Thursday's Murkage nights – a mix of dubstep electro and hip hop – break an otherwise uninterrupted indie schedule.

Taps Bar

NEW *Great Northern Tower, Watson Street, M3 4EE (819 5167, www.taps bar.co.uk) Metrolink St Peter's Square, or City Centre buses, or Oxford Road rail.* **Open** *noon-midnight Mon-Sat; noon-11pm Sun.* **Map** p58 C5 ⑩
The selling point here is that you can pour your own draught beer, from standard lagers to fruit brews such as Leifman's, from taps fitted to your table. Is it a gimmick? Well, yes, and you'll be paying over the odds for the pleasure, but it does at least offer plenty of opportunity for terrible 'on the pull' gags.

Tiger Lounge

5 Cooper Street, M2 2FW (236 6007). Metrolink St Peter's Square, or City Centre buses, or Oxford Road rail. **Open** *4.30-11pm (later on event nights) Mon-Thur; 4.30pm-3am Fri, Sat.* **Map** p59 D4 ㉛
Renamed after its eponymous Saturday nighter (the place was previously called 'Slice'), this eternally entertaining extravaganza puts on rock 'n' roll, soul, Detroit garage and kitsch covers in swell, although sweaty, leopard-print surroundings. Somewhere to play dress-up if you're so inclined – and the quirkier the outfit, the better.

Venue

29 Jacksons Row, M2 5WD (839 5915, www.thevenuenightclub.co.uk). Metrolink Deansgate-Castlefield, or City Centre buses, or Deansgate rail. **Open** *10pm-3am Wed, Fri, Sat.* **Map** p58 C4 ㉜
Indie-loving students are spoilt with yet another anthem-peddling club only spitting distance from the very similar 42nd Street. As well as the usual indie weekenders, the Venue provides a good-quality Wednesday night of retro classics from the '50s to the '90s.

Venus

42 Maybrook House, Blackfriars, M3 2EG (834 7288, www.venusmanchester. co.uk). Metrolink Market Street, or City Centre buses, or Salford Central rail. **Open** *11pm-5am Fri; 11pm-6am Sat.* **Map** p89 D3 ㉝
Venus's promoters pride themselves on providing their dressy, up-for-it crowd with a top-class club experience of Hed Kandi-esque funky, vocal house. This place is hot – literally. Clubbers keep cool with free ice pops and fans on request.

Arts & leisure

AMC Great Northern

Great Northern, Deansgate, M3 4EN (0870 755 5657, www.amccinemas. co.uk). Metrolink Deansgate-Castlefield, or City Centre buses, or Deansgate rail. **Map** p58 C5 ㉞
Screening standard movie fare in its 16 auditoria, the AMC cinema, which opened in 2001, is set apart by its location: a Victorian Grade II-listed building that was once a receiving warehouse for deliveries to Central Station (now Manchester Central; p64).

Odeon Manchester & IMAX

Printworks, Withy Grove, City Centre, M4 2BS (0871 224 4007, www.odeon. co.uk). Metrolink Shudehill, or City Centre buses, or Victoria rail. **Map** p59 E2 ㉟
If size really does matter, the Odeon beats every other City Centre cinema hands down, with 23 screens and an IMAX theatre. Its 'gallery' also gives cinephiles the chance for a more exclusive viewing experience. Here, intimate auditoria, large leather seats and an alcohol licence mean you need to book ahead to bag your spot by the bar.

Opera House

Quay Street, M3 3HP (0844 847 2295, www.manchesteroperahouse.org.uk). Metrolink St Peter's Square, or City Centre buses, or Oxford Road rail. **Map** p58 C4 ㊱

Opera House is a wonderfully ornate 2,000-capacity theatre whose output of West End musicals, comedy, ballet and drama is similar to its sister venue, the Palace Theatre. True to its name, though, this house is also home to regional and national opera, and often plays host to Manchester International Festival premières.

Portico Library & Gallery

57 Mosley Street, entrance on Charlotte Street, M2 3HY (236 6785, www.theportico.org.uk). Metrolink Mosley Street, or City Centre buses, or Piccadilly rail. **Open** 9.30am-4.30pm Mon-Wed, Fri; 9.30am-7.30pm Thur. **Map** p59 E4 **67**

Tucked unobtrusively away at the side of the Bank pub, and accessed via a buzzer system, the Portico recently celebrated 200 cerebral years of book lending (but you have to be a member to borrow from the collection) and arts events. Its tightly packed library, with creaking floorboards, leather-backed chairs and archaic section headings ('polite literature' is one), takes you right back to 19th-century Manchester – it remains a peaceful haven amid the bustle of town. A changing series of art exhibitions take place beneath a gorgeous Georgian glass dome ceiling, and literary events are held throughout the year. Note that steep entrance steps prevent full wheelchair access.

Royal Exchange

St Ann's Square, M2 7DH (833 9833, www.royalexchange.co.uk). Metrolink Market Street or St Peter's Square, or City Centre buses, or Victoria rail. **Map** p59 D3 **68**

The Exchange, once the world's biggest commercial trading floor, has its history writ large on its interior – literally, as cotton prices are still posted high on the walls. The Victorian building was converted into a theatre in 1976, and theatrical business was, for a while, brisk – until the 1996 IRA bomb forced its closure. Reopening in 1998 with a dedicated studio space for

new work, the theatre chose Stanley Houghton's play *Hindle Wakes* for its re-launch – the same work that had been running when the explosion took place. A symbol of the theatre's inde-fatigability, it was the perfect choice for a venue that, today, continues to stage some of the city's best theatre.

Sienna Spa Radisson Edwardian

Peter Street, M2 5GP (835 8964, www.siennaspa.com). Metrolink St Peter's Square, or City Centre buses, or Oxford Road rail. **Open** *Spa* 9am-9pm Mon-Fri; 10am-8pm Sat; 10am-6pm Sun. *Gym* 6.30am-9pm Mon-Fri; 8am-8pm Sat, Sun. **Map** p58 C5 **69**

This five-star day spa in the vaults of the former Free Trade Hall (it famously hosted gigs by Bob Dylan and the Sex Pistols, and was home to the Hallé for many years; it's now the Radisson Edwardian hotel; p176) has a gym, steamroom, sauna and swimming pool (check out the sauna's fibre-optic lighting – designed to look like a star-studded night sky) The towels are so thick you could use them as pillows, and the lighting is suitably forgiving. Expect top-of-the-range treatments (massages, manicures, body wraps, facials) from exclusive ranges, with prices to match.

Vertical Chill

North Face, 130 Deansgate, M3 2QS (837 6140, www.vertical-chill.com). Metrolink St Peter's Square, or City Centre buses, or Salford Central rail. **Open** 9.30am-4pm Mon-Sat; 11.30am-3.30pm Sun. **Map** p58 C3 **90**

Step inside clothing shop the North Face and you may be surprised to see a 23ft-high sheer wall of ice – known as the Saab Ice Wall – poking up between the fleeces and crampons. The -12°C monolith, operated by Vertical Chill, is perfect for practising climbing and ice-axe moves and, for those Edmund Hillary wannabes, there's an icy overhang to grapple with. Call for details of the various masterclasses.

Royal Exchange

Northern Quarter shops

Northern Quarter

To find Manchester's self-styled creative quarter, follow the stream of skinny-jean-clad kids heading up Oldham Street. The record shops, vintage boutiques and galleries exemplify the word 'independent'. It's defiantly chain-free – even the pubs are fiercely singular.

The action centers on Oldham Street, but explore the side lanes to fully uncover the eclectic shopping experience on offer. The friendly vibe is obvious at **Soup Kitchen**, where the close-knit creative community chows down. For more substantial fare, **Koffee Pot** does good-value breakfasts, or take your pick from the many curry places.

Part of the Northern Quarter's charm comes from its architecture – a slightly ramshackle collection of 18th- and 19th-century warehouses. Some have been beautifully restored (such as the building housing the **Buddhist Centre**), while others are, sadly, falling into a state of dilapidation. At the heart of the district is the impressive neo-Romanesque façade of the former **Smithfield Market**. Now surrounded by rather ugly flats, it fronts on to a small public square. In the same block sits the **Chinese Arts Centre** (its tiny café, serving Chinese tea, is a comfy retreat), while the market's sister building, now converted into the **Craft & Design Centre**, can be found on Oak Street. The centre is a hub of local design and industry; products available include prints, sculptures and leather goods.

Sights & museums

Chinese Arts Centre

Market Buildings, Thomas Street, M4 1EU (832 7271, www.chinese-arts-centre.org). Metrolink Shudehill, or City Centre buses, or Victoria rail. **Open** 10am-5pm Tue-Sat. **Admission** free. **Map** p91 B1 ❶

Established in 1986, this organisation occupies a specially designed building that was opened in 2003 and now acts as a national centre for the promotion of contemporary Chinese art. A changing programme of exhibitions and events celebrates a variety of international Chinese artists, and there is also a decent shop and specialist tearoom.

Greater Manchester Police Museum

57a Newton Street, M1 1ET (856 3287, www.gmp.police.uk). Metrolink Piccadilly Gardens, or City Centre buses, or Piccadilly rail. **Open** 10.30am-3.30pm Tue or by appt. **Admission** free. **Map** p91 C2 ❷

An easily overlooked curiosity, this converted former police station – far larger than it looks from the outside – contains early *CSI*-style case histories, the original prison cells, haunting Victorian mugshots and exhibits of grimly inventive confiscated weaponry, all overseen and explained by retired police officers.

Richard Goodall Gallery

59 Thomas Street, M4 1NA (832 3435, www.richardgoodallgallery. com). Metrolink Market Street, or City Centre buses, or Piccadilly rail. **Open** 11am-6pm Tue-Fri; 11am-5pm Sat. **Admission** free. **Map** p91 B1/B2 ❸

This commercial gallery's window display pulls in punters with its music and vintage posters and its so-hip-it-hurts illustrations, prints and graphic design. A second store round the corner on High Street focuses on higher-end rock photography and painting.

Eating & drinking

Abergeldie Café

40 Shudehill, M4 1EZ (834 5548). Metrolink Shudehill, or City Centre buses, or Victoria rail. **Open** 7am-5pm Mon-Sat; 8.30am-3.30pm Sun. **£**. **Café**. **Map** p91 B1 ❹

While the nation's obesity levels are now threatening to sink our little island, some may still find a dirty thrill

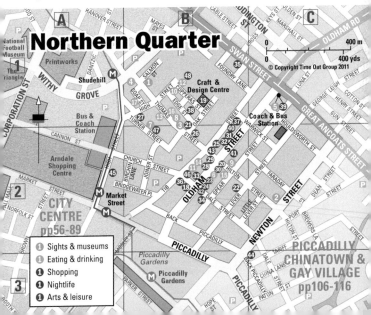

Northern Quarter

National Football Museum

Printworks

The Triangle

Shudehill

WITHY GROVE

Bus & Coach Station

CANNON ST

Arndale Shopping Centre

Market Street

CITY CENTRE pp56-89

Craft & Design Centre

Coach & Bus Station

WARWICK ST

OLDHAM RD

GREAT ANCOATS STREET

NEWTON STREET

PICCADILLY

Piccadilly Gardens

PICCADILLY CHINATOWN & GAY VILLAGE pp106-116

0   400 m
0   400 yds
© Copyright Time Out Group 2011

❶ Sights & museums
❶ Eating & drinking
❶ Shopping
❶ Nightlife
❶ Arts & leisure

in willingly eating fried foods. Greasy spoons such as the Abergeldie are now a dying breed, so enjoy the treasure of a traditional full English breakfast (a bargain at £3.20) while you still can.

Crown & Kettle

2 Oldham Road, M4 5FE (236 2923, www.crownandkettle.com). Metrolink Market Street, or City Centre buses, or Piccadilly rail. **Open** noon-midnight Fri, Sat; noon-10.30pm Sun. **Pub**. **Map** p91 C1 ⑤

Mothballed for some 20 years, this former haunt of hacks from the nearby Daily Express building has made a welcome return. Legend has it that it was originally intended as a law court, hence the intricate ceilings and mullioned windows, but the coloured plaster walls of its refit don't really do the place justice. There's more taste in the range of beers on offer, which includes ales from the local Boggart Hole Clough brewery.

Dry Bar

28-30 Oldham Street, M1 1JN (236 9840). Metrolink Piccadilly Gardens, or City Centre buses, or Piccadilly rail. **Open** 11am-midnight Mon-Thur, Sun; 11am-4am Fri, Sat. **Bar**. **Map** p91 B2 ⑥

A Northern Quarter mainstay long before the area's regeneration kicked in, this former Factory Records-owned bar was one of the first in the country. A must visit for any 'Madchester' or Haçienda veterans – order a beer at Dry and you'll be perching where countless Mancunian musicians have stood. It may be a shadow of its former self, an echo of Manchester music past, but the place still holds a certain charm.

Earth Café

16-20 Turner Street, M4 1DZ (834 1996, www.earthcafe.co). Metrolink Shudehill, or City Centre buses, or Victoria rail. **Open** 11am-4pm Mon-Fri; 10am-5pm Sat, Sun. **£**. **Café**. **Map** p91 B1/ B2 ⑦

This vegan café, in the basement of the Manchester Buddhist Centre (p105), serves food that's both fresh and, where possible, organic. The special platters are good value at £5 for rice, a heaped plate of the daily dish (butterbean casserole, for example) and two salads. There's a range of teas and smoothies.

57 Thomas Street

NEW *57 Thomas Street, M4 1NA (832 0521, www.marblebeers.co.uk). Metrolink Shudehill, or City Centre buses, or Victoria rail.* **Open** 11.30am-midnight daily. **Bar**. **Map** p91 B1 ⑧

This unassuming bar is the City Centre home of Manchester's best-known microbrewery, Marble Beers. Unlike the beautiful surrounds of the Marble Arch Inn (p146), 57 Thomas Street is sparsely decorated, with just one long table stretching the length of the bar, for starters. The strength of the place can be seen in its mantra of 'Beer & Food', which is exactly what it does – and does well. Hand-pumped real ale, imported beers and a mighty impressive cheeseboard offer a strangely satisfying no-frills ale experience.

Koffee Pot

21 Hilton Street, M1 1JJ (no phone, www.thekoffeepot.co.uk) Metrolink Market Street, or City Centre buses, or Piccadilly rail. **Open** 7am-3pm Mon-Fri; 9am-3pm Sat; 10am-2pm Sun. **£**. **Café**. **Map** p91 B2 ⑨

Home to arguably the best Full English in town, the Koffee Pot is where the city's creative types and bands head to when in need of a post-hangover fry-up. Breakfast and a brew come in at a fiver, and once you're sat in one of the wooden booths you'll find it hard to leave. The pot pies are also worth checking out. In fact, the only slight let-down with this place is its rather lacklustre coffee.

Market Restaurant

104 High Street, M4 1HQ (834 3743, www.market-restaurant.com). Metrolink Shudehill, or City Centre buses, or Victoria rail. **Open** 5-9.30pm Tue-Thur; noon-10pm Fri, Sat. **££**. **Modern British**. **Map** p91 B1 ⑩

The unprepossessing decor here may underwhelm, but, as is so often the case in Manchester, appearance should not be read as an indicator of quality. The Market has racked up over a quarter of a century of excellent cooking and has now refined its Modern British style to perfection. The beer list, in particular, comes highly recommended.

North Tea Power

NEW *36 Tib Street, M4 1LA (833 3073, www.northteapower.co.uk). Metrolink Market Street, or City Centre buses, or Victoria rail.* **Open** 8am-7pm Mon-Fri; 10am-7pm Sat; 11am-6pm Sun. **Café. Map** p91 B2 ⑪
The first café in Manchester to offer a 'tea espresso', North Tea Power has swiftly established itself as a tea and cake haven amid the heaving boutiques on its doorstep. Simple decor, coupled with a friendly and knowledgeable approach including its broad selection of teas, including arguably what is the best Lapsang Souchong in the city, make North Tea Power the perfect retreat (or, thanks to its free Wi-Fi, an excellent mobile office).

Northern Quarter Restaurant & Bar

108 High Street, M4 1HQ (832 7115, www.tnq.co.uk). Metrolink Shudehill, or City Centre buses, or Victoria rail. **Open** noon-10.30pm Mon-Sat; noon-7pm Sun. **£££. Modern European. Map** p91 B1 ⑫
Under the stewardship of head chef Anthony Fielden, the Northern Quarter has firmly established itself as a prime Modern British/European proposition. Lovely dishes such as lemon thyme, salsify and walnut gnocchi and roasted suckling pig have made the place an absolute must for any visiting foodies.

Odd

30-32 Thomas Street, M4 1ER (833 0070, www.oddbar.co.uk). Metrolink Shudehill, or City Centre buses, or Victoria rail. **Open** 11am-midnight

Mon-Thur, Sun; 11am-1.30am Fri, Sat. **Bar. Map** p91 B1 ⑬
A happy haven of eclectic quirkiness, Odd is the antithesis of corporate high-street drinking dens, and welcomes a mixed crowd. Even better than the DIY decor, tasty bar snacks, cocktails and continental beers is its background music: kooky jukebox by day, sets from forward-thinking indie advocates by night. The Odd empire now includes branches on Oxford Road (Odder) and in Chorlton (Oddest).

Simple

44 Tib Street, M4 1LA (835 2526, www.simplebar.co.uk). Metrolink Market Street, or City Centre buses, or Victoria rail. **Open** 11am-11pm Mon-Thur; 11am-midnight Fri; 11am-1am Sat; 11am-10.30pm Sun. **Bar-Restaurant. Map** p91 B2 ⑭
Established for almost a decade, Simple has the perfect combination of laid-back atmosphere and attentive staff. The cocktails are impressive but it's the food that really electrifies with everything – from waffles with scrambled egg and crispy bacon, to fennel and orange sea bass – made fresh in the bar's own kitchen. With a menu as varied and delicious as this, it's not unusual to find a brunch at Simple stretching into dinner.

Soup Kitchen

31-33 Spear Street, M1 1DF (236 5100, www.soup-kitchen.co.uk). Metrolink Market Street, or City Centre buses, or Piccadilly rail. **Open** 11am-3pm Mon-Wed; 11am-1am Thur-Sat; noon-5pm Sun. **£. Café. Map** p91 B2 ⑮
The idea behind Soup Kitchen is simple enough: after collecting your food from the counter, you transport your grub to one of the long benches and tables and say hello to fellow diners. Select large bowls of freshly made soup (which changes daily) and hunks of fresh bread for less than a fiver, or go for the daily hot special. A good, cheap and tasty lunch option, and now home to the excellent Good Grief 'zine shop.

Teacup

*53-55 Thomas Street, M4 1NA
(832 3233, www.teacupandcakes.com).
Metrolink Shudehill, or City Centre buses,
or Victoria rail.* **Open** *8.30am-5pm Mon;
8.30am-6pm Tue-Fri; 10am-7pm Sat;
10am-6pm Sun.* **£.** **Café.** **Map** p91 B1 ⑯
Manchester DJ Mr Scruff has long
been famous for his fondness for tea,
setting up a tea bar at all of his Keep It
Unreal club nights. It was a natural
next step to launch his own café;
Teacup stocks Scruff's own blends
alongside a loose-leaf menu that is 13
varieties long. Hungry? Try eggs six
ways, Pieminister pies, meatballs and
handmade cakes galore with your tea,
in this, one of the city's happiest cafés.

This & That

*3 Soap Street, M4 1EW (832 4971).
Metrolink Shudehill, or City Centre buses,
or Victoria rail.* **Open** *11am-4.30pm
Mon-Fri; 11am-8pm Sat; 11.30am-4pm
Sun.* **£.** **Curry.** **Map** p91 B1 ⑰
There's an enjoyable sense of the old
school canteen about this curry café,
with its plastic chairs and steaming
bain-marie (across which you place
your order). Asking for 'rice and three'
gets you a hearty plate of boiled rice
with three different curries mingling
joyously together on top. The offerings
vary daily, but you can expect a good
choice of meat (chicken and lamb) and
vegetable (from daal to cabbage) varieties, and for less than a fiver you'll get
a heap of spicy wholesome food, fresh
naan and a jug of mango lassi. The one
drawback is the hard-to-find location –
the place is tucked away in the sort of
alley that you might see featured on
Crimewatch reconstructions. But think
of the food that awaits, and be brave.

Shopping

The best place in the city to find
independent boutiques, quirky
one-off shops, vintage clothing and
cutting-edge styles, the Northern
Quarter attracts hip shoppers,

Alfresco art

Although the Northern Quarter is
better known for boutique shops
and bars, it also packs a visual
punch – if you're prepared to look.
Among the unofficial adornments
(such as a series of 'space
invader' tiles, the best of which
can be seen on Salmon Street),
Lemn Sissay's *Flags*, a poem
embedded into the pavement,
runs the length of Tib Street.
Although now fairly worn, the
stirring stone stanzas employ
a distinctive typeface created by
artist Tim Rushton; the same font
can be seen on the white-and-blue
street signs located throughout
the area. (Both were fired by local
ceramicists Majolica Works.)

Mosaics also feature around
Afflecks (p97). Although some
feared that the original artwork –
by artist Mark Kennedy – would be
lost during a recent refurbishment,
Kennedy was re-commissioned by
the developers. Alongside 12 new
works, a few of his old favourites
survive, among them the infamous
'And on the sixth day, God created
MANchester' quote.

Big Boys Toys, Peter Freeman's
neon sculpture atop the NCP car
park on Church Street, has lit up
the area since 1999. The lights
went out on this 12-metre-high
tower in 2005; a dispute over who
should pay for it was only recently
resolved and it's now switched on
daily from 9pm. Nearby, look out
for George Wylie's *New Broom*
(Hilton Street), as well as the
musical instrument-as-monster by
David Kemp that perches atop the
red-brick remains of a building on
Church Street, and a clutch of tiny
ceramic birds clinging to buildings
on Tib and Church streets.

MANCHESTER BY AREA

Afflecks

students and fashionistas who aren't afraid to wander between dodgy curry houses, garment warehouses and graffitied walls.

Afflecks

52 Church Street, M4 1PW (839 0718, www.afflecks.com). Metrolink Market Street, or City Centre buses, or Piccadilly rail. **Open** 10.30am-6pm Mon-Fri; 10am-6pm Sat; 11am-5pm Sun (ground floor only). **Map** p91 B2 ⓳
At weekends, this four-floor alternative shopping institution crawls with disaffected teens – for a leisurely browse, go midweek. You'll find new designers, clubwear, vintage, fancy dress, records, homewares, cute and kitsch gifts, posters and a vast range of black T-shirts. The building used to be Affleck & Brown's – the city's premier department store – and with careful purchasing, you can still emerge with gorgeous items at suitably teenage prices.

Craft & Design Centre

17 Oak Street, M4 5JD (832 4274, www.craftanddesign.com). Metrolink Market Street, or City Centre buses, or Piccadilly rail. **Open** 10am-5.30pm Mon-Sat. *Dec only* times vary Sun. **Map** p91 B1 ⓵⓽
This long-established creative hub continues to draw the best local talent. Each floor is lined with small shops and studios, and many traders design on site and sell their work fresh from the drawing bench, sewing machine or workbench. Products include one-off bags, intricate jewellery, large-scale photographic prints, paintings, sculpture and leather goods. There's also a pleasant café, and changing exhibitions throughout the year. And if you're after something really special, most of the artisans will work to commission.

Den Furniture

42-44 Oldham Street, M4 1LE (236 1112, www.denfurniture.co.uk). Metrolink Market Street, or City Centre buses, or Piccadilly rail. **Open** 10am-5.30pm Mon-Sat; Sun by appt. **Map** p91 B2 ⓴

The perfect antidote to chain shops, Den stocks a mixture of its own made-to-order furniture and individual (and often 're-loved') vintage finds – all made in Manchester. Chairs and much more besides come in every style, from King Louis boudoir to leather and chrome. And if you happen to own a bar that could do with a makeover, Den offers a 'complete bar design and refurbishment service'.

A Few Fine Things

7 Oak Street, M4 5JD (832 8400, www.afewfinethings.co.uk). Metrolink Market Street, or City Centre buses, or Piccadilly rail. **Open** 11am-6pm Thur-Sat; Mon-Wed, Sun by appt. **Map** p91 B1/B2 ㉑
You could be forgiven for thinking that a shop selling bespoke tweed and leather goods would be more at home in the Cotswolds, but A Few Fine Things' quality accessories are proving popular with stylish urbanites. Owners Stuart and Francesca make bags by hand in the basement of this charming corner shop; in fact, their 'handbag experience' voucher offers lucky recipients the chance to hang out in the workshop while a luxury made-to-measure bag is brought to life before their eyes. Understandably, expect to pay more than you would for a tatty vinyl number in one of the nearby vintage shops.

Fred Aldous

37 Lever Street, M1 1LW (236 4224, www.fredaldous.co.uk). Metrolink Piccadilly Gardens, or City Centre buses, or Piccadilly rail. **Open** 8.15am-5.15pm Mon-Sat; 11am-5pm Sun. **Map** p91 B2 ㉒
'Supplying the creative mind since 1861' states the sign. It doesn't sell opium, but Fred Aldous does offer a huge basement packed with everything the social sketcher, dedicated designer or committed craftsperson could ever want. Aisles groan with pens, paints, glue, paper, glitter and all the little bits and pieces you need to make jewellery, cards and felt things

Fancy dress

Kit yourself out for a night on the Village tiles.

The Gay Village promises a lively party for everyone, and a diverse bunch they are: on any night the pavements and clubs are teeming with every kind of partygoer. Never more so than on Wednesdays, which seem to unofficially be trans nights, when a host of venues offer drag cabarets and quizzes hosted by local 'showgirls' decked out to the nines. Wigs, glitter, sky-high heels, and disco classics are all in abundance as raucously mouthy drag queens take to the stages in the most flamboyant of outfits.

Unsurprisingly, there are some rather fabulous costumiers catering for them; if you want to get dressed up, head to the Northern Quarter. **House of Haynes**, at 32 Oldham Street (237 3775), offers a vast archive for accessorising any alter ego. Though you can buy outfits, they don't come cheap; generally, people hire instead. Even for a quick browse through their amazing gear, this shop is worth a stop.

It's not just the Village crowd getting in on the action. With some 75,000 students, this is a city that's big on fancy dress, and on any night out you're likely to bump into a gaggle of inexplicably dressed Smurfs or bell-bottomed '70s stars meandering along Oxford Road. For more affordable gear, head to the legendary **Attic Fancy Dress** store (832 3839) in Afflecks Palace. The amicable father and son who run it truly know their stuff and will take the time to kit you out properly. **Luvyababes** (819 5395), in the Arndale Centre, also has costumes for kids.

to sell at the church fête. Staff are immensely helpful, and it's easy to believe you're a successful artist simply by sniffing the creative air.

Magma

24 Oldham Street, M1 1JN (236 8777, www.magmabooks.com). Metrolink Piccadilly Gardens, or City Centre buses, or Piccadilly rail. **Open** 10am-6.30pm Mon-Sat; noon-6pm Sun. **Map** p91 B2 ㉓ Though this is a small chain, Magma retains the feel of an independent bookshop, with obscure and glossy photographic and art books. Some of the coffee-table books are the price of a, er, coffee table, but the wide range of magazines and journals offer a more affordable slice of print heaven. You can easily spend hours here, leafing through the volumes. There's also a selection of quirky postcards, T-shirts, graphic novels and gifts for those who find proper 'Art' too tiresome.

No Angel

20 Oldham Street, M1 1JN (236 8982, www.noangel.co.uk). Metrolink Piccadilly Gardens, or City Centre buses, or Piccadilly rail. **Open** 11am-6.30pm Mon-Sat; noon-5pm Sun. **Map** p91 B2 ㉔ With its hot-pink chaise longue, wooden floors and gargantuan mirror, No Angel could be a high-end boutique. It's much cooler than that, though – and much cheaper. Expect to find the latest garments and accessories from smaller, independent labels such as Motel and John Zack. Students and twentysomethings flock here for quirky glamour and Saturday-night glad rags. Don't forget to look inside the glass counter, stocked with handmade, affordable jewellery. No Angel also has a smaller shop in Afflecks (p97).

Northern Flower

58 Tib Street, M4 1LG (832 7731, www.northernflower.com). Metrolink Market Street, or City Centre buses, or Piccadilly rail. **Open** 9am-6pm Mon-Sat. **Map** p91 B2 ㉕

A flower shop with personal service and knowledgeable staff is something of a rarity in a world where the choice is often limited to wilted garage chrysanths and supermarket spider plants. At Northern Flower, you can believe that the blooms have just been picked by an elf skipping through a dew-drenched field. Find rare pot plants to liven up a dull office, get staff to make up a customised romantic bouquet or just pluck a few bold blooms to cheer yourself up on the way home.

Oi Polloi

63 Thomas Street, M4 1LQ (831 7781, www.oipolloi.com). Metrolink Market Street, or City Centre buses, or Piccadilly rail. **Open** 10am-6pm Mon-Sat; noon-5pm Sun. **Map** p91 B2 ㉖
Oi Polloi seems to have the menswear market nailed, as the recent move to a new (and bigger) store on Thomas Street would suggest. It offers a selection of upmarket casualwear labels such as Nigel Cabourn, Belstaff and Fred Perry, while classic footwear designs come from such brands as Converse and Spring Court.

Oklahoma

74-76 High Street, M4 1ES (834 1136). Metrolink Market Street, or City Centre buses, or Piccadilly rail. **Open** 10am-7pm Mon-Fri; 8am-7pm Sat; 10am-6pm Sun. **Map** p91 B1 ㉗
If a giant piñata were to explode in Manchester, the results might resemble Oklahoma. Defying categorisation, this airy, wooden-floored shop-cum-café stocks the best selection of retro and quirky cards in town, alongside bizarre and amusing cheap gifts, imported and designer homewares and a healthy dose of kitsch. If you're after Virgin Mary charm bracelets, or magic trees, you're in the right place. If you'd rather buy a subtitled Korean DVD and eat vegetarian chilli washed down with a banana smoothie, you're also catered for. Anyone who dares to leave this place disappointed is a joyless soul indeed.

Oxfam

8-10 Oldham Street, M1 1JQ (228 3797, www.oxfam.org.uk). Metrolink Piccadilly Gardens, or City Centre buses, or Piccadilly rail. **Open** 10am-6pm Mon-Sat; noon-5pm Sun. **Map** p91 B2 ㉘
This huge Oxfam is not a bargain-hunter's paradise – its City Centre location is reflected in the prices. But it does specialise in collectibles, and has a vinyl section that's well worth a peek, plus several shelves of rare books. Give it a miss for clothes, though, and go to Oxfam Originals up the road (Unit 8, Smithfield Building, 839 3160), which sells the fashionista's pick of the charity bundles, including cool bags and shoes from the 1960s to the '90s.

Piccadilly Records

53 Oldham Street, M1 1JR (839 8008, www.piccadillyrecords.com). Metrolink Piccadilly Gardens, or City Centre buses, or Piccadilly rail. **Open** 10am-6pm Mon-Sat; noon-5pm Sun. **Map** p91 B2 ㉙
A Manchester institution, Piccadilly is a much loved, old-fashioned independent record shop. As well as a huge choice of classic vinyl, it stocks the newest releases. Knowledgeable staff are happy to share news of forthcoming releases, or order that tricky-to-find edition. No wonder Piccadilly Records has survived into the age of the MP3.

Pop

34-36 Oldham Street, M1 1JN (236 5797, www.pop-boutique.com). Metrolink Piccadilly Gardens, or City Centre buses, or Piccadilly rail. **Open** 10am-6pm Mon-Sat; 11am-5pm Sun. **Map** p91 B2 ㉚
Pop is a student institution, selling original and recreated '60s and '70s styles upstairs, including jeans, cute tops and cotton dresses. The basement is crammed with original homewares, including Tretchikoff-style prints, tile-topped coffee tables and German lamps. An in-store branch of the Sweet Tooth Cupcakery, meanwhile, caters to the current taste for baked goods that

MANCHESTER BY AREA

look as good as they taste. For a quick, painless trip back in time, it's worth a visit – though if you're a retro purist, it may seem a bit sanitised.

Retro Rehab

91 Oldham Street, M4 1LW (839 2050). Metrolink Piccadilly Gardens, or City Centre buses, or Piccadilly rail. **Open** 10am-5.30pm Mon-Sat. **Map** p91 B2 ③①
This neat boutique stocks a good range of clothing dating from the '50s to the '80s, alongside its own reworked vintage garments. There's a great choice of accessories, jewellery and one-off bags, but dresses are the speciality here. The walls are lined with everything from mini to maxi frocks, all arranged in a handy colour-coded display.

Rockers

89 Oldham Street, M4 1LW (839 9202, www.rockersengland.co.uk). Metrolink Piccadilly Gardens, or City Centre buses, or Piccadilly rail. **Open** 11am-6pm Mon-Sat. **Map** p91 B2 ③②
Specialist shops can be unnerving but this one is notably down-to-earth, and has something for everyone who's ever eyed up a Harley. Having recently moved to new premises, the shop now has more room for racks of cool T-shirts, bags, jewellery, iron-on patches and spectacular '50s-style dresses. Staff live the dream with quiffs, chains and hefty turn-ups, but they welcome all comers, even if you're a lightweight who just fancies a skull-decorated lighter.

Thunder Egg

22 Oldham Street, M1 1JN (235 0606, www.thunderegg.co.uk). Metrolink Market Street, or City Centre buses, or Piccadilly rail. **Open** 10.30am-6pm Mon-Fri; 10am-6pm Sat; noon-5pm Sun. **Map** p91 B2 ③③
This funky little gift shop looks like the inside of a Japanese teenager's bedroom. It's packed with Hello Kitty ephemera, funny cards, cute bags and even crocheted Moomin dolls. Venture into the basement and find racks of

party dresses and boldly patterned clothing. It might be a little too visually exhausting for the over-thirties, but for a desirable and affordable gift for your cool mate, it's a great bet.

Travelling Man

4 Dale Street, M1 1JW (237 1877, www.travellingman.com). Metrolink Piccadilly Gardens, or City Centre buses, or Piccadilly rail. **Open** 10am-6pm Mon-Sat; 11am-4.30pm Sun. **Map** p91 B2 ③④
Are you male? Like the odd action adventure? Love computer games? Then you'll be drawn to this shop like a moth to a lightbulb. US and Japanese comics are displayed on ceiling-high racks, there are obscure board games featuring pneumatic vixens, computer quests, figurines from the crazed imaginations of reclusive animators and rare publications for the dedicated collector. They even host signings by graphic novelists and other nerdtacular special events. Your girlfriend may end up dumping you due to your newly developed geekiness – but you won't notice.

Nightlife

Band on the Wall

NEW *25 Swan Street, M4 5JZ (834 1786, www.bandonthewall.org). Metrolink Market Street, or City Centre buses, or Victoria rail.* **Open** times vary. **Map** p91 B1 ③⑤
See box p103.

Black Dog Ballroom

Corner of Tib Street & Church Street, M4 1JG (839 0664, www.blackdog ballroom.co.uk). Metrolink Market Street, or City Centre buses, or Victoria rail. **Open** noon-4am Mon-Fri, Sun; noon-5am Sat. **Map** p91 B2 ③⑥
With its exposed brickwork, softly lit booths and crimson-felted pool tables, this basement bar is like a little piece of New York's Lower East Side transported to the Northern Quarter. Black Dog Ballroom's real draw, though, is its generous opening times: the food

Common p102

menu, an appropriate mix of deli and diner, is served until 1am, while the booze flows well into the hours when decent folks should be soundly asleep.

Centro

74 Tib Street, M4 1LG (832 1325). Metrolink Market Street, or City Centre buses, or Victoria rail. **Open** 5pm-11.30pm Mon-Thur; 2pm-1am Fri, Sat; 2pm-midnight Sun. **Map** p91 B1/B2 **37**

A wide range of continental beers and munchable, reasonably priced bar food make up a small part of Centro's kaleidoscopic appeal. Split over two floors, this Northern Quarter stalwart makes for a relaxed retreat during the day and an unpretentious but hip hangout at night. Cool DJs make weekends go with an extra swing.

Common

39-41 Edge Street, M4 1HW (832 9245, www.aplacecalledcommon.co.uk). Metrolink Shudehill, or City Centre buses, or Victoria rail. **Open** 11am-midnight Mon-Wed; 11am-2am Thur-Sat; noon-midnight Sun. **Map** p91 B1 **38**

A sure-fire bet in the Northern Quarter for consistently friendly staff serving quality drinks in a down-to-earth and lively environment. There's an ever-changing mix of artwork on the walls, DJs spin records on Wednesdays and Saturdays, and the own-made food is served daily until 10pm.

Frog & Bucket

102 Oldham Street, M4 1LJ (236 9805, www.frogandbucket.com). Metrolink Market Street, or City Centre buses, or Victoria rail. **Open** 7pm-1am Mon; 7pm-2am Thur-Sat; 7pm-12.30am Sun. **Map** p91 C1 **39**

The Frog has given an early boost to such comedians as Dave Gorman, Peter Kay and the inimitable Johnny Vegas over the years – a list the venue hopes to add to through its 'Beat the Frog' amateur stand-up session held every Monday. Weekends at this welcoming old-school comedy club see more established names in charge of entertainment, after which a cheerfully cheesy disco ensues.

Matt & Phred's Jazz Club

64 Tib Street, M4 1LW (831 7002, www.mattandphreds.com). Metrolink Market Street, or City Centre buses, or Victoria rail. **Open** 5pm-2am Mon-Thur; 4pm-3am Fri, Sat. **Map** p91 B2 **40**

A much-loved Oldham Street staple and Manchester's only live jazz club, Matt & Phred's also provides legendarily good pizza and cocktails. The cosy interior is the perfect setting for music from local and international musicians.

Mint Lounge

46-50 Oldham Street, M4 1LE (228 1495, www.mintlounge.com). Metrolink Market Street, or City Centre buses, or Piccadilly rail. **Open** 10pm-3am Mon, Fri; 10.30pm-3.30am Sat. **Map** p91 B2 **41**

A venture of local promoters Electriks, Mint Lounge has grown from being the only burlesque bar in Manchester to a vibrant and varied club, popularly considered to be one of the coolest in the city. Clique on Fridays plays a selection of 21st-century disco and electro-pop, while Manchester's longest-running club night, Funkademia, is on Saturday. It's occasionally open Thursdays too.

Night & Day Café

26 Oldham Street, M1 1JN (236 4597, www.nightnday.org). Metrolink Market Street, or City Centre buses, or Piccadilly rail. **Open** 10am-2am Mon-Sat. **Map** p91 B2 **42**

Full of character, Night & Day is perfectly situated among Oldham Street's record shops: do some crate-digging, then head over for a relaxed beer and catch tomorrow's big act or cult faves hanging out, and – if you're lucky – playing intimate sets. Relaxed café-bar by day, world-class rock 'n' roll bar by night: no self-respecting music fan can claim a 'proper' trip to Manchester without a visit.

Back for good

Band on the Wall

Band on the Wall (p100), one of Manchester's best-loved music venues, has fought a long battle to get to where it is today. Although its musical pedigree dates back to the 1930s (its name derives from landlord Ernie Tyson's decision to mount a stage for musicians on the then-pub's wall), it really came into its own in 1975 when it was relaunched as a jazz venue. Later that decade it became the place where the Manchester punk scene first flamed into life (the likes of Joy Division, the Fall and the Buzzcocks all played here).

But by the millennium, Band on the Wall was struggling. The former Victorian pub it inhabited was crumbling and, in 2005, the dilapidated venue was forced to close. Owners Inner City Music focused on fundraising, but the sum they needed to put right the building's wrongs – £4 million – seemed so staggering that some began to wonder whether the closure might be permanent.

When it finally reopened in late 2009, after securing funds from the City Council, Arts Council and Heritage Lottery Fund, it was like welcoming back an old friend. The venue swiftly returned to business as usual and now hosts the sorts of live gigs, DJ sets and club nights that would otherwise go under-represented in the city.

Here, you can expect to see everything from jazz and world music to new folk, spoken word and experimental electronica. Eclectic, right-on (it's run on a not-for-profit basis and does as much for education groups as it does for musical hipsters), Band on the Wall is unlike any other music venue in Manchester. Its 19th-century features have been lovingly restored, while all the accoutrements of a 21st-century music hall – recording studio, superior acoustics, even its own interactive rooftop artwork – are happily in evidence. It may have been four years in the making (or 200 years, if you're being pedantic) but Band on the Wall is back, and this time it looks like it's back for good.

MANCHESTER BY AREA

Matt & Phred's Jazz Club p102

Northern

*56 Tib Street, M4 1LX (835 2548,
www.thenorthernpub.co.uk). Metrolink
Market Street, or City Centre buses,
or Piccadilly rail.* **Open** 8pm-3am Mon-
Wed; noon-4am Thur; noon-5am Fri, Sat;
noon-3am Sun. **Map** p91 B2 ❹❸

The Northern is a pub that emulates the
quarter's ethos as well as its name – it's
original, eclectic and innovative. The
variety of evening entertainment at this
smart bar is mind-boggling. Don't be
fooled by the unprepossessing grey
frontage or the elusive front door – with
everything from poetry to funk on offer,
this is a Northern Quarter essential.

Roadhouse

*8 Newton Street, M1 2AN (237 9789,
www.theroadhouselive.co.uk). Metrolink
Piccadilly Gardens, or City Centre buses,
or Piccadilly rail.* **Open** daily; times
vary. **Map** p91 B3/C3 ❹❹

Walking down the flight of steps into
the Roadhouse is akin to kicking open
the doors of a blast furnace: downstairs,
you're all but guaranteed the hottest
new talent in town. This ace Piccadilly
basement dive is the stopping-off point
for new bands, as well as home to
respected club nights such as indie
disco Revolver (Mondays).

Ruby Lounge

*28-34 High Street, M4 1QB (834 1392,
www.therubylounge.org). Metrolink
Market Street, or City Centre buses,
or Victoria rail.* **Open** times vary.
Map p91 A2 ❹❺

Straddling the border between the City
Centre and the more bohemian
Northern Quarter, Ruby Lounge has an
independent streak more in keeping
with the latter. The main attraction is
the eclectic range of live acts presented
throughout the week, though the venue
also hosts occasional club nights such
as Revolver. The L-shaped layout can
be frustrating, as music fans are
crammed into the scant space around
the stage – while the vast bar area
remains empty. Ruby Lounge is worth

it nevertheless, being one of the best
places in the city to catch bands before
they hit the big time.

Arts & leisure

Bikram Yoga Manchester

*Smithfield Building, 51 Church Street,
M4 1PD (834 7789, www.bikramyoga
manchester.co.uk). Metrolink Market
Street, or City centre buses, or Piccadilly
rail.* **Open** noon-9pm Mon-Sat.
Map p91 B2 ❹❻

Not for the faint-hearted, this studio
teaches Hatha yoga in a sweltering 40°C
(104°F) heated room, the high temper-
ature apparently protecting vulnerable
muscles against injury. Feel the burn!

Manchester Buddhist Centre

*16-20 Turner Street, M4 1DZ (834
9232, www.manchesterbuddhistcentre.
org.uk). Metrolink Shudehill, or City
Centre buses, or Victoria rail.* **Open**
10am-7pm Mon-Fri; 10am-5pm Sat.
Library by arrangement. **Map** p91 B2 ❹❼

One of the most beautifully refurbished
warehouses in the Northern Quarter
houses two shrine halls (one is open
throughout the day for drop-in medita-
tion), a library and bookshop. The
Bodywise centre offers everything
from yoga to shiatsu massage, while
the vegetarian Earth Café (p93) sates
both body and mind.

Satori Spa

*112 High Street, M4 1HQ (0845 224
6354, www.innersanctuaryspa.com).
Metrolink Market Street, or City Centre
buses, or Piccadilly rail.* **Open** 9am-8pm
Mon-Fri; 9am-6pm Sat; 10am-5pm Sun.
Map p91 B1 ❹❽

Originally established as the Inner
Sanctuary Spa in 2002, Satori is a small
but perfectly formed day spa tucked
away in the heart of the Northern
Quarter. It offers everything from hot
stone massage to spray tans, and from
Chinese acupuncture to the more usual
facials, manicures and pedicures.

MANCHESTER BY AREA

Chinatown

Piccadilly, Chinatown & the Gay Village

Strolling down **Canal Street** can sometimes feel a little like walking on to the set of *Queer as Folk*, the late-'90s TV show that propelled it into the national consciousness. Bars, clubs and restaurants cluster around the canal, and sitting out on this traffic-free street to watch life's parade pass by is a treat. **Tribeca**, **Taurus** and **Manto** are good places to start the night, while the large choice of clubs means you don't need to stop until sunrise. Canal Street is also the focal point of Manchester Pride – ten days of parades, picnics, sport, comedy, live music and partying that culminates in the Pride Parade.

Close by sits the civic centrepiece of **Piccadilly Gardens**, remodelled in 2002. Tadao Ando's concrete 'bunker' at its foot provides a barrier to the fuming buses at the interchange beyond, making for a more pleasant open-air experience.

A fountain attracts kids – daring each other to race through – and bars, cafés and regular public events provide distraction from the ugly office block that sits to the east.

A few minutes' walk away, a towering, multi-tiered **Chinese Imperial Arch** marks the start of **Chinatown**. Built in 1987 as a gift from the Chinese people, the arch was the first of its kind in Europe. Chinatown is lively all year round, but Chinese New Year is celebrated with particular vigour. Fireworks, food and an enormous dancing dragon top off the festivities, while institutions such as **Yang Sing** serve top-class Chinese food.

Sights & museums

Alan Turing Memorial
Sackville Park, Sackville Street. Metrolink Piccadilly Gardens, or City Centre buses, or Piccadilly rail. **Map** p107 B2 ❶

Turing, a hero of the World War II Bletchley Park codebreakers, came to Manchester and helped to found one of the world's first computers (a copy of which can be seen at MOSI; p129). His story ended tragically – he committed suicide in 1954, two years after his arrest for a then-illegal homosexual relationship. This statue, unveiled in 2001, sits at the heart of the city's gay village.

Imperial Chinese Archway

Faulkner Street, M1. Metrolink St Peter's Square, or City Centre buses, or Oxford Road rail. **Map** p107 B2 **❷**
Manchester is home to one of Europe's largest Chinese communities, and this striking piece of architecture commemorating the fact – a gift to the city from the people of China – sits in the middle of a rather shabby square, surrounded on all sides by bustling human and vehicular traffic. A ten-minute walk away, the Chinese Arts Centre (p90) provides a more serene appreciation of the nation's culture and art.

International 3

8 Fairfield Street, M1 3GF (237 3336, www.international3.com). Metrolink Piccadilly Gardens, or City Centre buses, or Piccadilly rail. **Open** (during exhibitions) noon-5pm Wed-Sat. **Admission** free. **Map** p107 C3 **❸**
An independent artist-run space, this one-room gallery presents a changing programme of high-quality contemporary and conceptual art.

Piccadilly Gardens

Metrolink Piccadilly Gardens, or City Centre buses, or Piccadilly rail. **Map** p107 B1 **❹**
Donated for public use more than two centuries ago, the land that is now Piccadilly Gardens first housed an infirmary, demolished in 1909. The present-day city council loosely interpreted the original intentions by selling off the Portland Street corner for commercial development (it has now brought to life thanks to a clutch of decent bars and eateries) in order to

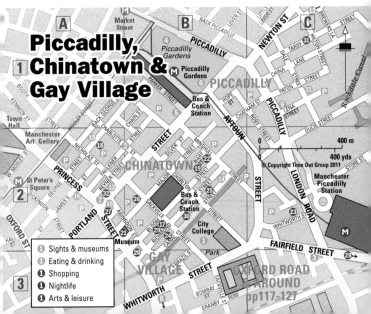

- ❶ Sights & museums
- ❶ Eating & drinking
- ❶ Shopping
- ❶ Nightlife
- ❶ Arts & leisure

finance the 2002 overhaul of the rest of the gardens. The area now contains a popular walk-through fountain, a thoughtful metal tree sculpture commemorating the World War II civilian dead, a controversial concrete wall courtesy of Japanese architect Tadao Ando and, from late 2011, a new, giant 'Wheel of Manchester'.

Visitor Information Centre

NEW *Piccadilly Plaza, Portland Street, M1 4BT (0871 222 8223, www.visit manchester.com). Metrolink St Peter's Square, or City Centre buses, or Oxford Road rail.* **Open** 9.30am-5.30pm Mon-Sat; 10.30am-4.30pm Sun. **Admission** free. **Map** p107 B1 ❺

This all-new centre provides a 21st-century means of finding out about Manchester: interactive maps, touch-screen panels and live Twitter feeds supply up-to-the-second information, although staff are also on hand to provide an old-fashioned welcome. It's from here that you can book the seemingly never-ending range of official guided walks around the city.

Eating & drinking

Barburrito

1 Piccadilly Gardens, M1 1RG (228 6479, www.barburrito.co.uk). Metrolink Piccadilly Gardens, or City Centre buses, or Piccadilly rail. **Open** 11am-9pm Mon-Wed; 11am-10pm Thur-Sat; noon-8pm Sun. **£. Mexican. Map** p107 B1 ❻

Barburrito recently won the Manchester Food and Drink Festival Award for Best Casual Dining Venue, and their principle of compile-your-own burrito appears to have caught on, so much so that a second outlet has opened across town (on Deansgate) to keep up with demand. The fiery veggie burrito with extra hot sauce is hard to beat as a quick lunchtime treat.

Circus Tavern

86 Portland Street, M1 4GX (no phone). Metrolink St Peter's Square, or City Centre buses, or Oxford Road rail. **Open** 11am-11pm daily. **Pub**. **Map** p107 A2 ❼

A listed boozer that dates back to the 1790s, when the place is said to have been the hangout of choice for performers from the city's then-permanent circus. One of Tetley's heritage pubs, it's popular with football fans – despite its diminutive size – and there's a good smattering of United and City paraphernalia on the walls. There's no food and no music, but bags of atmosphere.

EastZEast

Ibis Hotel, Princess Street, M1 7DG (244 5353, www.eastzeast.com). Metrolink St Peter's Square, or City Centre buses, or Oxford Road rail. **Open** 5-11.30pm Mon-Thur; 5pm-midnight Fri, Sat; 5-11pm Sun. **££**. **Indian. Map** off p107 B3 ❽

Although you might be tempted by the Curry Mile's bright lights, be warned: it's rare to find good food amid the gaudiness. Punjabi specialist EastZEast, however, is an altogether classier proposition. The family behind this hotel-restaurant worked in Bradford for over 50 years, and that experience shows in the superb service, delicious *karahi* dishes and gargantuan naan breads.

Michael Caines Restaurant at Abode

107 Piccadilly, M1 2DB (247 7744, www.abodehotels.co.uk). Metrolink Piccadilly Gardens, or City Centre buses, or Piccadilly rail. **Open** noon-2.30pm, 6-10pm Mon-Sat. **££££. Modern European. Map** p107 C1 ❾

Ignore the fact that this restaurant is stuffed into a hotel basement. Under the leadership of executive chef Ian Matfin and double Michelin star holder Michael Caines, it is arguably one of Manchester's best eateries. The tasting menu – starring locally sourced truffles and saddle of venison – with matching wine list (not to mention the champagne bar) are among the not-to-be-missed fine dining features on offer here.

Piccadilly Station

Yang Sing p112

101 Brasserie

Macdonald Townhouse, 101 Portland Street, M1 6DF (236 5122, www.macdonaldhotels.co.uk/townhouse-manchester). Metrolink St Peter's Square, or City Centre buses, or Oxford Road rail. **Open** noon-9.30pm daily. **£££**. **International**. **Map** p107 A2 ⑩

Head chef Tim Davies has settled on a simple, local, flavoursome approach at 101 Brasserie. Regionally sourced ingredients are combined in a no-nonsense fashion – though don't take that as a placeholder for invention. Braised leg of Cumbria marsh lamb sits alongside sweet potato and spinach korma on the à la carte menu, to be enjoyed while overlooking the bustle of Portland Street.

An Outlet

Carver's Warehouse, 77 Dale Street, M1 2HG (236 3043, www.anoutlet.net). Metrolink Piccadilly Station, or City Centre buses, or Piccadilly rail. **Open** 8am-5pm Mon-Fri; 11am-5am Sat. **£**. **Deli-café**. **Map** p107 C1 ⑪

Housed inside a beautifully converted warehouse (by the architects behind No.1 Deansgate), An Outlet specialises in simple but well-sourced deli food and drinks in a relaxed atmosphere. Enjoy a Parma ham, artichoke and olive salad with oatcakes, washed down by an international bottled beer or 'coffeetail' (a late-night take on the usual caffeine fix) while checking out the book exchange, newspapers or free Wi-Fi.

Port Street Beer House

NEW *Port Street, M1 2EQ (www.portstreetbeerhouse.co.uk). Metrolink Piccadilly Gardens, or City Centre buses, or Piccadilly rail.* **Open** noon-1am Mon-Thur, Sun; noon-2.30am Fri, Sat. **Pub**. **Map** off p107 C1 ⑫

The newest addition to Manchester's burgeoning real-ale scene, Port Street Beer House provides the perfect environment in which to appreciate the ever-expanding world of craft brewing. From the brains behind the award-winning

(and fiercely independent) Common (p102), the Beer House is home to one of the most extensive selections of rare American beers and local ales in the city. To add to its beery charm, it also offers 'thirds', the seasoned ale-festival drinker's measure of choice.

Red Chilli

70-72 Portland Street, M1 4GU (236 2888, www.redchillirestaurant.co.uk). Metrolink St Peter's Square, or City Centre buses, or Oxford Road rail. **Open** noon-11pm Mon-Thur, Sun; noon-midnight Fri, Sat. **££**. **Chinese**. **Map** p107 A2 ⑬

Most Chinese restaurants focus on Cantonese dishes, but Red Chilli differentiates itself by offering cooking from Sichuan and Beijing. As a result, the menu may seem unfamiliar, listing dishes such as the curious offal-based baked intestine with green chilli, and an excellent deep-fried sea bass. The presentation makes a real impact and the flavours are equally impressive.

Taurus

1 Canal Street, M1 3HE (236 4593, www.taurus-bar.co.uk). Metrolink Piccadilly Gardens, or City Centre buses, or Piccadilly rail. **Open** noon-11pm Mon-Thur; noon-1am Fri, Sat; noon-10.30pm Sun. **Bar**. **Map** p107 B2 ⑭

Owned and run by Canal Street stalwarts Mike 'Polly' Pollard and Iain Scott, Taurus owes its success to the twin tenets of excellent service and a sense of mischievousness. The decor is homely rather than super stylish, but who cares when the food, cocktails and company are this good? A night out here is always bags of fun. The bar has also recently been licensed to perform civil partnerships.

Teppanyaki

Connaught Building, 58-60 George Street, M1 4HF (228 2219, www.teppanyaki-manchester.co.uk). Metrolink St Peter's Square, or City Centre buses, or Oxford Road rail. **Open** 5.30-11pm

MANCHESTER BY AREA

Mon, Tue; noon-2pm, 5.30-11pm Wed-Fri; 6-11pm Sat; noon-7pm Sun. **££££**.
Japanese. Map p107 A2 ⓯
Teppanyaki is the Japanese style of cooking that originated among Samurai warriors cooking on the battlefield, using the inside of their metal armour as a sizzling hot pan. Here, awesome chefs prepare the ingredients in the kitchen and then cook them in front of your eyes, so that you can see the skill and fresh ingredients that go into your dish. With excellent sushi and sashimi as a further draw, it's worth splashing out at Teppanyaki.

Yang Sing
34 Princess Street, M1 4JY (236 2200, www.yang-sing.com). Metrolink St Peter's Square, or City Centre buses, or Oxford Road rail. **Open** noon-11pm Mon-Thur; noon-midnight Fri, Sat; noon-10.30pm Sun. **£££**. **Chinese**. Map p107 A2 ⓰
This fantastically glamorous Chinese restaurant has had a colourful 34-year history. Through everything, it's kept a consistency in the kitchen that would shame many other restaurants. Don't bother with the menu: simply explain to your waiter what you like and don't like, agree a price per head, and then your banquet will be devised for you.

Shopping

Shopping opportunities in and around Piccadilly are largely limited to functional stores such as Superdrug, M&S and Somerfield. The area doesn't offer much in the way of browsing, but there are a few specialist stores worth seeking out.

Clone Zone
36-38 Sackville Street, M1 3WA (236 1398, www.clonezone.co.uk). Metrolink Piccadilly Gardens, or City Centre buses, or Piccadilly rail. **Open** 11am-8pm Mon-Thur; 11am-9pm Fri, Sat; 11am-7pm Sun. **Map** p107 B2 ⓱
A Gay Village institution, Clone Zone stocks a wide range of gay and lesbian

publications – such as obscure, arty and erotic magazines – and, most famously, rubber and fetish gear and toys that are much admired by clubbers, bedroom poseurs and experimental lovers.

Woo Sang Chinese Supermarket
19-21 George Street, M1 4HE (236 4353, www.woosang.co.uk). Metrolink St Peter's Square, or City Centre buses, or Oxford Road rail. **Open** 10.30am-7pm Mon-Fri, Sun; 10.30am-7.30pm Sat. **Map** p107 A2 ⓲
Air-dried meats, exotic vegetables, incense sticks, and over 90 varieties of instant packet noodles – a visit to the Woo Sang is nearly as good as a quick whisk around Hong Kong. Fabulous packaging, fascinating ingredients you won't find at Tesco, and the odd but rewarding experience of being immersed in a completely different culture for 15 minutes, are all draws at this supermarket. If you can't afford the cost of a long-haul flight to China, this option is second-best.

Nightlife

Charlie's Karaoke Bar
1 Harter Street, M1 6HY (237 9898). Metrolink Piccadilly Gardens, or City Centre buses, or Oxford Road rail. **Open** 10pm-4am Mon-Sat. **Map** p107 B2 ⓳
Tatty but charming, Charlie's occasionally mutates from karaoke hangout into club proper. Decadent cabaret soirée the Whim Wham Club is on the first Friday of every month, while all other nights are based around karaoke. If you've spent the day shopping for vintage garb in the Northern Quarter's quirky boutiques, this is the place in which to show it off.

Club Alter Ego
105-107 Princess Street, M1 6DD (237 1749). Metrolink Piccadilly Gardens, or City Centre buses, or Oxford Road rail. **Open** 11.30pm-4.30am Tue, Sat; times vary Fri. **Map** p107 B3 ⓴

If the bland Gay Village soundscape of homogenised house turns your shimmy into a shudder then take refuge at Club Alter Ego, home of evergreen innovative indie shindig Poptastic. Its two weekly sessions are the venue's main draw, with a new Friday club night bringing a more dance-focused crowd into the mix.

Cruz 101

101 Princess Street, M1 6DD (950 0101, www.cruz101.com). Metrolink Piccadilly Gardens, or City Centre buses, or Oxford Road rail. **Open** 11pm-4am Mon, Wed, Sun; 11pm-5.15am Thur; 11pm-6am Fri, Sat. **Map** p107 A2 **㉑**
Really two clubs in one, with a large main room and smaller lower level, Cruz is Manchester's oldest gay club – but the (mostly) bright young things on its dancefloors each week keep its appeal fresh. Though it started as a gay disco (think Chic and Donna Summer), Cruz's music policy has since evolved, and now features a more varied mix of funky house, pop, trance and R&B.

Essential

8 Minshull Street, M1 3EF (236 0077, www.essentialmanchester.com). Metrolink Piccadilly Gardens, or City Centre buses, or Piccadilly rail. **Open** 11pm-4am Thur, Sun; 11pm-5am Fri; 11pm-6am Sat. **Map** p107 B2 **㉒**
Opened by Take That's former manager and de facto king of camp Nigel Martyn Smith, Manchester's first gay superclub took Canal Street by storm when it burst on to the scene over a decade ago. Visits by such gay deities as Kylie Minogue have kept the buzz going, and on a scene defined by the new and fresh, the longevity of the biggest gay club outside the capital seems assured.

Legends

4-6 Whitworth Street, M1 3QW (236 5400, www.legendsmanchester.com). Metrolink Piccadilly, or City Centre buses, or Piccadilly rail. **Open** *Legends* varies depending on the event; usually

Gay karaoke

Canal Street isn't all that quiet at the best of times. However, the trend for karaoke nights in and around the Gay Village means that even early in the week, there's always music (of sorts) in the air. You'll find amazingly supportive crowds at the various karaoke nights, just waiting to join in on the chorus. And, best of all, you won't have to pay for your three minutes of fame: most events are free, and some even offer prizes for the best crooner.

Tuesday is a big night for karaoke in the Village, and few places are able to better the **New Union** at 111 Princess Street (228 1492, www.new unionhotel.com, 9pm-2am), one of the area's oldest gay pubs: along with public adoration, it offers a prize of £30 for the top singer of the night. If you manage to grab the moolah, you can spend it the following night at **Charlie's Karaoke Bar** (see left), which dedicates almost every night to amateur singalongs, or wait a week for perhaps the most outrageous experience of them all: Trannyoke Tuesdays (9pm-2am) at fab **Queer** (p114), a fabulously outré mix of singing, cabaret and pop anthems.

And if none of those takes your fancy, there's always **Lammars** at 57 Hilton Street (237 9058, www.lammars.co.uk). Voted Manchester's best bar for two years running (in the Pride of Manchester Awards), its live-mic night (9pm-1am Wed) ups the ante by giving budding musicians a stage amid the bar's quirkily glamorous surroundings.

10pm-4am Fri, Sat. *Outpost* 11am-11pm Mon-Thur; 11am-2am Fri; noon-2am Sat; 1-11pm Sun. **Map** p107 C2 ㉓

A brilliantly disorienting labyrinthine set-up on the site of seminal '60s night-spot the Twisted Wheel. Legends plays host to the original antidote to gay Canal Street clubbing, HomoElectric. Run by Electriks, the people behind Electric Chair, this awesome club night famously welcomes enthusiastic 'homos, hetros, lesbos, don't knows and disko asbos' into its sweaty, occasional embrace. The Legends venture includes the Outpost bar next door.

Manto

46 Canal Street, M1 3WD (236 2667, www.mantobar.com). Metrolink Piccadilly Gardens, or City Centre buses, or Piccadilly rail. **Open** noon-midnight Mon-Wed, Sun; noon-1am Thur; noon-2am Fri; noon-3am Sat. **Map** 105 B2 ㉔

Manto was one of the catalysts for Manchester's now-established bar scene, proudly showcasing the cre-ativity and vibrancy of the gay scene behind a glass front for the first time. Now more institution than rebellious innovator, it's nevertheless still a big draw. With a '90s night on Thursdays, DJs on Fridays and Saturdays and bar-gain cocktails, Manto can be depended upon for a lively night.

Queer

4 Canal Street, M1 3HE (228 1360, www.queer-manchester.com). Metrolink Piccadilly Gardens, or City Centre buses, or Piccadilly rail. **Open** 11am-1am Mon-Thur; 11am-late Fri-Sun; *After hours party* 4am-10am Sun. **Map** p107 B2 ㉕

A glamorous bar that's a favoured spot in which to warm up before moving on to Essential (p113). Queer serves food accompanied by a chilled soundtrack during the day, with resident DJs and a full-on club vibe later at night.

Retro Bar

78 Sackville Street, M1 3NJ (274 4892). Metrolink Piccadilly Gardens, or City Centre buses, or Piccadilly rail. **Open** *Pub* 9am-2am Mon-Thur, Sun; 9am-3am Fri, Sat. *Club* 8pm/9pm-3am daily. **Map** p107 B2 ㉖

A mere stone's throw from the Canal Street strip but a million miles away in terms of outlook, Retro is – as its name suggests – a defiantly run-down yet charming little venue. The place hosts a variety of off-the-wall underground indie nights, typically run by young, up-and-coming promoters. The upstairs pub keeps the same late hours as the club and is home to a good, if overpriced, jukebox and something that has become an endangered species in Manchester – a pool table.

Satan's Hollow

101 Princess Street, M1 6DD (236 0666). Metrolink Piccadilly Gardens, or City Centre buses, or Oxford Road rail. **Open** *Club nights* (days vary) 10pm-3am. **Map** p107 A2 ㉗

Gothic decor, wilfully eclectic club nights – including bhangra, rock and pop – and regular gigs define this the-atrical set-up. But despite its devilish architecture, fearsome lighting and at times oddly styled bar staff, this is one venue that never takes itself too seri-ously. Note that the entrance is tucked away on Silver Street.

Star & Garter

18-20 Fairfield Street, M1 2QF (273 6726, www.starandgarter.co.uk). Metrolink Piccadilly, or City Centre buses, or Piccadilly rail. **Open** *Club nights* 9pm-3am selected Fri, Sat. **Map** p107 C3 ㉘

This Piccadilly bolthole is a contender for the title of most indie venue in Manchester, with disco monthlies ded-icated to the Smiths and Belle and Sebastian, plus regular up-and-coming and unsigned gigs. Though the dance-floor is dark, sticky and the size of a postage stamp, the Star & Garter is where the cutest and kookiest of vin-tage threads are flaunted. Gladioli and hearing aids are optional.

Essential p113

Dark days, bright nights

Monopolising the city's after-hours into the winter.

Since 2006, if you asked for the ultimate Manchester clubbing destination, you likely got one answer: the **Warehouse Project**. Its phenomenal success – it was voted best UK club by *Mixmag* in 2007 – propelled it from its original venue into a vast disused space in the underbelly of Manchester Piccadilly station.

This 2,000-strong party kicks off for only 12 weeks a year (Sept-Dec), culminating in an explosive New Year's Day finale, yet creates a storm of anticipation. Tickets for the Friday and Saturday sessions (until 6am), and midweek gigs, run about £20 and sell out fast.

This sweaty cavern is a far cry from the glitz and glamour at other clubs. The walls are sticky, the toilets little more than portaloos and, bizarrely, there's a burger van parked in the smoking area. The underground, industrial feel of the venue evokes an unlicensed rave, but with three bars selling an array of cocktails, sweaty ravers downing bottles of water Ibiza-style, an awesome sound and light show, and top DJs on the decks, the atmosphere is electric.

And it's growing: 2010 saw a larger chill-out area equipped with deckchairs, squishy beanbags and even a cinema screen. The line-up included US hip hop legend MF Doom and brooding Mancunian star Ian Brown. For an authentic taste of Manchester nightlife, WHP is unmissable.

■ www.thewarehouseproject.com

Vanilla

39-41 Richmond Street, M1 3WB (228 2727, www.vanillagirls.co.uk). Metrolink Piccadilly Gardens, or City Centre buses, or Piccadilly rail. **Open** 5pm-late Tue-Thur; 4pm-4am Fri; 3pm-4am Sat; 3pm-late Sun. **Map** p107 B2 ㉙

Vanilla is the only bar on Canal Street with a female focus, and one of the most famous in the country. DJ nights through the week offer everything from pop to indie rock and funky house. In possession of a Y chromosome? Then take a female chaperone or you won't get in.

Via

28-30 Canal Street, M1 3EZ (236 6523, www.via-bar.co.uk). Metrolink Piccadilly Gardens, or City Centre buses, or Piccadilly rail. **Open** noon-2am Mon-Thur; noon-3am Fri, Sat; noon-1am Sun. **Map** p107 B2 ㉚

Built like an Escher painting, Via hosts DJs playing house and Ibiza anthems at weekends (Thur-Sun), while Monday is karaoke night. Open from noon, this labyrinthine venue serves everything from a late breakfast to supper.

Arts & leisure

Basement

18 Tariff Street, Piccadilly, M1 2FN (236 8131, www.basementcomplex. co.uk). Metrolink Piccadilly Gardens, or City Centre buses, or Piccadilly rail. **Open** 24hrs daily. **Map** p107 C1 ㉛

A gay-owned and gay-run sauna that has a round-the-clock licence.

Colin Jellicoe Gallery

82 Portland Street, M1 4QX (236 2716, www.colinjellicoe.co.uk). Metrolink St Peter's Square, or City Centre buses, or Oxford Road rail. **Open** noon-5pm Tue-Fri; 1-5pm Sat. **Map** p107 A2 ㉜

A 40-odd-year-old commercial art gallery that is still run by proprietor Colin Jellicoe. Primarily showcasing Jellicoe's own work, the gallery also puts on decent group exhibitions.

MANCHESTER BY AREA

Pure Space p121

Oxford Road & Around

Infamous for its thundering traffic, Oxford Road nevertheless packs in so many galleries, museums and theatres that locals have christened it Manchester's 'cultural corridor'. It's also home to two universities (the University of Manchester and Manchester Metropolitan), whose 71,000 students inevitably lend a raucous flavour.

At the northern end sits **Cornerhouse**, the city's arthouse film and contemporary art complex, while at the other, at the start of the **Curry Mile**, sits the Victorian redbrick **Whitworth Art Gallery** and historic **Whitworth Park**. Along with a mix of contemporary and historic artwork, textiles and wallpapers, the Whitworth squeezes in an award-winning café serving locally sourced sustenance.

In between Cornerhouse and the Whitworth you'll find theatres, the **Manchester Museum**,

the **University of Manchester**'s collegiate campus (a quadrangle of Gothic buildings designed by Alfred Waterhouse; check out the atmospheric Christie Bistro inside), edgy music venue the **Deaf Institute** and two Danish-inspired **Kro** bars. Halfway up the road, **Grosvenor Park** occupies the site of a former church. In summer, this grassy retreat is reassuringly dotted with sun-loving students.

Rumours of large-scale redevelopment may yet solve Oxford Road's traffic problems; until then, don't let the honking and spluttering jams put you off exploring this area of the city.

Sights & museums

CUBE Gallery
113-115 Portland Street, M1 6DW (237 5525, www.cube.org.uk). Metrolink St Peter's Square, or City Centre buses,

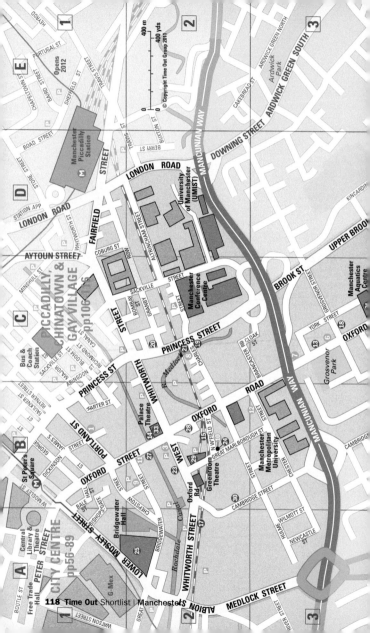

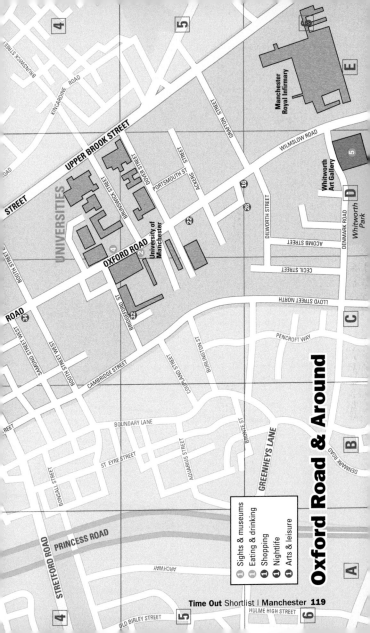

or *Oxford Road rail*. **Open** noon-5.30pm Mon-Fri; noon-5pm Sat. **Admission** free. **Map** p118 B1 ❶

The once patchy Centre for the Urban Built Environment has improved in recent years, staging a series of cerebral exhibitions that range from conceptual art to building design – with the place now revelling in its role as the city's only gallery dedicated to interrogating an urban environment we so often take for granted.

Manchester Museum

University of Manchester, Oxford Road, M13 9PL (275 2634, www.manchester.ac.uk/museum). Metrolink St Peter's Square, or bus 11, 16, 41, 42, 47, 147, 190, 191, or Oxford Road rail. **Open** 11am-4pm Mon, Sun; 10am-5pm Tue-Sat. **Admission** free. **Map** p119 D5 ❷

Once a rather dusty example of a museum in the old-school mould, this building (designed in 1890 by Alfred Waterhouse, the architect of London's Natural History Museum) received a refit in 2003, allowing much-needed daylight to reach its murky corners – although its corridor layout would still confound a tomb raider. Persevere, though, for highlights that include a notable collection of Egyptian mummies, the recently revamped Mammals Hall and a full-size replica of a Tyrannosaurus skeleton (named Stan), posed in full hunting mode.

Refuge Assurance Building

Oxford Street, City Centre, M60 7HA. Metrolink St Peter's Square, or City Centre buses, or Oxford Road rail. **Map** p118 B2 ❸

Designed by Alfred Waterhouse for the Refuge Assurance Company, this late-19th-century Grade II-listed building is a landmark in Manchester, with its distinctive red brickwork and 217ft (66m) clock tower. It was converted to a hotel in the mid 1990s and, after a £7 million refurbishment in 2005, now houses the Palace Hotel (p176).

University of Manchester

Oxford Road, M13 9PL (306 6000, www.manchester.ac.uk). Metrolink St Peter's Square, or bus 16, 41, 42, 47, 190, 191, or Oxford Road rail. **Map** (Visitors Centre) p119 D4 ❹

This sprawling academic complex is one of the country's largest educational establishments. Amid the beautiful collection of red-brick buildings and theatre venues (Martin Harris Centre, the John Thaw Studio Theatre), history abounds – the golden generation of British alternative comedy (Ben Elton, Rik Mayall, Ade Edmondson) studied here, Ernest Rutherford's research led to the splitting of the atom, while 'the Baby', one of the world's first computers, was built here in 1948.

Whitworth Art Gallery

Oxford Road, M15 6ER (275 7450, www.manchester.ac.uk/whitworth). Metrolink St Peter's Square, or bus 15, 16, 41-45a, 47, 48, 50, 87, 111, 141-145, 157, or Oxford Road rail. **Open** 10am-5pm Mon-Sat; noon-4pm Sun. **Admission** free. **Map** p119 D6 ❺

The Whitworth has undergone something of a revolution of late. A new director has shaken up the old institution, fusing a rich, historic collection (of particular note are its watercolours, textiles and wallpapers) with work by some of the world's most exciting contemporary artists. The fence that separated gallery from adjacent park has been torn down, and the gallery has high hopes that plans to extend the building into the park will go ahead. For now, make the most of its light-flooded galleries and excellent café.

Eating & drinking

Abdul's

133-135 Oxford Road, M1 7DY (273 7339, www.abduls.net). Metrolink St Peter's Square, or bus 15, 16, 41-45a, 47, 48, 50, 87, 111, 141-145, 157, or Oxford Road rail. **Open** 11am-3am daily. **£**. **Kebabs**. **Map** p118 C3 ❻

When people leave Manchester, Abdul's often appears on the list of things that they'll miss. This is no mere nostalgia-driven regret – the food here is in a different galaxy to the standard greasy post-pub kebab. Think spicy-tikka chunks of flame-grilled chicken served in fresh naan with salad and sauces. Manchester loves Abdul's – and with good reason.

Kro 2

Oxford House, Oxford Road, M1 7ED (236 1048, www.kro.co.uk). Metrolink St Peter's Square, or bus 15, 16, 41-45a, 47, 48, 50, 87, 111, 141-145, 157, or Oxford Road rail. **Open** 8.30am-midnight Mon-Fri; 9.30pm-1am Sat; 9.30-11pm Sun. **Bar**. **Map** p118 C3 ⑦

The largest of the home-grown chain of Kro bars, Kro 2 pays the strongest homage to Danish minimalism, and is all the more loved for it. The bar's abundance of glass gives it an inside-out feel – and also provides some of the best people-watching opportunities in the city. Kro 2 also has one of Manchester's largest beer gardens, and the presence (and effectiveness) of the plentiful outdoor heaters means it's still a viable choice even on a crisp November afternoon.

Lass O'Gowrie

36 Charles Street, M1 7DB (273 6932, www.thelass.co.uk). Metrolink St Peter's Square, or City Centre buses, or Oxford Road rail. **Open** noon-midnight daily. **£**. **Gastropub**. **Map** p118 C2 ⑧

The Lass is a Manchester institution; since being taken over in 2005, its stated aim has been to create the perfect village inn. The simple food ably assists that aim with brilliant own-made pies and artisan-made sausages. There are eight ales on tap, including three guest beers, which sometimes make an appearance on the food menu, too, as in the steak and Black Sheep Ale pie.

Peveril of the Peak

127 Great Bridgewater Street, M1 5JQ (236 6364). Metrolink Deansgate-Castlefield, or City Centre buses, or Deansgate rail. **Open** noon-2.30pm, 5-11pm Mon-Fri; 4-11pm Sat; 4-10.30pm Sun. **Pub**. **Map** p118 B2 ⑨

This Grade II-listed building, named after a stagecoach renowned for the speed at which it made its trips from Derbyshire, is arguably Manchester's most distinctive pub. Once you've passed the green-tiled exterior, you can see all sorts of people inside, at all times, but it gets particularly packed on Fridays and Saturdays, and Manchester United fans are in abundance on match days. The pub is also said to have its very own ghost. The brews vary, but favourites include Boddingtons, Marston's Pedigree, Timothy Taylor Landlord and Bombardier. There's a pool table in the cramped back room, and darts and table-football in the front. Look out for occasional folk nights.

Pure Space

11 New Wakefield Street, M1 5NP (236 4899, www.purespacecafebar. co.uk). Metrolink St Peter's Square, or City Centre buses, or Oxford Road rail. **Open** 4.30pm-2am Wed-Sat. **Bar**. **Map** p118 B2 ⑩

With a roof terrace that offers punters protection from the elements during Manchester's rainy season – so, essentially, all year round, apart from a week or so in July or August – Pure Space is a hidden gem. Stylish without being pretentious, the bar is one of those trusted choices that unites a range of different tastes.

Temple

100 Great Bridgewater Street, M1 5JW (278 1610). Metrolink St Peter's Square, or City Centre buses, or Oxford Road rail. **Open** noon-midnight Mon-Thur; noon-1am Fri, Sat; noon-11pm Sun. **Bar**. **Map** p118 B2 ⑪

MANCHESTER BY AREA

This place spent a former incarnation as a public lavatory and is now one of Manchester's trendier, albeit more cramped, boozers. Home to one of the finest jukeboxes in town and occasional haunt of local rock royalty (in the form of Elbow front man Guy Garvey), this bar is the place to head for if you prefer your beer to be strong, continental and bottled.

Zouk Tea Bar & Grill

Unit 5, The Quadrangle, M1 5QS (233 1090, www.zoukteabar.co.uk). Metrolink St Peter's Square, or City Centre buses, or Oxford Road rail. **Open** noon-midnight daily. **££.** **Pakistani. Map** p118 B3 ⑫

Zouk cost a cool million to fit out, and it shows – inside, it's all luxurious seating and glittering chandeliers. But it's the open-plan kitchen that forms the restaurant's centrepiece, neatly illustrating that great cooking is at the heart of the Zouk experience. Try the delicately spiced king prawn *karahi* – one curry you definitely won't live to regret come morning.

Shopping

Dominated by students, Oxford Road is functional, full of bars and cafés, and lacking in one-offs and individual shops. It's essential to take a trip out of the City Centre to Rusholme, otherwise known as the 'Curry Mile', where the endless (though variable) eateries are punctuated by Asian stores selling exotic groceries, saris, books, music and gold jewellery.

Johnny Roadhouse

123 Oxford Road, M1 7DU (273 1111, www.johnnyroadhouse. co.uk). Metrolink St Peter's Square, or bus 14, 16, 41-45a, 47, 48, 50, 87, 111, 140, 142, 143, 147, 157, 197, 250, 291, or Oxford Road rail. **Open** 9.30am-5.30pm Mon-Sat. **Map** p118 C3 ⑬

Trading from the same premises for over 50 years, Johnny Roadhouse is a rite of passage for every Manc musician and wannabe. Johnny himself passed away in 2009, with tributes from many famous patrons flooding in, but the much-loved music superstore lives on, offering three floors of brass, string and percussion instruments and effects. The Smiths were regulars here and the shop is featured in the LS Lowry-style video for Oasis's 'The Masterplan'.

Venus

95 Oxford Street, St James' Building, M1 6ET (228 7000, www.venusin manchester.co.uk). Metrolink St Peter's Square, or City Centre buses, or Oxford Road rail. **Open** 8am-6pm Mon-Fri; 9am-5pm Sat. **Map** p118 B2 ⑭

One of the first designer flower shops in the city, Venus continues its modern floral revolution. Don't expect to find any feeble carnations here; there's just lush, verdant bursts of tropical colour, spiky, graphic shapes and imaginative arrangements.

Nightlife

Attic

50 New Wakefield Street, M1 5NP (236 6071, www.thirstyscholar.co.uk). Metrolink St Peter's Square, or City Centre buses, or Oxford Road rail. **Open** 10pm-3am Thur; 10pm-4am Fri, Sat. **Map** p118 B2 ⑮

Climb the rickety spiral staircase to reach this small club under a railway arch. Attic is home to some of the city's best underground club nights – expect to find electro, house, drum 'n' bass and more from local and international DJs. On big nights and for special events, promoters take over both floors (once the pub downstairs closes).

Big Hands

296 Oxford Road, M13 9NS (272 7309). Metrolink St Peter's Square, or bus 16, 41-48, 50, 111, 142, 143, 147, 157,

Literary lifestyle

The written word plays a big role on the cultural scene.

Carol Ann Duffy

Where once Manchester was known solely for its music (and, perhaps, its football), the city has in recent years forged a reputation in the wider cultural arena. And while the big-name performances of the **Manchester International Festival** (p40) tend to dominate the headlines, the city today is as much a hotbed of literary activity as it is of artistic endeavour.

The **Manchester Literature Festival** occurs during the autumn festival season and focuses both on literary luminaries – enticing the likes of Seamus Heaney to the city for a rare public appearance, or letting Jeanette Winterson loose in Manchester Cathedral – and on newer forms of the written word, such as the **Manchester Blog Awards** (every October). It also supports local publishers such as Comma Press (whose author, David Constantine, won the 2010 BBC National Short Story Award).

The presence in the city of two international writing schools supports the burgeoning scene: alumni of the **Centre for New Writing** (for three years led by Martin Amis, and from late 2011 fronted by Colm Tóibín) include Not the Booker nominee Jenn Ashworth, while Tóibín himself is expected to lead regular public debates (check the University of Manchester website for details of events featuring Tóibín, alongside readings from the likes of Will Self and John Banville).

Close by, MMU's **Manchester Writing School** is buoyed by the Poet Laureate, Carol Ann Duffy, who, like Tóibín (and Amis before him), frequently hosts public events. The school also runs the annual £10,000 **Manchester Writing Competition**, as well as the biennial **Manchester Children's Book Festival**.

Theatre plays its part, thanks to the **Bruntwood Playwriting Competition**, Britain's largest such contest, which gives writers the chance see their work performed at the **Royal Exchange Theatre** (p88). **Contact Theatre** (p125), meanwhile, hosts the city's most dynamic spoken-word events, although offbeat venues such as the **Deaf Institute** (p124) also stage edgy reading and open-mic nights. And it's not all about the new: the **International Anthony Burgess Foundation** (p127) celebrates the city's most famous literary son, while the **Elizabeth Gaskell House** (p151) provides insight into the life of the 19th-century 'industrial' novelist. All in all, literature-lovers in Manchester have rarely had it so good.

197, 250, 291, or Oxford Road rail.
Open 10am-2am Mon-Thur; 10am-3am
Fri; 11am-3am Sat; 6pm-1am Sun.
Map p119 D5/D6 **16**

The musical smarts of Big Hands'
defiantly independent crowd – com-
pounded by regular after-gig visits
from touring musicians – have made
this bar an essential indie hangout for
those in the know. Stop off here for a
pre-Academy pint, and warm your ears
up with an eclectic variety of tunes.
The music policy ranges from reggae
to northern soul. The closing times get
extended on busier nights.

Brickhouse

Arch 66, Whitworth Street West,
M1 5WQ (236 4418, www.brickhouse-
nightclub.com). Metrolink St Peter's
Square, or City Centre buses, or Oxford
Road rail. **Open** 11pm-3am Fri, Sat.
Map p118 A2 **17**

Tucked under a railway arch, the
Brickhouse is easy to overlook, but a
shame to miss if you're looking for fun
and nostalgia. The Blur-vs-Oasis-era
music weeklies papering its corru-
gated walls set the tone for Friday's
'90s indie night. Saturday's Mixtape
braves the present day, albeit with one
foot in the past, playing a mix of new
indie releases and retro rock 'n' roll.
Look out for the after-show parties
held after local gigs.

Deaf Institute

135 Grosvenor Street, M1 7HE
(276 9350, www.thedeafinstitute.
co.uk). Metrolink St Peter's Square,
or bus 41- 48, 50, 85, 86, 111, 142,
143, 147, 157, 197, 250, 291, or
Oxford Road rail. **Open** 10am-2am
Mon-Thur, Sun; 10am-3am Fri, Sat.
Map p118 C3 **18**

The Deaf Institute – aka Trof 3 – is the
third bar in the Trof empire, following
Trof 2 in the Northern Quarter and the
original in Fallowfield, called simply
Trof (p158). The Grade II-listed Deaf
and Dumb Institute has been converted
into a cavernous café-bar and music

hall to rival the best of the City Centre
venues. Weekend club nights rotate
and include indie favourite Up the
Racket, the innovative Now Wave DJs,
and hip pop party Guilty Pleasures.
Tuesday's Gold Teeth night brings
gangsta rap to the main bar, with
grunge and punk in the basement.

FAC251: The Factory

NEW *112-118 Princess Street,*
M1 7EN (272 7251, www.factory
manchester.com). Metrolink St Peter's
Square, or City Centre buses, or Oxford
Road rail. **Open** 11pm-3.30am Mon;
11pm-3am Tue-Thur; 9pm-3am Fri, Sat.
Map p118 C2 **19**

In 2010, FAC251: The Factory opened
in the former head office of Factory
Communications, the site that's been
credited with the birth of that whole
'Madchester' thing. Co-owned by
Peter Hook of New Order and in a
building proclaimed to be both the
labour of love and bête noir of 'Mr
Manchester', Tony Wilson, the club is
steeped in die-hard Factory folklore.
However, far from being a rehashing
of Factory branded offerings,
FAC251's musical menu is refresh-
ingly varied. Three floors open six
nights a week to the sounds of dubstep, Motown, tropical, hip hop, indie,
experimental, disco and more.

5th Avenue

121 Princess Street, M1 7AG (236
2754, www.5thavenuemanchester.com).
Metrolink St Peter's Square, or City
Centre buses, or Oxford Road rail.
Open 10pm-2.30am Mon, Wed; 10pm-
3am Thur-Sat. **Map** p118 C2 **20**

This popular, student-friendly club
features the usual cheap drinks and
draws dancers to the floor with its
revamped sound and light systems, and
indie tunes most nights of the week.

Joshua Brooks

106 Princess Street, M1 6NG
(273 7336, www.joshuabrooks.co.uk).
Metrolink St Peter's Square, or City

Centre buses, or Oxford Road rail.
Open 11am-3am Mon-Wed; 11am-4am
Thur, Fri; noon-4am Sat; noon-3am Sun.
Map p118 C2 ㉑
This lo-fi student hangout manages to
keep everyone happy, with match
screenings, a lively early evening drinking atmosphere, and a basement space
after dark for clubbers. Independently
promoted events rotate monthly.

Manchester Academy 1/2/3 & Club Academy

*Manchester University Students
Union, Oxford Road, M13 9PR (275
2930, www.manchesteracademy.net).
Metrolink St Peter's Square, or bus 16,
41- 48, 50, 111, 142, 143, 147, 157,
197, 250, 291, or Oxford Road rail.*
Map p119 D5 ㉒
Three spaces on the university campus accommodate acts across all gen-
res, from unsigned to well-established.
The Academy now includes Club
Academy, home to a range of student-
oriented evenings.

Ritz

*100 Whitworth Street West, M1
5NQ (236 4355, www.ritznightclub.
co.uk). Metrolink St Peter's Square,
or City Centre buses, or Oxford
Road rail.* **Open** 10pm-3am Sat.
Map p118 B2 ㉓
This ex-ballroom's sprung dancefloor
has been graced by generations of
Mancunians. Mondays and Saturdays
are popular student sessions. Even better (and worth keeping an ear out for)
are the occasional gigs from acts such
as Elbow that temporarily realise the
club's true potential.

Sub Space

*New Wakefield Street, M1 5NP (236
4899, www.purespacecafebar.co.uk).
Metrolink St Peter's Square, or City
Centre buses, or Oxford Road rail.*
Open 10.30pm-2.30am Thur-Sat.
Map p118 B2 ㉔
A late-night counterpart to the Pure
Space bar (p121), basement venue Sub

Space runs busy club sessions.
Specialising in soul and funk, the
nightclub is popular with a mixed,
friendly crowd.

Arts & leisure

Bridgewater Hall

*Lower Mosley Street, M2 3WS (907
9000, www.bridgewater-hall.co.uk).
Metrolink Deansgate-Castlefield, or
City Centre buses, or Deansgate rail.*
Map p118 A2 ㉕
With such impressive musical accoutrements as a 5,500-pipe organ, and a
menu of 300-plus events every year,
there's no better place to tune into classical, jazz, pop and world music. The
decade-old concert hall is also the performing home of the Hallé and the BBC
Philharmonic orchestras.

Contact Theatre

*Devas Street, off Oxford Road,
M15 6JA (274 0600, www.contact-
theatre.org). Bus 16, 41, 42, 47, 48,
50, 111, 157 or Oxford Road rail.*
Map p119 D6 ㉖
With its castles-in-the-air façade, hip-
hop director Baba Israel at the helm
and regular showcases of new theatre,
spoken word, dance and music events,
Contact has the advantage when it
comes to attracting a younger crowd.

Cornerhouse

*70 Oxford Street, M1 5NH (200
1500, www.cornerhouse.org). Metrolink
St Peter's Square, or City Centre buses,
or Oxford Road rail.* **Map** p118 B2 ㉗
For a quarter of a century, Cornerhouse
has championed independent art and
film in the city, with a cinema and festivals programme that is arguably the
best in town. As a result, its slightly
cramped galleries, arthouse cinemas,
bookshop and chichi café-bars are regularly packed out, particularly in the
evenings and at weekends – a situa-
tion that should be alleviated by its
move, in 2014, to a purpose-built new
home just up the road.

MANCHESTER BY AREA

Greenroom

Dancehouse

10 Oxford Road, M1 5QA (237 9753, www.thedancehouse.co.uk). Metrolink St Peter's Square, or City Centre buses, or Oxford Road rail. **Map** p118 B2 ㉓
Although best known for its comedy nights, this art deco former cinema puts on dance, drama and music gigs, and is the home of the Northern Ballet School.

Greenroom

54-56 Whitworth Street West, M1 5WW (615 0500, www.greenroom arts.org). Metrolink Deansgate-Castlefield, or City Centre buses, or Oxford Road rail. **Map** p118 B2 ㉙
A champion of experimental theatre, live art, dance and spoken-word events that expects the audience to muck in too. You have been warned…

International Anthony Burgess Foundation

NEW *Chorlton Mill, Cambridge Street, M1 5BY (235 0776, www.anthony burgess.org). Metrolink Deansgate-Castlefield, or bus 101, 104, 109, or Oxford Road rail.* **Open** *Café* 8am-5pm Mon-Fri; 9am-5pm Sat; 10am-4pm Sun. **Admission** free. **Map** p118 B2 ㉚
The Foundation opened in 2010 as a repository for a vast collection of Burgess ephemera, from the author's musical instruments and typewriters to his manuscripts and library. The city's most famous author is perhaps also its most infamous – a love-hate relationship evident on both sides. 'As a piece of civic planning, or rather unplanning, I think it's terrible,' he once said of the city – and yet Burgess remained proud of his northern roots. The Foundation also hosts regular cultural events, and has a decent café.

Manchester Aquatics Centre

2 Booth Street East, M13 9SS (275 9450). Bus 16, 41, 42 or Oxford Road rail. **Open** 6.30am-10pm Mon-Fri; 7am-6pm Sat; 7am-10pm Sun. **Map** p118 C3 ㉛

Built for the 2002 Commonwealth Games, and central Manchester's only public swimming pool, this facility is home to two 50-metre pools, as well as fitness studios.

Martin Harris Centre for Music & Drama

University of Manchester, Bridgeford Street, M13 9PL (275 8951, www.manchester.ac.uk). Bus 16, 41, 42, or Oxford Road rail. **Map** p119 C5 ㉜
This venue quietly hosts some of the city's best literary events. Its concert hall is home to the Quatuor Danel string quartet (which often gives free lunchtime concerts), while the John Thaw Studio Theatre holds a reading series that has in the past featured such literary luminaries as Will Self, John Banville and Martin Amis.

Palace Theatre

Oxford Street, M1 6FT (0844 847 2275, www.manchesterpalace.org.uk). Metrolink St Peter's Square, or City Centre buses, or Oxford Road rail. **Map** p118 B2 ㉝
Massive musicals, big-name comedians and celeb-stuffed Christmas pantos regularly play to a packed house. The theatre also stages dance, from highbrow English National Ballet productions to the more popular *Riverdance*.

Royal Northern College of Music (RNCM)

Oxford Road, M13 9PL (907 5200, www.rncm.ac.uk). Metrolink St Peter's Square, or bus 15, 16, 41-45a, 47, 48, 50, 87, 111, 141-145, 157, or Oxford Road rail. **Map** p119 C4 ㉞
One of the UK's leading conservatoires, the RNCM balances a fierce reputation for teaching against an international reputation for top-notch performance. If mention of student musicians conjures up images of amateurs, think again. Only the very gifted study here. It also pulls in international players for festivals such as its annual festival of brass.

Castlefield & Deansgate Locks

With its atmospheric railway arches, cleaned-up canals and seemingly endless supply of tiered locks and cobblestones, **Castlefield** remains one of the city's loveliest outdoor spots. Even the 47-storey **Beetham Tower** nearby doesn't detract from the 150-odd-year-old industrial architecture. Though it can be quiet on weekdays, Castlefield offers something that the rest of the city is often missing: peace and tranquillity.

Overlooked by a vast Victorian viaduct, the main draws in the neighbourhood are the sprawling **MOSI** (Museum of Science and Industry), a **Roman Fort**, an outdoor arena (at which residents burst into a spontaneous rendition of Monty Python's 'Always Look on the Bright Side of Life' when they heard news of Manchester's second failed Olympic bid). For many, the highlight is simply sitting outside **Dukes 92** tucking into man-size slabs of cheese and bread. Frequent outdoor events bring Castlefield to life during the summer, from screenings of football matches to music festivals.

Closer to the centre of town, **Deansgate Locks** hosts a series of bars frequented by the tanned and brash, as well as the excellent **Comedy Store**, each of which is tucked inside a railway arch and facing on to the canal. Just behind the red-brick entrance to Deansgate Station is one of the city's better contemporary art spaces – **Castlefield Gallery**.

Sights & museums

Beetham Tower

301-303 Deansgate, M3 4LQ.
Metrolink Deansgate-Castlefield,
or City Centre buses, or Deansgate
rail. **Map** p129 C2 ❶

Beetham Tower is one of the most prominent additions to Manchester in recent years. Its fame rests chiefly on its height – the 47-storey tower soars 561ft (171m), making it by far the tallest building in the city, and the tallest in the UK outside London. Split as it is between residential apartments (the Olympian penthouse is occupied by the building's architect, Ian Simpson), offices and the Hilton hotel (p175), there's little here for the casual tourist except the pricey Cloud 23 (p133), a 'sky bar' with outstanding views across the city and the surrounding countryside. See box p130.

Castlefield Gallery

2 Hewitt Street, Knott Mill, M15 4GB (832 8034, www.castlefieldgallery.co.uk). Metrolink Deansgate-Castlefield, or City Centre buses, or Deansgate rail. **Open** 1-6pm Wed-Sun. **Admission** free.
Map p129 C2 ❷
An artist-run gallery specialising in the conceptual end of the creative

scale, Castlefield Gallery frequently showcases emerging practitioners and new media. The twin-level building reopened in its current (and somewhat hidden) location in 2002 and has steadily been building its reputation ever since then.

MOSI (Museum of Science & Industry)

Liverpool Road, M3 4FP (832 2244, www.mosi.org.uk). Metrolink Deansgate-Castlefield, or City Centre buses, or Deansgate rail. **Open** 10am-5pm daily. **Admission** free.
Map p129 B1 ❸
This family-friendly playground of vintage technology is set among the converted remains of the world's oldest surviving passenger railway station. Recently refurbished to the tune of £9 million, MOSI's highlights include a children's interactive gallery (where kids can lift up a car or play with a tornado machine), the huge Power Hall of thrusting, steaming turbines like

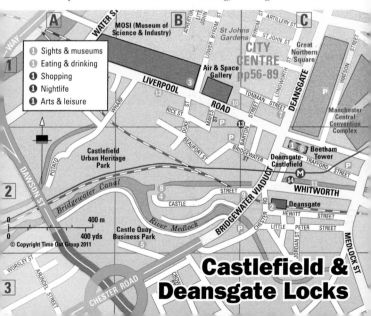

Castlefield & Deansgate Locks

© Copyright Time Out Group 2011

Scaling new heights

Beetham Tower

Make no bones about it: the £150 million **Beetham Tower** (p128), on Deansgate, truly divided Mancunian opinion when it was completed in 2006. Many have now been swayed by the skyscraper, and are proud that the city is currently home to the UK's tallest building outside London; others still consider it to be a monolithic blot on the landscape. One thing's for sure: with 47 floors and a height of 561 feet (171 metres), you can't miss it.

Half **Hilton** hotel (p175) and half residential apartments, the tower stands on the site of a railway viaduct that crossed Deansgate and connected with Central Station

(what is now the junction of Great Bridgewater Street and Liverpool Road). The viaduct was demolished in the mid 1960s by an explosives demolition contractor called Simpson, assisted by his boy Ian; the lad from Heywood grew up to become the renowned architect of Manchester-based Ian Simpson Architects. The firm designed the tower for Liverpudlian developers the Beetham Organisation, which has also commissioned several other eponymous towers (some of which have been completed, while others are still in the pipeline) in Liverpool, Birmingham and the capital. London's tower, planned for the South Bank, will be the tallest, with a planned height of 590 feet (180 metres).

With its glass and steel envelope, vertical louvres and polished-concrete podium, the Beetham Tower does feel more than a touch last-century, and will not be to every taste. Yet even those who dislike the tower might concede that it turns something of a corner for Manchester. The city has no waterfront and little topography, and needs to rewrite itself from time to time. The Town Hall (p67) did it in the 1870s; Sunlight House did it in the 1930s; CIS did it in the 1960s; and now it could well be the turn of the Beetham Tower. All those strained necks and squinting eyes are looking at something. In some intuitive way, the lad from Heywood and his team have made a quintessentially Manchester building. And even if you don't like the tower itself, you're sure to be impressed by the fabulous views afforded from the Hilton's **Cloud 23** bar (p133).

Cloud 23. See p133

Scientific endeavour

The revamped Museum of Science & Industry.

MOSI

As the heart of the Industrial Revolution and the birthplace of nuclear physics, Manchester has a long history of scientific and technological endeavour. But as the 21st century got underway, the museum dedicated to showcasing these achievements, **MOSI** (Museum of Science & Industry), was looking decidedly old-tech. Built on the site of the world's oldest surviving passenger railway station, the sprawling museum and its unparalleled collection of early steam trains and vintage planes was still pulling in visitors, albeit with rumblings of discontent. Placards were peeling, dust was gathering and some interactive exhibits were so old they belonged behind glass themselves.

Fortunately, in 2009 the museum was given an £9 million funding injection. It promptly embarked on a dizzying redevelopment programme to overhaul the main entrance, fit extensive conference facilities and a new restaurant, and improve what is secretly everyone's favourite part of any museum: the gift shop. Alongside these enhancements,

work was undertaken on two exhibition galleries, one long-standing and one completely new.

Now, in the refurbished family-favourite Experiment! gallery, kids can lift an entire Mini using only a crank, see how many of Manchester's homes can be lit by using rubbish as power and measure their reactions against the flapping of a fly's wings. The new Revolution Manchester gallery, meanwhile, is designed to help visitors navigate their way around the five listed buildings, some 16 galleries and working steam train (which plies a short stretch of track dating back to 1830) that make up MOSI. Featuring a gargantuan, 50-screen 'media wall', Revolution Manchester brings the museum experience bang up to date, with digital displays, exciting games and an intriguing collection of historic items on display for the first time. With the technological innovation celebrated in the museum finally reflected in MOSI's own development, science and industry have found their way back home.
■ Listings p129.

something from the feverish dreams of Brunel, and the Air and Space Hall, featuring a pantheon of airborne greats including a colossal Shackleton bomber. See box, left.

Eating & drinking

Albert's Shed

20 Castle Street, M3 4LZ
(839 9818, www.albertsshed.com).
Metrolink Deansgate-Castlefield,
or City Centre buses, or Deansgate
rail. **Open** noon-3pm, 5-10pm Mon-Thur; noon-3pm, 5-10.30pm Fri; noon-4.30pm, 5-11pm Sat; noon-4.30pm, 5-9.30pm Sun. **£££. Modern International**. Map p129 B2 ❹
Hearty fish stew, penne with Italian sausage, Lancashire cheese and onion pie – the only complicated thing about the menu at this converted quayside tool-shed is that you'll have a hard time working out what you should choose to eat. There is another equally brilliant, if less architecturally interesting, branch of the restaurant simply called Albert's located in West Didsbury, on Barlow Moor Road.

Choice Bar & Restaurant

Castle Quay, M15 4NT (833 3400,
www.choicebarandrestaurant.co.uk).
Metrolink Deansgate-Castlefield,
or City Centre buses, or Deansgate
rail. **Open** noon-10pm Tue-Sat; noon-9pm Sun. **£££. Modern British**. Map p129 B2 ❺
Choice has won several awards since launching in 2001, and its cuisine should suit those with a taste for refined flavours and an eye for outstanding presentation. The British tapas menu offers a unique twist on traditional Spanish plates, with chorizo making way for Cumberland sausage, for example.

Cloud 23

Hilton, 303 Deansgate, M3 4LQ (870
1600, www.hilton.co.uk). Metrolink
Deansgate-Castlefield, or City Centre

buses, or Deansgate rail. **Open** 5pm-1am Mon-Thur, Sun; 5pm-2am Fri, Sat. **Bar**. Map p129 C2 ❻
Set on the 23rd floor of the Hilton Deansgate (p175), this luxe 'sky bar' is one of the most talked-about venues in the city (so book to avoid disappointment), offering incredible panoramic views from its floor-to-ceiling windows. It's also the highest point in Manchester at which you can order a cosmopolitan – that's got to be worth drinking to. See box p130.

Dimitri's

Campfield Arcade, Tonman Street,
M3 4FN (839 3319, www.dimitris.
co.uk). Metrolink Deansgate-Castlefield,
or City Centre buses, or Deansgate rail.
Open 11am-11pm daily. **££. Greek**.
Map p129 C1 ❼
No prizes for guessing that there's a Greek lineage lurking at this lively restaurant. The menu is alive with tasty meze dishes, great for soaking up the ouzo. If you can tolerate the crime against language, order the Kalamata Plata – a feast of sharing nibbles.

Dukes 92

18-25 Castle Street, M3 4LZ (839
8646, www.dukes92.com). Metrolink
Deansgate-Castlefield, or City Centre
buses, or Deansgate rail. **Open** 11.30am-11pm Mon-Wed; 11.30am-midnight Thur; 11.30am-1am Fri, Sat; noon-10.30pm Sun. **Pub**. Map p129 B2 ❽
The canalside patio of the enduringly popular Dukes 92 is one of the best outdoor spots from which you can enjoy a summer pint and share a cheese and pâté plate; choose from over 30 types of cheese from Britain and around Europe.

Knott

374 Deansgate, M3 4LY (839 9229).
Metrolink Deansgate-Castlefield,
or City Centre buses, or Deansgate
rail. **Open** noon-11.30pm Mon-Wed, Sun; noon-12.30am Thur-Sat. **Bar**.
Map p129 C2 ❾

The Knott has been squeezed in beneath railway arches and shakes violently whenever a loco rumbles overhead (slightly unnerving the first time it happens). An excellent food menu complements the fine range of organic bottled beers and the output of Marble Brewery and guest breweries.

Ox

71 Liverpool Road, M3 4NQ (839 7740, www.theox.co.uk). Metrolink Deansgate-Castlefield, or City Centre buses, or Deansgate rail. **Open** noon-9.30pm Mon-Sat; 9.30am-11am, noon-7pm Sun. **££. Gastropub. Map** p129 B1 ⑩

An award-winning gastropub with a largely British menu garnished with Asian twists. There's a mishmash of furniture dotted around the dark interior and a raft of well-kept real ales. For those who can't face the journey home – or afford the Hilton, opposite – there are nine guest rooms upstairs (p179).

Revolution

Arch 7, Whitworth Street West, M1 5LH (839 7558, www.revolution-bars.co.uk/deansgate). Metrolink Deansgate-Castlefield, or City Centre buses, or Deansgate rail. **Open** 10am-2am Mon-Thur, Sun; 10am-3am Fri, Sat. **Bar/restaurant. Map** p129 C2 ⑪

Revolution's exposed brick walls and leather seating draw a young urbane crowd for after-work drinks and (in the basement club) late-night dancing. It's also popular for food – though the menu of upscale pub grub might not be particularly adventurous, for lunch or dinner on Deansgate Locks it's the pick of the bunch. And with ongoing two-for-one offers running all day on Monday (gourmet burgers) and Tuesday (stonebaked pizzas), you can get a decent meal and a glass of wine for under a tenner.

Sapporo Teppanyaki ⑫

91 Liverpool Road, M3 4JN (831 9888, www.sapporo.co.uk). Metrolink Deansgate-Castlefield, or City Centre buses, or Deansgate rail. **Open** noon-11pm daily. **££. Japanese. Map** p129 B1 ⑫

Proving there's more to Japanese cuisine than slowly rotating trays of raw fish, Sapporo Teppanyaki offers a spectacle as well as a dining experience. Order a meal and watch as the 'show chef' tosses, dices and grills it before your eyes. Best for group outings – the tossing may prove too much during intimate meals.

Nightlife

Cask

29 Liverpool Road, M3 4NQ (819 2527). Metrolink Deansgate-Castlefield, or City Centre buses, or Deansgate rail. **Open** noon-11pm Mon-Sat; noon-10.30pm Sun. **Map** p129 C1 ⑬

Blink and you'll miss Cask's eggshell-blue frontage. Apart from an impressive selection of beers in a cosy environment, what might catch your attention is the sign that says 'Bring your own food'. With limited space on the premises – and one of the best chip shops in Manchester next door – this is not as strange as it seems.

Comedy Store

Arches 3 & 4, Deansgate Locks, Whitworth Street West, M1 5LH (839 9595, www.thecomedystore.co.uk). Metrolink Deansgate-Castlefield, or City Centre buses, or MetroShuttle Circular No.2 free bus, or Deansgate rail. **Open** Regular shows from 8pm. **Map** p129 C2 ⑭

This venue, the northern outpost of the long-running London laughter-factory, is at the heart of Manchester's current comedy renaissance, with big names from the stand-up circuit regularly dropping by to win audiences in its theatre-style auditorium. Launched in 2000, and propping up one end of the bustling Deansgate Locks cluster, the Comedy Store is a good option for drinks, dinner and a show.

Lowry p142

Salford & Salford Quays

Salford

Let's get one thing straight: Salford isn't in Manchester. There's nothing that will rile the locals more than mistaking the two – on both sides of the divide. Manchester and Salford are two separate cities that just happen to share a border.

Salfordians are proud of their industrial heritage and tight-knit communities, and the Smiths' *The Queen is Dead* album cover (shot at **Salford Lads Club**) put Salford on the musical map. In recent times, the cultural focus has shifted to Chapel Street and nearby **Islington Mill**, a converted warehouse that includes gallery and gig space. It hosts the Sounds from the Other City music festival, which sprawls out from the Mill to take over pubs and even churches along Chapel Street.

As well as a number of superb traditional pubs, there is now some

fine dining in Salford, which comes courtesy of the Lowry Hotel's **River Restaurant**, while fine drinking can be had at the hard-to-find **Corridor** cocktail bar.

Sights & museums

Ordsall Hall

Ordsall Lane, Salford, M5 3AN (872 0251, www.salford.gov.uk). Metrolink Exchange Quay, or bus 71, 73, 84, 92. **Map** off p137 A3 ❶
Ordsall is an unlikely setting for this splendid Grade-I listed house, which comprises elements of medieval, Tudor, Stuart and Victorian construction. The building has been undergoing a £12 million redevelopment, which has seen the restoration of many of its original features: the original chandelier, oak timbers and wall sconces in the Great Hall will, for example, be on display when the hall reopens to the public in mid-2011.

St Philip's with St Stephen

St Philip's Place, Salford, M3 6FJ (834 2041, www.salfordchurch.org). Bus 36, 37, or Salford Central rail. **Open** *Holy Communion* 7pm Tue; noon-2pm Wed; 9.45am Sun. **Admission** free. **Map** off p137 A2 ❷

St Philip's, a neoclassical Anglican church dating back to the 1820s, is one of a handful of 19th-century buildings to survive the neglect faced by many of its Chapel Street neighbours. Built by Robert Smirke (who also designed the British Museum in London), the church is distinctive thanks to a colonnaded entrance topped by a perpendicular bell tower. And, under the stewardship of the Reverend Andy Salmon, this is one forward-thinking place of worship. As at the nearby Sacred Trinity, regular concerts are held here (particularly during music festivals Sounds from the Other City and Un-convention), ranging from genre-defying Florence and the Machine to the slightly more sedate BBC Philharmonic Orchestra.

Salford Lads Club

St Ignatius Walk, Salford, M5 3RX (872 3767, www.salfordladsclub.org.uk). Bus 33, or Deansgate rail. **Open** by appt. **Admission** free. **Map** off p137 A2 ❸

Featured on the cover of the Smiths' *The Queen is Dead* album, this registered charity, established in 1903, still fulfils its original function as a sports club and community centre, although it's now open to both boys and girls. The spot is a magnet for Smiths devotees, and the surrounding streets host regular pilgrimages of often rather worried-looking foreign fans. Inside, the club has a specific room devoted to the band, where you'll find all sorts of memorabilia, as well as a collection of images that fans have sent in of themselves in the classic cover pose. If you would like to visit the room, email info@salfordladsclub.org.uk to arrange an appointment.

Salford Museum & Art Gallery

Peel Park, The Crescent, Salford, M5 4WU (778 0800, www.salford.gov.uk). Bus 7, 8, 12, 26, 31, 32, 36, 37, 67, 68, 100, or Salford Crescent rail. **Open** 10am-4.45pm Mon-Fri; 1-5pm Sat, Sun. **Admission** free. **Map** off p137 A2 ❹

Inevitably overshadowed by its more prestigious neighbours both up and down the road (its Lowry collection has been transferred to the Lowry; p142), this gallery nevertheless has a good selection of Victorian art, including Dollman's striking *Famine* painting and an exquisite Burne-Jones drawing of a woman's head. The recreated Victorian Street, Lark Hill Place, is crammed with vivid period sights and sounds.

Eating & drinking

Corridor

Barlow's Croft, Salford, M3 5DY (832 6699, www.corridorbar.co.uk). Bus 67, 100, or Salford Central rail. **Open** 5pm-2am Wed, Thur; 5pm-4am Fri; 7pm-4am Sat; 7pm-1am Sun. **Bar**. **Map** p137 B2 ❺

Despite its obscure back-alley location and a wilful lack of external signage, Corridor is arguably Salford's finest gin-mill. Inside, low lights, leather booths and sparse decor leave plenty of room to admire the main event: an expertly put-together cocktail list that has, quite rightly, won several industry awards. A cocktail menu boasting some 40-plus varieties, fine spirits that include Seagram's gin and Luksusowa vodka, and a laid-back feel make this an after-hours drinking den that's worth setting your sat-nav for.

Crescent

18-21 The Crescent, Salford, M5 4PF (736 5600). Bus 7, 8, 12, 26, 31, 32, 36, 37, 67, 68, 100, or Salford Crescent rail. **Open** noon-11pm Mon-Thur, Sun; noon-midnight Fri, Sat. **Pub**. **Map** p137 A2 ❻

Don't be put off by the grey exterior and basic furniture: it's the beer that counts at the Crescent, one of Salford's older pubs, dating back to the mid 19th century. You'll fight for a seat with CAMRA types and eggheads from the nearby University of Salford (who really should be doing other things), all of whom crowd in for cask ales, with up to ten available at any one time. Beers from the Pictish Brewing Company are particularly good, as is the Hawthorn Hobble from the Goose Eye Brewery. Regular quiz nights, a great jukebox (at least if Led Zeppelin is your idea of great music) and frequent beer festivals are additional highlights. A recently renovated live-music room adds a new dimension to the space.

King's Arms

11 Bloom Street, Salford, M3 6AN (832 3605, www.studiosalford.com). Bus 3, 7, 8, 10, 12, 25-27, 31, 32, 36, 37, 67, 68, 71, 93, 98, 100, 137, 138, or Salford Central rail. **Open** noon-11pm Mon-Thur; noon-midnight Fri, Sat. **Pub**. Map p137 A2 ⑦

This is a real gem, an alcopop-free zone sitting pretty in the no-man's-land between Manchester and Salford (it's an easy stroll from the City Centre). Beers include offerings from the excellent Saltaire Brewery, among others, with Timothy Taylor a staple. In the snug you can join the Knitting Club, while the fantastic vaulted room upstairs (home to Studio Salford) hosts regular band nights and plays. All told, it's hard to fault this pub – even the jukebox has won awards.

Mark Addy

Stanley Street, Salford, M3 5EJ (832 4080, www.markaddy.co.uk). Bus 36, 37, or Salford Central rail. **Open** noon-11pm Mon-Sat; noon-10.30pm Sun. **£££**. **Classic British**. Map p137 A3 ⑧

Head chef Robert Owen Brown's food is the stuff of legend among Manchester foodies. His latest venture has seen him transform the previously under-whelming riverside Mark Addy into a sumptuous dining experience. In the

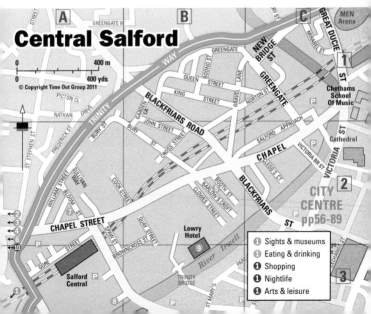

Central Salford

0 — 400 m
0 — 400 yds
© Copyright Time Out Group 2011

GREENGATE W

TRINITY WAY

NEW BRIDGE ST

GREENGATE

GREAT DUCIE ST

MEN Arena

Chethams School Of Music

Cathedral

CITY CENTRE pp56-89

BLACKFRIARS ROAD

CHAPEL ST

BLACKFRIARS ST

VICTORIA ST

CHAPEL STREET

Lowry Hotel ⑨

River Irwell

Salford Central

TRINITY BRIDGE

❶ Sights & museums
❷ Eating & drinking
❸ Shopping
❹ Nightlife
❺ Arts & leisure

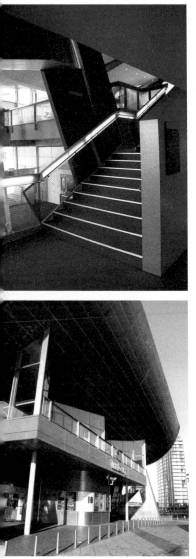

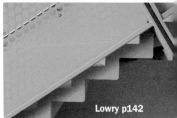

Lowry p142

bare brick dining room of this former boat landing station, you can sit back and watch the river flow by while enjoying the signature black pudding potato cake with poached egg (£5.75) or the monthly six-course Gourmet Evenings (£30, last Wed of the month). Locally sourced ingredients are paired with the best produce from microbreweries and an extensive wine-list that more than matches the quality of the food.

River Restaurant

Lowry Hotel, 50 Dearmans Place, Salford, M3 5LH (827 4041, www.the lowryhotel.com). Bus 1, 2, 7, 8, 10, 12, 25-27, 31, 32, 36, 37, 67, 68, 70, 71, 93, 98, 100, 137, 138, X34, or Salford Central rail. **Open** noon-2pm, 2.15-4pm, 6-10.30pm Mon-Fri; 11.30am-2pm, 2.15-4pm, 6-10.30pm Sat; 12.30-3pm, 3.15-5pm, 7-10pm Sun. **£££**. **Modern British**. Map p137 B3 ⑨

Oliver Thomas took on the mantle of head chef here in the wake of Eyck Zimmer's departure in 2008. It can't have been easy – Zimmer won multiple awards while in Salford, among them National Chef of the Year – but Thomas wisely marked his appointment by shifting the menu firmly into traditional British territory. So, meat-heavy dishes, such as braised pig's cheek and calf's liver, jostle for space alongside Dover sole and Scottish salmon. There's also an outstanding British cheese selection and a filling brunch menu. Whether Thomas's unconventional career path (as a butcher, a baker and a miner) has anything to do with his approach is anyone's guess, but he is at least unafraid of shaking things up at this riverside eaterie.

Arts & leisure

Islington Mill

James Street, Salford, M3 5HW (07947 649896, www.islingtonmill. com). Bus 36, 37, or Salford Central rail. **Open** noon-midnight Thur, Fri. **Admission** free. **Map** off p137 A3 ⑩

Islington Mill, a converted cotton warehouse, has led something akin to a cultural revolution in Salford over the past decade. The building, just a few minutes' walk from Manchester City Centre, houses 50 artists' studios, a gallery and art school, recording studio, gig space, B&B and more besides. It's home to the annual Sounds from the Other City music festival and has close links to Chapel Street, a mile-long stretch of Victorian pubs, university buildings and churches just a stone's throw away. A recent refurb means the Mill is now open every Thursday and Friday, although regular music and art events run throughout the week. And while Chapel Street and its surroundings are still a very long way from the scrubbed-up glamour of Manchester, Islington Mill, the epitome of art-school cool, offers the kind of edgy underground entertainment you'd kick yourself if you missed.

Salford Quays

Salford may have taken longer to redevelop than Manchester, but 2011 sees it play its trump card: **Media City** (or MediaCityUK, to be true to the branding gurus), the new northern home of the BBC that opens along the Quays' spectacular waterfront during 2011.

A 15-minute tram hop west of the City Centre, and with its own hotels, apartments, waterside park and shops, this £650 million media island is the new home of ITV, five BBC departments and the BBC Philharmonic Orchestra, as well as innumerable digital, TV and film companies.

Media City opens with the promise of public events in its vast central plaza, which, with a capacity of 5,000 and access to an enormous digital screen, is likely to showcase everything from live music and film screenings to markets and arts events.

MANCHESTER BY AREA

Media City forms a triangle of attractions now open at Salford Quays, the former industrial docks whose regeneration began in earnest over a decade ago. The **Lowry** arts centre sits close by, surrounded by made-for-footballer apartments and an outlet shopping mall, while a gleaming new footbridge spanning the Manchester Ship Canal connects Media City to **Imperial War Museum North** on the opposite shore. Strictly speaking, the museum isn't in Salford: it's in the borough of Trafford. We just thought we'd better set the record straight before you start asking for directions.

Sights & museums

Imperial War Museum North

The Quays, Trafford Wharf Road, M17 1TZ (836 4000, http://north.iwm. org.uk). Metrolink Media City, or bus 205. **Open** *Summer* 10am-6pm daily. *Winter* 10am-5pm daily. **Admission** free. *Air Shard* £1.20. **Map** p141 A2 ⓫ Surely Manchester's most striking building of the past decade, the brain-boggling design of the museum is based on star architect Daniel Libeskind's concept of a shattered globe (representing the world divided by conflict). Inside, floors and walls gently slope and disorient museumgoers. More a museum of peace than a museum of war, the place works hard at being an entertaining and educational multimedia-led venue. Its permanent displays, which include artillery, audio-visual shows and hands-on exhibits, are supplemented by temporary shows, such as 2011's 'War Correspondent', the UK's largest ever exhibition about wartime journalism. A new quayside entrance, seating and outdoor performance area has been created to mark the opening of Media City (it meets the footbridge that now connects the two). The tower offers an impressive, if vertiginous, view.

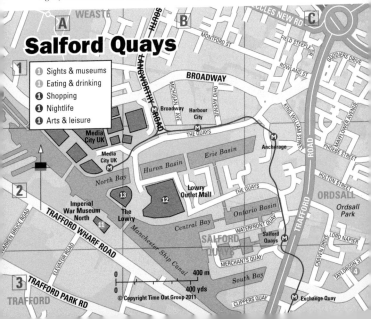

Eating & drinking

Convenience and a choice of reputable chains are the prevailing themes of the Salford Quays drinking and dining experience. The Lowry Outlet Mall's 'plaza restaurants' include some of the more interesting of the franchises – Bella Italia and Café Rouge among them – while the food court hosts Subway, Burger King and the like.

Close to the Salford Quays Metrolink station are yet more franchise options – Frankie & Benny's, Chiquito and Arbuckle's all provide you with an opportunity to take on ballast before strolling along the waterside and browsing the area's shops and attractions.

The Lowry and Imperial War Museum North's cafés – or a packed lunch or takeaway – are currently your best options if you want to see the water while you eat. Unfortunately, many of the other restaurants are woefully tilted away from the view.

A smart, waterside, foodie haven and some decent bar life are what's lacking here – a missed opportunity in such a good-looking spot. However, as developments at Media City progress, it promises to bring more variety with it: expect to see some dramatic changes as new offerings open up to serve the newcomers to Salford Quays.

Shopping

Lowry Outlet Mall

The Quays, Salford, M50 3AH (848 1850, www.lowrydesigneroutlet.com). Metrolink Media City, or bus 69. **Open** 10am-6pm Mon-Wed, Fri; 10am-8pm Thur; 10am-7pm Sat; 11am-5pm Sun. **Map** p141 B2 ⑫
This indoor factory outlet offers clothes, books, gifts and homewares at discounts of between 25% and 75%. What you'll get depends largely on how happy you are to devote hours to rummaging. The selection of shops is patchy, although the Flannels, Gap and Whistles stores usually make a trip worthwhile. Cinemas and a range of chain eateries, including Pizza Express and Café Rouge, enable you to make a day of it.

Arts & leisure

Lowry

Pier 8, Salford Quays, M50 3AZ (0843 208 6005, www.thelowry.com). Metrolink Media City, or bus 69, 290, 291. **Open** *Galleries* 11am-5pm Mon-Fri, Sun; 10am-5pm Sat. **Admission** *Galleries* free. **Map** p141 A2/B2 ⑬
A long way from the grimly functional mill buildings so often captured by its eponymous subject and raison d'être, the Lowry marked a tipping point for the previously isolated Salford Quays development when it opened in spring 2000. This landmark waterside building now houses the world's largest collection of LS Lowry's art, with its galleries regularly presenting themed exhibitions of the 'matchstick' man's work.

Lowry is only half of the story, however, as the centre brings together an amazing variety of visual and performing arts projects under one roof. As well as the contemporary exhibitions in its galleries (displaying everything from photography to conceptual art), the steel-clad wonder has also hosted more award-winning theatre productions than any other regional venue. Its two theatres and additional performing arts space receive blockbuster musicals, dance, opera, comedy, ballet, children's shows, jazz, folk and popular music acts and West End productions. The restaurant and terrace bar situated in the south side of the building, meanwhile, both serve breathtaking views along with sustenance, while its close proximity to Imperial War Museum North (p141) make a trip to Salford Quays doubly worthwhile.

City of Manchester Stadium

North Manchester

Sometimes overlooked in favour of South Manchester's more affluent suburbs, the north races ahead of its southern sister when it comes to international sporting facilities. Two miles from the centre, Sportcity is a sprawling complex that houses the National Squash Centre, a 6,000-seat athletics arena, the Regional Tennis Centre and the **Manchester Velodrome**.

Sportcity is part of the legacy of the 2002 Commonwealth Games, an event that did much to reverse economic decline in north-east Manchester. The city tackled the huge event with gusto, pulling off a 'best ever' Games and in the process creating some of the best sporting facilities in the country. Sportcity continues to host national and international fixtures, from badminton, cycling and squash championships to niche events such as the National Taekwondo Championships. No tour of Sportcity

would be complete without a visit to Manchester City's football ground – the **City of Manchester Stadium**. The 48,000-capacity stadium is a match for United's 'theatre of dreams', and arguably draws a more loyal and local crowd. From spring 2012, Sportcity will be connected to the centre by a new Metrolink line.

Further north, **Heaton Park** continues the sporting theme. As well as 600 acres of parkland, an 18th-century house and farm centre, Heaton Park has four championship-standard bowling greens built for – you guessed it – the Commonwealth Games.

It's not all sport in this part of town, though: the philanthropic legacy of the Industrial Revolution is clearly evident in the ambitious architecture and artworks scattered across North Manchester, from the impressive Edwardian **Bury Art Gallery** to the understated grandeur of **Bolton Town Hall**.

Sights & museums

Bolton Town Hall

*Victoria Square, Bolton, BL1 1RU
(01204 333333, www.bolton.gov.uk).
Bus 8, 36, 37, or Bolton rail.* **Open**
Tours by appt; call 01204 331090.
Admission *Tours free.*
Bolton has never been content to sit in
Manchester's shadow. Its Town Hall,
completed in 1873 and dominating the
town centre, easily has enough grandeur
to rival its Manchester counterpart. The
neoclassical design, featuring a grand
Corinthian portico and sweeping staircase, reveals how important Bolton was
during the 'Cottonopolis' era – it was
once one of the most productive centres
of cotton spinning in the world. Today,
as then, culture plays a part in daily life,
with the curving sweep of Le Mans
Crescent at the rear of the building providing a home not only for the Town
Hall (and its theatre venue, the Albert
Halls) but also for a museum, art gallery,
library and aquarium to boot.

Bury Art Gallery, Museum & Archives

*Moss Street, Bury, BL9 0DR (253
5878, www.bury.gov.uk). Metrolink Bury,
or bus 135.* **Open** *10am-5pm Tue-Fri;
10am-4.30pm Sat.* **Admission** *free.*
A grand Edwardian building, the Bury
Art Gallery is worth a visit to see
founder Thomas Wrigley's collection of
200 or so artworks, including paintings
by Turner, Constable and Landseer.
The gallery also stages contemporary
exhibitions and is keen on kids: a table
set in the middle of the main gallery
encourages reading, role play and
colouring-in. Nearby, East Lancashire
Railway's working steam trains, and the
new Fusiliers Museum (whose collection dates back to Napoleonic times),
round out a Bury cultural day-trip.

Heaton Park

*Off Middleton Road, Prestwich,
M25 2SW (773 1085, www.heaton
park.org.uk). Metrolink Heaton Park,*
or bus 56, 59, 64, 64a, 89, 137, 138,
150, 151, 167, 484, 495. **Open** *8am-
4.30pm daily.* **Admission** *free.*
Nestled in the foothills of the Pennines,
Heaton Park is one of Europe's largest
municipal parks. It contains eight
English Heritage listed buildings, a
boating lake, four championship-
standard bowling greens, a golf course,
a herd of highland cattle and a petting
farm. The park hosts numerous concerts throughout the year. At its heart
is Heaton Hall, an elegant neoclassical
country house designed by James
Wyatt in the late 18th century, the former home of the Earls of Wilton.
Although partially restored, the house
is currently closed to the public.

Heaton Park Tram Museum

*Heaton Park, Prestwich, M25 2SW
(740 1919, www.mtms.org.uk).
Metrolink Heaton Park, or bus 56, 59,
64, 64a, 89, 137, 138, 150, 151, 167,
484, 495.* **Open** *Winter noon-4pm Sun.
Summer noon-5pm Sun.* **Admission**
free. Tram fare £1; 50p reductions.
Run by volunteers, this small but lovely
museum is housed in an old tram shelter, from which restored vehicles run all
year. The original system fell into dis-
use in the 1930s, and the park's tram-
lines were released from beneath a layer
of tarmac only in the late '70s. The
building includes transport memorabilia, demonstration models, a shop and
a maintenance pit where you can see
the trams undergoing restoration.

Manchester Jewish Museum

*190 Cheetham Hill Road, Cheetham, M8
8LW (834 9879, www.manchesterjewish
museum.com). Metrolink Victoria, or
bus 59, 89, 135, 167, or Victoria rail.*
Open *10.30am-4pm Mon-Thur; 1-5pm
Sun. Closed Jewish hols.* **Admission**
£3.95; £2.95 reductions; £9.50 family.
Just beyond the outskirts of the City
Centre lies the Jewish Museum, in an
old synagogue founded in 1874.
Downstairs is the fully restored former

place of worship. Upstairs, the ladies' gallery houses a permanent display cataloguing the history of the still prominent local Jewish community. Helpful guides explain the ritual and history.

Manchester Museum of Transport

Boyle Street, Cheetham, M8 8UW (205 2122, www.gmts.co.uk). Metrolink Victoria, or bus 53, 54, 59, 88, 89, 135, 151, 167, or Victoria rail. **Open** 10am-4.30pm Wed, Sat, Sun. **Admission** £4; free-£2 reductions.
Two halls house over a century's worth of lovingly restored public transport history; the collection is one of the largest of its kind. The timeline starts with a 19th-century horse-drawn carriage and concludes with a Metrolink tram.

Strangeways

1 Southall Street, Manchester, M60 9AH (817 5600). Metrolink Victoria, or bus 134, 135, or Victoria rail.
The intriguingly named Strangeways – officially HM Prison Manchester since the 1990s – owes its fame to the Smiths' 1987 album *Strangeways, Here We Come* and to the 1990 riot that led to extensive rebuilding. It was designed by Manchester Town Hall architect Alfred Waterhouse in the 1860s; only the most disastrous of tourist excursions will end up within its walls, but its panopticon 234ft (71m) tower makes it one of the city centre periphery's more distinctive landmarks.

Eating & drinking

Aumbry

NEW *2 Church Lane, Prestwich, M25 1AJ (798 5841, www.aumbryrestaurant. co.uk). Metrolink Prestwich, or bus X43.* **Open** noon-2.30pm, 7-9.30pm Wed-Sat; noon-3.30pm Sun. **£££**. **Modern international**.
Aumbry is a contender for one of Manchester's best eateries – both the restaurant itself and chef Mary-Ellen McTague have won accolades. Looking like a Cotswold holiday home out front and resembling the dining room at a Lake District guesthouse inside, Aumbry's main visual appeal comes from the food itself – soused herring or roasted duck arranged as artfully as a Turner Prize entry. And, as you might imagine, it tastes pretty incredible too.

Lamb Hotel

33 Regent Street, Eccles, M30 0BP (no phone). Metrolink Eccles, or bus 10, 33, 63, 67, 68, 70, or Eccles rail. **Open** 11.30am-11pm Mon-Thur; 11.30am-11.30pm Fri, Sat; noon-11pm Sun. **Pub**.
As good as it gets when it comes to original pub decor. Built in 1906, this is a pretty much unspoilt Grade II-listed Holts pub, with a superb wood-panelled billiards room, complete with full-size table. Other features include exquisite glazed tiles, a clutch of high-ceilinged rooms and a huge mahogany bar, enclosed with thick acid-etched glass. Some of the regulars can be a bit intimidating; it's best to visit during the day.

Marble Arch Inn

73 Rochdale Road, Manchester, M4 4HY (832 5914). Metrolink Victoria, or bus 17, 17a, 24, 51, 56, 64, 65, 74-78, 80-83, 89, 112, 113, 118, 123, 124, 131, 163, 180-184, or Victoria rail. **Open** noon-11.30pm Mon-Thur; noon-midnight Fri, Sat; noon-10.30pm Sun. **Pub**.
Victorian tiling and a sloping floor give this place a historic feel. The brewery at the back makes it a magnet for real-ale aficionados. Guest beers from Marston's, Bazens' and Greene King supplement the brewery's own. Traditional pub food is available, and there's a decent jukebox.

Slattery

197 Bury New Road, Whitefield, M45 6GE (767 7761, www.slattery.co.uk). Metrolink Whitefield, or bus 90, 95, 98, 135, 484, or Whitefield rail. **Open** *Dining room* 9am-4pm Mon-Fri; 9am-3.30pm Sat. *Shop* 9am-5.30pm Mon-Fri; 9am-5pm Sat. **££**. **Tea room**.

Open all hours

The club that's raising the stakes for after-hours venues.

Sankeys

Following a radical refit that mirrored the regeneration of its industrial surroundings, Mancunian institution **Sankeys** (formerly Sankeys Soap) is proof that serious clubbing in Manchester is not solely about the mega-club experience. Situated in a landmark building, and featuring impressive line-ups, the club commands a substantial slice of the action and has now achieved recognition on the world stage.

The Beehive Mill-based club was refurbished back in 2006. A third room was added, the sound and light bolstered, the music policy reinvented and the grimy interior radically overhauled to create a brand new club space primed for futuristic fun. Clubbers responded favourably – in 2010, Sankeys was voted the number-one club in the world in *DJ Magazine*'s Top 100 Clubs poll.

'We're aiming to be the most forward-thinking venue north of Fabric [in London],' says owner David Vincent. '85 per cent of the DJs we've got booked have never played Manchester before, and that's always good for the scene. It helps music move forward and evolve.'

The club is neither superclub nor purely underground, but creates a boutique clubbers' experience from the best aspects of both. Because of this, and thanks to its year-round, five nights a week opening, Sankeys provides a more easily accessible Manchester club experience than the seasonal and often sold-out Warehouse Project (see box p116). Some nights, such as electro stalwart Bugged Out, are well established; others, such as underground house and Latin night Carnival, are more recent. The 2006 refurbishment undoubtedly gave Sankeys a slicker image, but it still continues to push the musical envelope after hours.

■ Listings p148.

The Slattery family have been baking since 1967, and crafting chocolates since 1991. They now run a dining room that serves breakfasts and lunches, as well as a range of chocolate-based goodies – their beautiful Swiss hot chocolate is simply orgasmic. They'll even teach you the arts of chocolate-making.

Nightlife

Sankeys

Beehive Mill, Radium Street, Ancoats, M4 6JG (236 5444, www.sankeys.info). Metrolink Market Street, or bus 75-78, 80, 82, 83, 89, 180-182, 184, 216-218, 231-237, or Piccadilly rail. **Open** 11pm-3am Tue-Thur; 11pm-5am Fri, Sat; 7pm-1am Sun. **Admission** varies.
See box p147.

Arts & leisure

Manchester City Football Club

Sportcity, M11 3FF (0870 062 1894, www.mcfc.co.uk). Bus 216, 217, 230, X36, X37, or Manchester Piccadilly rail. **Open** *Tours* 11am, 1.30pm, 3.30pm Mon-Sat; 11.45am, 1.45pm, 3.30pm Sun. **Admission** *Tours* £8.50; £6 reductions.
The 48,000-capacity City of Manchester Stadium hosted the 2002 Commonwealth Games before being converted for the city's less glamorous but more endearing second football club, Manchester City, in 2003. On site you'll find a club shop, a restaurant, a museum, athletics track and squash courts. Tours are available (£8.50, £6 reductions); call to book. On top of Manchester City home games, the stadium occasionally hosts big-name concerts and other events.

Manchester Climbing Centre

Bennett Street, West Gorton, M12 5ND (230 7006, www.manchesterclimbing centre.com). Bus 205, 206, or Ardwick rail. **Open** *Climbing wall* 10am-10pm Mon-Fri; 10am-6pm Sat, Sun. *Café* noon-9.30pm Mon-Fri; 10am-5.30pm Sat, Sun.
Practice your belaying and leading in this Grade-II listed church, which now houses one of the largest climbing walls in Europe. Hang around under the huge stained-glass windows on the 75 tied routes and two bouldering walls, or brush up on your rope skills with specialist courses. All levels are catered for here, from complete beginners (including children) to experienced climbers. Get to grips with the mezzanine-level Basecamp Café (good cakes, Wi-Fi access), with its great viewing gallery from which to watch the action.

Manchester Velodrome

Stuart Street, Philips Park, M11 4DQ (223 2244 Velodrome, 0843 208 1840 Revolution, www. manchestervelodrome.com). Metrolink Piccadilly, or bus 217, 219, 53, or Piccadilly rail. **Open** 8am-10pm daily.
As the home of the British Cycling Team, the Velodrome's track is one of the best in the world, but the place still welcomes all levels of ability. If riding a fixed-gear bike appeals, hour-long taster sessions provide full kit and advice on riding the steep banking (and how to stop a bike without brakes). 'Revolution' events held during the winter season pull in crowds of 3,000-plus with a 'night at the races' combo of sprinting and endurance races, music, food and booze. Basketball, netball, spinning classes and badminton are also on offer.

Octagon Theatre

Howell Croft South, Bolton, BL1 1SB (01204 529407, www.octagon bolton.co.uk). Bus 8, 12, 36, 37, 68, or Bolton rail.
This multi-award-winning and perennially popular theatre takes its name from its octagonal auditorium. This isn't the result of architectural whimsy: clever design means directors can choose from theatre-in-the-round, traditional end-on or 'thrust', depending on the production, and audiences are guaranteed excellent sightlines.

Octagon Theatre

Manchester United Football Club p165

South Manchester & Stockport

South Manchester

Manchester's wealthier communities are most populous in its southern reaches, whose suburban boutiques, eateries and gardens make the short trip out of the centre worth the effort. Though non-southern Mancunians tend to roll their eyes at mention of the organic-buying media types who populate **Didsbury** and **Chorlton** (rumour has it that one newsagent in Chorlton sells more *Guardian* newspapers than anywhere else in the UK), there is much to recommend these suburbs.

While the City Centre isn't particularly rich in open space, the southern suburbs have enough of the green stuff to make up for it. From **Fletcher Moss** in Didsbury to **Tatton Park** further out of town, there's enough parkland to get you pink-cheeked after overindulging in the city's more urban pursuits.

Heading south along the Oxford Road takes you towards Rusholme's **Curry Mile**, a riotous strip of neon lights, booming bhangra, swishing saris and curry houses so tightly packed that it'd be rude not to stop off and sample a bhuna or balti (the curries aren't always great, but the experience is). The traffic here can be horrendous during early evening.

Fallowfield is primarily a student stomping ground with little to recommend it; instead, head over to **Gorton** in the south-east to visit the **Manchester Monastery**, or down to **Withington**, **West Didsbury** and **Didsbury Village**. West Didsbury's **Burton Road** has become an eating destination for urbanites, with pubs such as the **Metropolitan** dishing up reliable, hearty fare. Across the road, **Greens** regularly serves staggering veggie dishes capable of sating even the most hardened of carnivores. Further west, though there's little else in leafy **Urmston**, is **Isinglass**, a superb restaurant serving English dishes and showcasing local produce.

Further south, along Princess Parkway, the dramatic **Hulme Arch Bridge** straddles the carriageway, a symbol of the area's impressive regeneration. Once a concrete jungle of dank flats and gloomy walkways, Hulme was rebuilt in the 1990s with smart red-brick townhouses and green spaces that replaced the 1960s high-rises.

Comfy boozers abound in the south, and it's easy to lose a Sunday afternoon switching between the papers and downing pints of locally brewed or organic beer. Chorlton's **Marble Beer House** is a good bet, while Withington's **Red Lion**, complete with beer garden and bowling green, is the perfect place to relax if the sun shines.

Those seeking retail therapy will be delighted by the quirky boutiques and independent record stores that clutter the streets in West Didsbury and Chorlton. Burton Road is again the place to head for in the former, while Chorlton's equivalent is **Beech Road**. Here, boutiques and boozers vie for space between delis and restaurants, although Beech Road's charms have been threatened by newer shops and bars opening in and around the Wilbraham and Barlow Moor crossroads – such as eclectic bar **Electrik** or the wonderfully kitsch **Wowie Zowie!**

As with the north, this slice of Greater Manchester is awash with sports venues. **Old Trafford** is home to Manchester United's 'theatre of dreams', as well as to **Lancashire County Cricket Club**'s ground.

Sights & museums

Elizabeth Gaskell House
84 Plymouth Grove, Ardwick, M13 9LW (01663 744 233, www.elizabeth gaskellhouse.org). Bus 50, 113, 130, 147, 191, 197, or Ardwick rail. **Open** noon-4pm 1st Sun of mth. **Admission** free (donations welcome).

After years of neglect, initial restoration of the home of Elizabeth Gaskell is now complete. One of Manchester's most esteemed novelists, Gaskell wrote in the 'industrial' genre made famous by such literary visitors to the house as Charles Dickens. With the Regency-style villa now saved from collapse – restoration was as much structural as to reveal original features – it now regularly opens to the public. Fundraising for further development continues.

Fletcher Moss Gardens
Wilmslow Road, Didsbury, M20 2SW (998 2117, www.manchester.gov.uk). Bus 42, 42a, 196, or East Didsbury rail. **Open** dawn-dusk (times vary). **Admission** free.

Donated to the public by Alderman Moss in 1914, these lovely gardens – stretching across some 21 acres in the suburbs – are notable for their rare plant species that bloom throughout the year. A nature trail winds through woods before opening on to the River Mersey, but the real draw is the tiered rock garden overlooking the tennis courts. A tiny teahouse opens sporadically (afternoons only) for tea and ice-cream.

Gallery of Costume
NEW *Platt Hall, Rusholme, M14 5LL (245 7245, www.manchestergalleries.org). Bus 41-44, 46-48, 54, 140-143, 145, 157, 158.* **Open** 1.30-4.30pm Wed-Sat. **Admission** free.

Housed in an 18th-century textile merchant's home and the recent recipient of a major makeover, this collection is the largest of its type in Britain (but with only a fraction of the 20,000-plus items on display). High fashion from the 17th century to the present is represented, and the contrasting selections of working attire from the neighbouring South Asian community are also interesting.

MANCHESTER BY AREA

Rehabilitating an old soak

Restoration of the Victoria Baths continues apace.

Victoria Baths

Victoria Baths, that fragile old dame of splashing and swimming, celebrated her 100th birthday in 2006 with the news that long-overdue restoration work was going ahead. Although one of Manchester's most sumptuous Grade II-listed Victorian remnants, the baths closed in 1993, and for ten years its future looked bleak.

Thanks to local campaigners, the baths claimed the attention of *Restoration*, the BBC TV show about buildings on the verge of collapse. Charming its way into first place, the Baths won the hearts of the voting public – and £3.5 million. Although not insubstantial, this initial funding, topped up by an extra £1 million in 2009, is around only a quarter of what the building needs for a complete restoration.

In the meantime, however, much good work has been done: a new roof tops the gala pool, the front block has been improved, and the stained glass, mosaic floors

and Turkish baths have been brought back to their former glory.

So now is a good time to pay a visit to this watery wonder. A multicoloured brick exterior gives way to floor-to-ceiling tiled rooms. Original signs still hang, while grand stained glass-windows gleam. The echoes of a noble past resonate across now-empty pools.

Best of all, because the building is now structurally sound, visitors are better catered for, with weekly tours (2pm Wed) and open days on the first Sunday of each month (Apr-Oct only). Although the building still lacks the mod cons you'd expect of a museum (a lack of heating, for example, forces the baths to close during winter), the volunteer staff pull out the stops to give a warm welcome. And as fundraising continues, the tours, gift shop and refreshments – not to mention occasional vintage fairs and art and music events – provide the icing on this particular architectural cake.
■ Listings, see right.

Manchester Monastery

Gorton Lane, Gorton, M12 5WF (223 3211, www.themonastery.co.uk). Bus 205, 206, or Ashburys rail. **Open** noon-4pm Sun. **Admission** free. *Tours* from £5. Designed by Edward Pugin and built between 1863 and 1867, this spectacular piece of ecclesiastical architecture, which was originally the Monastery of St Francis, served as a focus for the local community for over a century. Falling attendances (and declining numbers of monks) meant it was abandoned by the Franciscan order in 1989, and thereafter stripped of its contents by successive property developers, vandals and art thieves. A decade later, it was on the World Monuments Fund list of the globe's 100 most endangered sites. Much of the pilfered statuary has since been recovered, and a £6.5 million renovation in 2007 saw the building restored to its former glory. It now houses concerts, weddings and conferences, and runs regular tours.

Pankhurst Centre

60-62 Nelson Street, Chorlton-on-Medlock, M13 9WP (273 5673, www.thepankhurst centre.org.uk). Bus 15, 16, 41-44, 46-48, 50, 111, 113, 140-143. **Open** 10am-4pm Mon-Thur. **Admission** free. Saved from demolition in 1979, this Georgian house is where the remarkable Emmeline Pankhurst brought up her daughters Sylvia, Christabel and Adela, all active Suffragettes. She founded the militant Women's Social and Political Union here in 1903. Today, the Pankhurst Centre functions on two levels: as a women-only space for workshops, and as a bookshop and exhibition room (men admitted) recreating Pankhurst's parlour.

Tatton Park

Knutsford, Cheshire (01625 374400, www.tattonpark.org.uk). Bus 26, 27, 289, or Knutsford rail. **Open** *Park* late Mar-early Oct 10am-7pm daily. Early Oct-late Mar 11am-5pm Tue-Sun. *Mansion, garden, farm, Old Hall* varies;

see website for details. **Admission** *Mansion, garden or farm* £5; £3 reductions; £13 family. *Combined ticket* £8; £4 reductions; £20 family. *Park entry* (per car) £5.

Get lost in the Cheshire countryside in this 1,000-acre park with free-roaming deer, lakes and a farm. A walled garden has fruit trees and fig houses; sample some of this fresh produce in the on-site restaurant. The 200-year-old Mansion features unchanged state rooms, but the real attractions are outside – the gardens include an 1850s fernery and Japanese landscaping. Keep an eye out for garden-based artwork in 2012 when the Tatton Park Biennial returns.

Victoria Baths

Hathersage Road, Chorlton-on-Medlock, M13 OFE (224 2020, www.victoria baths.org.uk). Bus 191, 197, or Ardwick rail. **Open** *Apr-Nov* 2pm Wed; noon-4pm 1st Sun of mth. **Admission** £2. *Tours* £5. The winner of the BBC's *Restoration* programme in 2003, Victoria Baths is finally approaching a functional state after around £4.5 million-worth of development: walls, roof, windows and floors have all been restored. Regular vintage fairs, and art and music events are held here. See box, left.

Wythenshawe Hall & Gardens

Wythenshawe Park, Northenden, M23 0AB (998 2117, www.manchester. gov.uk). Bus 41. **Open** *Hall* June-Sept 11am-5.30pm Sat, Sun. *Gardens* daily (times vary). **Admission** free. Many of Wythenshaw Hall's original Tudor timbers – it was built in 1540 – survived a Parliamentarian assault when it held out as a Royalist stronghold during the English Civil War (hence the listed Oliver Cromwell statue opposite). The hall stands in 250-acre Wythenshawe Park, whose mix of meadows, formal gardens and woodlands is supplemented by a petting farm, horse-riding facilities and a horticultural centre.

Asian Fusion

489-491 Barlow Moor Road, Chorlton, M21 8ER (881 7200, www.asianfusionltd. co.uk). Bus 22, 23, 23a, 46, 47, 84, 85, 270, 297. **Open** 5-11.30pm Mon-Thur, Sun; 5pm-midnight Fri, Sat. **££. Asian**.
It's interesting to watch the chefs, led by Salim Ahmed, at work in this open-plan restaurant. Asian Fusion is a welcoming place, which is perhaps why it's always filled with families, couples and groups. Balti bangla – sizzling chunks of chicken topped with red onions – is a popular, medium-strength dish.

Café Jem&I

1C School Lane, Didsbury, M20 6RD (445 3996, www.jemandirestaurant. co.uk). Bus 23a, 42, 142, 157, 158, 171, 196, 370, or East Didsbury rail. **Open** noon-2pm, 5.30-10pm Mon-Thur; noon-2pm, 6-10pm Fri, Sat; noon-3pm, 6-10pm Sun. **££. Modern British**.
This popular Didsbury restaurant, run by the gifted Jem Sullivan (previously of the Lime Tree, p157), has been awarded the Michelin Bib Gourmand – a prize that identifies establishments that represent good value for money. Expect dishes such as pumpkin, asparagus and petit pois risotto for not much more than a tenner.

Gabriel's Kitchen

NEW *265 Upper Brook Street, M13 0HR (276 0911, www.themoderncaterer.co.uk).* Bus 50, 54, 113, 130, 147. **Open** 8am-5pm Mon-Thur; 8am-9pm Fri; 9am-9pm Sat; 10am-5pm Sun. **£. Café**.
Gabriel's Kitchen is an unfussy, wood-clad diner set off the Oxford Road corridor. Whether you opt for the steak salad with tangy dressing, mutton shoulder hotpot or one of the sublime cooked breakfasts, it's all regionally sourced good eating.

Greens

43 Lapwing Lane, Didsbury, M20 2NT (434 4259, www.greensdidsbury.co.uk). Bus 46, 47, 111, 169, 178, 179, or East Didsbury rail. **Open** 5.30-10.30pm Mon, Sat; noon-2pm, 5.30-10.30pm Tue-Fri; 12.30-3.30pm Sun. **££. Vegetarian**.
After a visit to Greens, it's more or less compulsory for carnivores to declare: 'I loved it, and I'm not even vegetarian.' The short set menu (three courses for £17, Wed-Fri and Sun lunch) provides brilliant value, but if you're out on a Saturday night, we recommend the roasted aubergine, beetroot and butter bean cottage pie with sauerkraut. Oh, and be sure to save a little room for the white chocolate cheesecake topped with dark chocolate sauce.

Horse & Jockey

NEW *9 The Green, Chorlton, M21 9HS (860 7794, www.horseandjockey chorlton.com).* Metrolink Chorlton, or bus 23, 86. **Open** noon-11pm Mon-Wed; noon-11.30pm Thur; 11am-midnight Fri, Sat; 11am-11pm Sun. **££. Gastropub**.
Beloved of Chorlton natives, the recently overhauled Horse & Jockey is a pub with great food, genuine heart and a mind blowing rotation of guest cask ales; in the space of just six weeks it racked up over 50 different brews. If you'd rather not indulge in an alcoholic beverage, though, it also has a coffee machine the size of the Death Star.

Isinglass

46 Flixton Road, Urmston, M41 5AB (749 8400). Bus 22, 23, 23a, 46, 47, 84, 85, 270, 297, or Urmston rail. **Open** noon-2.30pm, 6-10pm Mon-Thur; 6-11pm Fri, Sat; 6-10pm Sun. **££. Modern British**.
Suburban Urmston is the unlikely home of Isinglass, one of Manchester's most impressive restaurants. The name refers to a gelatin-like substance made from fish bladders used to clarify beer and wine – but don't let that put you off. This idiosyncratic establishment takes the oft-empty promise of using only local ingredients, and shows what can be achieved when experts hold themselves to it. Salad leaves from Chat

Manchester Monastery p153

Suburban deli delights

Gabriel's Deli

Like food? Then you'll love the southern suburbs, whose supply of fine food continues to expand like a waistband at Christmas. Despite incursions by the likes of supermarket giant Tesco, Chorlton remains a stronghold of independent eating. The gastronomic charge is led by Polish bakery **Barbakan** (Manchester Road), whose outstanding loaves (over 50 varieties, including a Chorlton sourdough) are matched by an extensive cheese and meats counter. Its baked charms are recognised elsewhere too: it supplies shops and restaurants across Manchester, including big names such as **Selfridges** (p82).

Unicorn Grocery (p161) is the city's only vegan supermarket, and stocks a range of organic produce, fruit and veg. Its organic wines and beers are recommended, although rumours that going organic may avoid a Saturday-morning hangover have been greatly exaggerated.

Traditionalists should head to the award-winning Chorlton fishmonger **Out of the Blue** (Wilbraham Road) – its fish pie mix offers particularly good value – as well as Didsbury's **Evans** (Barlow Moor Road), for fish, meat and poultry, or drop into the excellent (and, again, award-winning) **Cheese Hamlet** (Wilmslow Road). Traditional, too, is the tiny **JB Richardson's** bakery on Beech Road: expect old-school florentines, strawberry cream tarts and divine Eccles cakes that scream 'master confectioner' (as well as 'eat me now!'). You'll find cakes galore at **And the Dish Ran Away with the Spoon** (Burton Road), whose cupcakes, brownies and slices of sweetness can be sampled in the on-site café, or at the City Centre's **Real Food Market** (p68).

Still hungry? Fill up at **Gabriel's Deli** (Wilbraham Road). Home-cooked meals by the team behind **Gabriel's Kitchen** (p154) and the café at the **Whitworth Art Gallery** (p120) are sold alongside excellent cakes, coffee and limited fresh produce. Decent meals and sublime coffee are also on offer at the **Horse & Jockey** gastropub (p154), where even dogs get the chance to sup the very best: its canine beer (real beer with alcohol removed and beef flavour added) is, so we are told, something of a draw for those with four legs and a shaggy disposition.

Moss, rich Dunham Massey ice-cream, meat from Knutsford… the menu doubles up as a local geography guide. Most impressive of all, the evident quality comes at very affordable prices.

Jai Kathmandu

45 Palatine Road, Northenden, M22 4FY (946 0501). Bus 41, 43, 48, 105. **Open** noon-2.30pm, 6-11.30pm Mon-Thur; noon-2.30pm, 6pm-midnight Fri, Sat; 6-11pm Sun. **££. Nepalese**.
Although this restaurant (unconnected to West Didsbury's Great Kathmandu) may not appear to be much from the outside, inside, the Nepalese-centred cooking is a cut above most curry house fare. Spicy kidney kebabs and a rich bhuna gosht stand out on the menu.

Lime Tree

8 Lapwing Lane, West Didsbury, M20 2WS (445 1217, www.thelimetree restaurant.co.uk). Bus 46, 47, 111, 169, 178, 179, or East Didsbury rail. **Open** noon-2.30pm, 5.30-10.15pm Tue-Fri, Sun; 5.30-10.15pm Mon, Sat. **£££. Modern French**.
Patrick Hannity's refined operation has loyal customers who can border on the fanatical in their evangelising, but their fervour is well placed. The Lime Tree wears its French influences lightly, so dishes of calf's liver are accompanied by (a delicious) bubble and squeak.

Marble Beer House

57 Manchester Road, Chorlton, M21 9PW (881 9206). Metrolink Chorlton, or bus 84, 86, 270. **Open** noon-11pm Mon-Wed; noon-11.30pm Thur, Sun; noon-midnight Fri, Sat. **Pub**.
Small and intimate, this pub has a nice line in reclaimed furniture and an ever-changing choice of guest beers. There's a well-stocked chiller, with some mighty strong Belgian bottles. Snacks come by the bowl courtesy of Chorlton's famous organic grocers Unicorn, across the road. There's a sister branch of the pub – 57 Thomas Street (p93) – in the Northern Quarter.

Metropolitan

2 Lapwing Lane, West Didsbury, M20 2WS (374 9559, www.the-metropolitan. co.uk). Bus 46, 47, 111, 169, 178, 179, or East Didsbury rail. **Open** 11.30am-11.30pm Mon-Wed; 11.30am-midnight Thur-Sat; noon-11.30pm Sun. **£££. Pub**.
This sprawling, loveable pub is a prime venue in which to enjoy a traditional roast dinner – but booking is advisable. With its assortment of large tables and ramshackle bookshelves, the Met is a great venue for a lost Sunday. Evening dishes tend towards high-quality pub fare (Thai green curry, chicken suprême).

Petra Restaurant

267 Upper Brook Street, M13 0HR (274 4441, www.petra2eat.co.uk). Bus 50, 54, 113, 130, 147. **Open** 11.30am-2.30pm, 5-11pm Mon-Fri; 5-11pm Sat, Sun. **££. Middle Eastern**.
This unlicensed restaurant off a busy main road has a tasty take on Middle Eastern cuisine, from the delightful baba ganoush – an aubergine and garlic dip sweetened with pomegranate – to the range of delicately spiced kebabs. For a small corkage fee you can bring your own beer or wine.

POD

NEW *30 Albert Road, Levenshulme, M19 2FP (248 7990, www.pod-deli.co.uk). Bus 67, 191, 192, 193, 197, or Levenshulme rail.* **Open** 8am-10.30pm Mon-Thur, Sun; 8am-midnight Fri, Sat. **Deli**.
Introducing a much needed alternative to the fast food restaurants that dominate the Levenshulme culinary landscape, POD (an acronym of Post Office Deli rather than a reference to capsule-like dimensions) serves a host of boards and platters ideal for sharing. Or order a whole home-made corned beef hash, ideal for selfishly finishing yourself.

Red Lion

532 Wilmslow Road, Withington, M20 4BT (434 2441, www.redlionpub manchester.co.uk). Bus 50, 113, 130,

MANCHESTER BY AREA

147, or Burnage rail. **Open** 11am-11pm Mon-Wed; 11am-11.30pm Thur; 11am-12.30am Fri, Sat; noon-11.30pm Sun. **Pub**.

A cavernous pub with a whitewashed 200-year-old façade, the prevailing beer of choice here is Matson's. It's one of the most popular boozers in the area, especially during the summer, with bonuses being the long-running Monday-night quiz and a tremendous chippy (Andy's) opposite, to satisfy those post-pub munchies.

Royal Oak

729 Wilmslow Road, Didsbury, M20 6WF (434 4788). Bus 23, 42, 42a, 142, 157, 158, 171, 196, 370. **Open** 11am-11pm Mon-Wed; 11am-11.30pm Thur; 11am-midnight Fri, Sat; noon-11.30pm Sun. **Pub**.

Among the glitz and neon of the numerous chains that have taken over south Manchester's most affluent suburb, this place is a haven for traditionalists, being one of the few remaining places where you can quaff a pint of dark mild. Drama buffs will love the theatrical posters and memorabilia.

Solomon Grundy

449 Wilmslow Road, Withington, M20 4AN (445 0353). Bus 50, 113, 130, 147, or Burnage rail. **Open** 11am-midnight Mon-Thur; 10am-midnight Fri, Sat; 10am-11pm Sun. **Bar**.

With a friendly atmosphere that belies its hipster aesthetic, it's almost as if this place knows it's not as cool as it pretends to be – even the menu, mockingly subtitled 'world famous', is self-effacing. By night, Solomon Grundy goes into bar mode; over a glass or two of reasonably priced Rioja, students rub shoulders, and occasionally more, with locals.

Trof

2A Landcross Road, Fallowfield, M14 6NA (224 0467, www.trof. co.uk). Bus 41, 42, 43, 48, 142. **Open** 10am-midnight Mon-Thur; 10am-2am Fri; 9am-2am Sat; 9am-midnight Sun. **£**. **Café-bar**.

This café is a stone's throw from Fallowfield's many boozers, so most of the customers will be students eating off a hangover with a hearty breakfast, or, more likely, a hefty Trof burger. The chocolate milkshakes are a joy.

Shopping

Belly Button Cards & Gifts

240 Burton Road, West Didsbury, M20 2LW (434 4236, www.bellybutton designs.com). Bus 23, 42, 46, 111, 142, 157, 158, 171, 196, 370. **Open** 10.30am-6pm Mon-Sat; noon-4pm Sun.

This Manchester-based company sells its unique greetings cards all over the world, but its shop remains closer to home. There are no naff floral designs or lengthy poems here, just simple, quirky designs that are printed on high-quality paper. There's also a good range of blank cards, wrapping paper, notebooks and gifts.

Kingbee Records

519 Wilbraham Road, Chorlton, M21 0UF (860 4762, www.kingbeerecords. co.uk). Metrolink Chorlton, or bus 16, 46, 47, 85, 86, 168, 276. **Open** 10am-5.30pm Mon-Sat.

Record shops are ten a penny in Manchester – but some still achieve legendary status. Despite sitting on an anonymous suburban drag, Kingbee is the worst-kept secret in town. DJs, obsessives and musicians (both famous and aspiring) make regular visits here to stock their collections with rare, deleted and obscure 45s, and albums from the annals of ska, soul, rock and psychobilly.

Longsight Market

Dickenson Road, Longsight, M13 0WG (225 9859). Bus 53, 54, 168, 170, 173, 191, 192, 196, 197, or Levenshulme rail. **Open** 9am-4pm Tue; 9am-4.30pm Wed, Fri; 9am-5pm Sat.

See box p68.

McQueen p161

Lancashire County Cricket Club p165

McQueen

54 Beech Road, Chorlton, M21 9EG
(881 4718). Metrolink Chorlton, or bus
16, 46, 47, 85, 86, 168, 276. **Open**
10.30am-6pm Mon-Sat; noon-5pm Sun.
Not to be confused with the late fashion designer, McQueen is a small, independent boutique with hand-picked stock featuring up-and-coming labels, established designers and quirky one-offs for men and women. Shoes and bags add to the offerings, and while the shop can sometimes resemble a Primrose Hill-set jumble sale (with prices to match), it is delightfully British.

Pixie

6 Albert Hill Street, Didsbury, M20
6RF (445 5230, www.pixiechildrens
wear.com). Bus 23, 42, 142, 157, 158,
171, 196, 370, or East Didsbury rail.
Open 10am-5.30pm Mon-Sat.
A place like this could probably only work in Didsbury – the flashy, mon-eyed part of Manchester – as it appeals to mothers who don't believe in cheap and cheerful when it comes to dressing their children. It sells clothes, shoes and gifts for under-tens, as well as a range of yummy-mummy ready womenswear.

Sifters

177 Fog Lane, Burnage, M20 6FJ
(445 8697). Bus 44, 50, 130, 145,
169, 170, 179, 196, or Burnage rail.
Open 9.30am-5.30pm Mon, Tue, Thur-Sat; 9.30am-1pm Wed.
Enjoying the timeless publicity of a mention in an Oasis song (Mr Sifter in 'Shakermaker'), this small second-hand record shop emits a high-pitched whistling noise that only obsessive collectors – generally young men in studenty jackets – are able to hear. Not that 'normal' people won't find anything great – Sifters has everything from Loretta Lynn to Les Negresses Vertes – it's just that they'll need sharp elbows to snatch up that rare Nirvana import.

Trafford Centre

M60 junctions 9, 10, Manchester, M17
8AA (746 7777, www.traffordcentre.
co.uk). Metrolink Stretford, or bus 23,
23a, 250. **Open** 10am-10pm Mon-Fri;
10am-8pm Sat; noon-6pm Sun.
This huge, shiny mall caters for every whim and is, therefore, generally pulsing at the seams with bag-laden shoppers. All the major fashion names are here, plus John Lewis and Selfridges. In between are smaller chains, gift stores, endless cafés and a vast food court, topped with a multi-screen cinema. Barton Arcade hosts homeware stores such as Dwell and Habitat. The decor has an incongruous neoclassical theme, with sweeping marble halls, frolicking nymph murals and Romanesque busts surveying the retail frenzy.

Unicorn Grocery

89 Albany Road, Chorlton, M21 0BN
(861 0010, www.unicorn-grocery.co.uk).
Metrolink Chorlton, or bus 84, 86, 270.
Open 9.30am-7pm Tue-Fri; 9am-6pm
Sat; 11am-5pm Sun.
A large vegan grocery store selling everything the environmentally conscious shopper could wish for. The produce is locally sourced, organic and/or GM-free, and all household products can be guaranteed not to kill fish or turn squirrels radioactive. There's also a wide range of dairy-free, gluten-free and sugar-free items.

Wowie Zowie!

107 Manchester Road, Chorlton, M21
9GA (860 6470, www.wowiezowie-online.
com). Metrolink Chorlton, or bus 84, 86,
270. **Open** 1pm-7pm Mon; 11am-7pm
Tue-Fri; 11am-6pm Sat; 11am-5pm Sun.
Few shops have an exclamation mark in their title, but few shops are like Wowie Zowie! Right at home in bohemian Chorlton, this tiny delight is jam-packed with pristine vintage homewares, records, clothing and accessories. Everything is hand-selected, from Ladybird books to jewel-coloured glassware. Once you

MANCHESTER BY AREA

get over feeling suddenly old, you'll probably be tempted to buy your very own piece of 1970s nostalgia.

Nightlife

Electrik

559a Wilbraham Road, Chorlton, M21 0AE (881 3315, www.electrikbar.co.uk). Metrolink Chorlton, or bus 84-86, 168. **Open** 3pm-midnight Mon; noon-midnight Tue-Thur, Sun; noon-1am Fri, Sat.

Before Electrik, Chorlton's barlife was obstinately focused on the salubrious but secluded Beech Road area. Electrik heralded a shift back to the arterial centre, and a lively crowd packed up against its patio doors is now a prominent feature of the Chorlton weekend. Opened by the collective behind Manchester's Electric Chair club, Electrik hosts DJs at the weekend and a painstakingly curated jukebox on weekdays. An intimate, lively setting, it also has decent daytime coffee and food.

Fuel Café Bar

448 Wilmslow Road, Withington, M20 3BW (448 9702). Bus 23, 41-44, 142, 143. **Open** 11am-midnight Mon-Thur; 11am-2am Fri; 10am-2am Sat; 10am-midnight Sun.

A relaxed vegetarian café-bar by day, Fuel hosts a diverse programme of nightlife events by independent promoters. Monthly regulars include live acts from local label Debt Records, and a friendly and eclectic open-mic night. Look out for occasional readings and film screening nights.

Iguana Bar

115-117 Manchester Road, Chorlton, M21 9PG (881 9338, www.iguanabar. co.uk). Metrolink Chorlton, or bus 84-86, 270. **Open** noon-12.30am Mon-Thur, Sun; noon-2am Fri; Sat.

This unpretentious, welcoming set-up has seen a number of additions and improvements to its already eclectic schedule. Stop in for long-running weekly stand-up session Mirth on Mondays, wave your glow sticks at Wednesday's Chorlton 'n' Cheese night, or bop to quirky indie beats with DJ Camille on the last two Fridays of the month. Different world music events rotate throughout the month.

Manchester Apollo

Stockport Road, Ardwick Green, M12 6AP (0870 401 8000, www.carling. com/music). Bus 192, or Ardwick rail. **Open** varies.

A staple of the Manchester gig circuit, and just a short walk from Piccadilly, this former theatre turned mid-sized concert venue is packed nightly by music fans seeking hip hop, dance, rock or cheesy pop. Pay more for a civilised seat on the balcony, or grab a piece of the action on the dancefloor. It's also known as the Carling Apollo.

Rampant Lion

17 Anson Road, Victoria Park, M14 5BZ (225 9925, www.rampantlionpub.co.uk). Bus 50, 130. **Open** noon-midnight Mon-Thur, Sun; noon-1am Fri, Sat.

Established for years as cosy boozer for the student halls next door, the Rampant Lion reopened in 2009 with stylish new decor, a gastropub menu and a varied events calendar. The main bar is a bright, friendly drinking and dining space, while the basement venue hosts bands and DJs.

Arts & leisure

Belle Vue Greyhound Stadium

Kirkmanshulme Lane, Gorton, M18 7BA (0870 840 7550, www.lovethedogs.co.uk). Bus 201, 203, 204, or Belle Vue rail. **Open** 6.30pm Thur-Sat. **Admission** £3-£5; £3 12-17s; free under-11s.

Three race meetings a week, every week, featuring one of the world's fastest animals – the greyhound. Choose from trackside bellowing and fast food or the more refined option of three courses and polite cheering in the Grandstand restaurant.

Mountain excitement

Chill Factore

Anyone familiar with the UK's swelling ranks of indoor ski slopes knows that they can be far from atmospheric – more akin to sliding around a refrigerated aircraft hangar than cruising through mountains. It's a problem that owners of the £31 million **Chill Factore**, the UK's longest real-snow indoor ski slope, have been determined to address. Real snowflakes are produced here every night (using a mix of compressed air and water), thus ensuring a crisp covering of around 16 tonnes of fresh snow on the slopes each morning.

It may be just across from the Trafford Centre, but the ambience of the place has been as carefully controlled as the climate, with a series of themed 'mountain village' restaurants lining the centre's Alpine Street, although the range on offer – JD Wetherspoon's, Costa Coffee, Nando's – are really only as alpine as their wood-panelled decor. Shops fare better: Snow+Rock, the North Face and Quicksilver are all credible snow-brands.

But it's the facilities here that will impress the most: as well as all that snow, the main slope, coming in at a 15-degree rake and 180 metres long, is suitable for experienced skiers (it's equivalent to an outdoor red run), while a 40-metre nursery slope, 60-metre luge and supervised snow-play crèche, not to mention a packed programme of ski and snowboard lessons, will help any would-be skier improve their runs.

The cost of maintaining this sub-zero installation means that hour-by-hour skiing is priced higher than even the priciest of Alpine paradises at roughly £25 per two-hour session. But, of course, it saves you the price of a flight – and the environmental impact. And though snow-making is never going to be green, Chill Factore is at least trying to be responsible, using environmentally sound refrigerant, plus renewable energy sources. Pre-booking, particularly at evenings and weekends, is recommended.

■ www.chillfactore.com

A night at the Plaza

Stockport's art deco cinema is enjoying a new heyday.

Stockport Plaza

Elegance isn't a word often associated with a night at the flicks, but patrons at the **Stockport Plaza** expect to step into another era, and to do so with a bit of class. From usherettes with doily headdresses to Pathé newsreels played before the main feature, the Plaza delights in its position as a 1930s Super Cinema, a Grade-II listed building and much-loved urban anachronism in the heart of Stockport.

Built in 1932, at the height of the Depression and during the switchover from silent movies to 'talkies', the Plaza served as an escape for people used to the hard life of a northern industrial town. From 1967 to 1999, the building was a Mecca bingo hall, but was converted back to a cinema by a charitable trust in 2000, and fully restored, to the tune of £3.2 million, in 2009. Featuring a single screen with an impressive 1,200-seat capacity, the Plaza certainly knows its clientele: several recent screenings could have sold out three times over. When it's not screening films, the venue serves as a variety theatre showing classic plays that appeal to both a nostalgic older crowd and young urbanites with a thing for Bette Davis.

And then there's the Compton organ, which is kept in pristine condition so that the likes of Radio 2's Nigel Ogden can accompany the occasional silent movie double bills. Organ music also precedes regular classic movie screenings, and the house organist delivers a rousing rendition of the national anthem at the end of the night.
■ Listings p166.

Lancashire County Cricket Club

Talbot Road, Old Trafford, M16 0PX (0844 499 9666, 874 3333 Lodge, www.lccc.co.uk). Metrolink Old Trafford, or bus 114, 252, 253, 254, 255, 256, 257, 263, 264. **Open** *Office* 9am-5pm Mon-Fri. Closed in winter.

The home of Lancashire County Cricket Club for 150 years, the pavilion at Old Trafford is now looking a little tatty. On the cards is a controversial £70 million modernisation programme, which will include expansion, although at time of writing the future of the scheme was uncertain. The Lodge, a 68-room hotel overlooking the pitch, provides a place to stay for die-hard fans, while a small museum (open on 1st XI and International match days) displays 200 years' worth of cricketing memorabilia.

Manchester United Football Club

Sir Matt Busby Way, Old Trafford, M16 0RA (868 8000, www.manutd. com). Metrolink Old Trafford, or bus 256, 263. **Open** (excluding match days) *Museum* 9.30am-5pm daily. *Tours* 9.40am-4.30pm daily. **Admission** *Museum* £10.50; £8.50 reductions; £34 family. *Museum & tour* £13.50; £10 reductions; £44 family.

The stadium of the world's most famous football team may not be in the most glamorous of locations, but it nevertheless has the Premier League's largest capacity, recently expanded to 76,000. If you can't get your mitts on a match-day ticket (they're extremely hard to get hold of without a season ticket), console yourself in United's impressive museum. Kids can try to kick the ball as hard as Wayne Rooney (a high-tech machine measures maximum velocity – they'll have to top 77mph to beat United's star players), or trot down the players' tunnel as part of the popular behind-the-scenes tour (book in advance; tickets can be bought via the website).

Stockport

Stockport may be seen as a plainer, less fashionable sister to Manchester, but it still manages to hold its own. The vast borough is made up of eight districts and reaches from Manchester to the Peak District. Visitors can head out to **Mellor** and **Marple** for pubs and walks, **Bramhall** and **Lyme Park** (p168) for their historic houses, or into **Heaton Moor** for drinks and dinner. Stockport town centre itself is a mix of high-street shops and meandering cobbled streets, with a splendid 15th-century market place and Victorian covered hall at the top of town. It's also home to the landmark brick viaduct, as painted by Lowry, and the UK's first (and only!) hat museum.

Sights & museums

Hatworks

Wellington Mill, Wellington Road South, Stockport, SK3 0EU (355 7770, www. hatworks.org.uk). Bus 42, 173, 192, 203, or Stockport rail. **Open** (last entry 4pm) 10am-5pm Tue-Sat; 11am-5pm Sun. **Admission** free. *Tours* £2.65; £7 family. Proudly describing itself as 'the UK's only museum devoted solely to the hatting industry', Hatworks is a quaint experience, displaying machinery and memorabilia from local hatting factories (once the town's prime trade, hence Stockport County FC's nickname of the Hatters). A second floor is crammed with headwear donated by everyone from Vivienne Westwood to Fred Dibnah, plus there's an extensive family area where kids can play dress-up.

Staircase House

30-31 Market Place, Stockport, SK1 1ES (480 1460, www.staircasehouse. org.uk). Bus 42, 173, 192, 203, or Stockport rail. **Open** 1-5pm Tue-Fri; 10am-5pm Sat; 11am-5pm Sun. **Admission** £4; £3 reductions.

Located behind the tourist information office, and extensively restored following a major fire in 1995, Staircase House is a very modern presentation of the city's architectural history told through the surviving layers of this impressive building. Dating back to the 15th century, and continuously occupied until shortly after World War II, its rooms are filled with replica period furnishings and artefacts, most of which can be handled.

Stockport War Memorial & Art Gallery

Wellington Road South, Stockport, SK3 8AB (474 4453, www.stockport.gov.uk). Bus 42, 173, 192, 203, or Stockport rail. **Open** 1-5pm Tue-Fri; 10am-5pm Sat; 11am-5pm Sun. **Admission** free.

In contrast to the grand colonnaded entry, the gallery space that hosts a changing programme of art exhibitions consists of just a pair of drab, functional rooms. Beyond is a more impressive and imposing statue of Britannia, with a kneeling warrior beneath a beautiful glass-domed ceiling, surrounded by engraved lists of the fallen. Upstairs, the memorial hall acts as the main gallery.

Eating & drinking

Damson

113 Heaton Moor Road, Stockport, SK4 4HY (432 4666, www.damson restaurant.co.uk). Bus 42, 173, 192, 203, or Stockport rail. **Open** noon-3pm, 5-10.30pm Mon-Sat; noon-7.30pm Sun. **£££**. **Modern British**.

Out on Heaton Moor is one of the most talked-about restaurants in south Manchester. It's from the team behind Sam's Chop House (p74), so you can expect the same great quality, albeit with significantly subtler flavours – lobster, mussel and crab risotto is one of the menu's many delights.

Swan with Two Necks

36 Princes Street, Stockport, SK1 1RY (480 2341). Bus 42,

173, 192, 203, or Stockport rail. **Open** 11am-11pm daily. **Pub**.

Built in 1926, this is a long, narrow Robinson's pub, and one of several in Stockport town centre that have made it into CAMRA's *Inventory of Historic Pub Interiors* (the nearby Queen's Head is another). There's a snug, a vault and a comforting amount of wood and glass. The food is traditional pub grub, with huge portions followed by a small bill. You can sometimes smell the beer at the nearby Robinson's brewery.

Nightlife

Blue Cat Café

17 Shaw Road, Heaton Moor, Stockport, SK4 4AG (432 2117, www.bluecatcafe. co.uk). Bus 142, or Heaton Chapel rail. **Open** 7pm-midnight daily.

The Blue Cat is a little enclave of city bohemia picked up and transplanted to the 'burbs. It proudly showcases the best new bands, both local and touring, operating a policy of original music only, with no tribute or cover bands allowed. Past highlights include Johnny Marr and Viva Stereo. Most bands can be seen without having to pay a cover.

Arts & leisure

Sale Sharks

Edgeley Park, Hardcastle Road, Stockport, SK3 9DD (286 8926, www.salesharks. com). Bus 11, 28, 192, 309, 310, 368, 369, 371, X69, or Stockport rail.

One of the oldest clubs in English Rugby history, the Sale Sharks are currently playing their best-ever matches. They play at the home of Stockport County FC – a League Two side that offers a refreshing antidote to English football's over-priced Premiership.

Stockport Plaza

The Plaza, Mersey Square, Stockport, SK1 1SP (477 7779, www.stockport plaza.co.uk). Bus 42, 191, 192, or Stockport rail.
See box p164.

Alderley Edge

Days Out

The listings in this guidebook cover only the central portion of Greater Manchester. In this chapter, you'll find highlights of the wider urban area, along with trips that dip into the beautiful countryside that surrounds the city.

Alderley Edge

About 15 miles south of Manchester, into the footballer belt, the plush little town of Alderley Edge is something of a magnet for the Cheshire set. The town centre is full of boutiques, bijou restaurants and amusingly expensive charity shops; aim for the junction of London Road and Stevens Street for the most browsable.

You can pass a happy hour indulging in material pursuits here, but what distinguishes Alderley Edge from other wealthy satellite towns is the primeval geological feature that gives the town its name. Just over a mile away via the B5087 (Macclesfield Road), the edge itself is a red sandstone escarpment

some 600 feet (185 metres) high, thought to be the result of a cataclysmic prehistoric flood. On a clear day, you can see for miles across the Cheshire plain.

The land is owned by the National Trust and, on certain days (call 01625 584412 for details), you can turn up for a guided walk that will point out the geological history as well as a wealth of intriguing features, including the site of a beacon that was to be used to alert the country to the arrival of the Spanish Armada, a hermit's refuge and the face of a wizard carved into the rock. This face is relatively recent, but does draw attention to the folklore that formed the basis for Alan Garner's brilliant Edge-set 1960 children's novel *The Weirdstone of Brisingamen*.

Take a refreshment break at the Wizard tearoom situated next to the car park. Then, if you're driving, take in Nether Alderley Mill (Congleton Road, Nether Alderley, SK10 4TW, 01625 445853, www.nationaltrust.org.uk), but plan ahead: it's open only to pre-booked groups. A gem of an Elizabethan corn-mill, complete with working water-wheel, it's a mile south on the A34.

Getting there: Take the train from Manchester Piccadilly to Alderley Edge, or, by car, take the A34 directly from the City Centre.

Lyme Park

Disley, Stockport, Cheshire, SK12 2NX (01663 762023, www.nationaltrust. org.uk). **Open & admission** days & times vary; check website for details. This attractive country house on the threshold of the Peak District has much to recommend it, but owes its recent fame to being the setting for Colin Firth's memorable appearance from the lake in the 1995 BBC adaptation of *Pride and Prejudice*. As well as that happy memory, visitors will be treated to roaming herds of red and fallow deer on the numerous country walks. If you're on foot, note that the park entrance is over a mile from the hall and buildings; a shuttle bus operates when the house is open, in the spring and summer.

Lyme Hall dates back to Tudor times, and Tudor elements survive, although most of the present-day building dates from extravagant 18th-century conversions. It's surrounded by an elegant series of Victorian conservatories and gardens. All the usual National Trust facilities – café, knowledgeable guides, a shop – are present and correct, and there's also an adventure playground.

For a taste of the Peak District proper, nip across the Derbyshire border five miles away to the rambler-friendly village of Hayfield. It's a big draw for walkers here, as one of the best access points to the rugged moor-land and mountain of Kinder Scout, the historic site of the 1932 mass tres-pass that ultimately led to today's right to roam. Should Kinder prove a little too ambitious, then the village of Little Hayfield is a mile away on paths and minor roads, or you could follow one of the paths on the Sett Valley trail (follow signs from Hayfield station

car park or call in to the information centre on Station Road; 01663 746222).

For a meal, try the Pack Horse (3-5 Market Street, SK22 2EP, 01663 740074, www.thepackhorsehayfield.com); it's a handsome pub offering locally sourced meat dishes and good veggie options.

Getting there: Lyme Park is on the A6, 12 miles south of Manchester. To reach Hayfield, continue on the A6, then go left on the A6015 once through Disley. Disley train station is half a mile from the park gates; the line (or a bus, or a mile's walk) also connects to New Mills, from where you can get a bus to Hayfield.

Quarry Bank Mill

Quarry Bank Road, Styal, Wilmslow, Cheshire, SK9 4LA (01625 527468, www.quarrybankmill.org.uk). **Open** days & times vary; check website for details. **Admission** £14.20; £7.05 reductions; £35.40 family.

One of the industrial jewels in the National Trust's crown, Quarry Bank Mill is an impressively preserved 18th-century mill building, the centre of a working colony established by Samuel Greg that was both socially and techno-logically revolutionary for its time. Set in a wooded country estate, it stands as a living portal to the past, as well as a pretty setting for rambles and picnics.

Approached down a hill, the vast red-brick building stands next to the river (the first mill was powered by water wheel, a stunning example of which is still active). The damp local climate was ideal for cotton processing – too dry, and the cotton would not stretch – and the mill stands as a reminder of what made the region the industrial powerhouse it was. At the start of the walkthrough tour, museum inter-preters in period dress show you early spinning techniques before taking you into halls of still-operative machinery – the deafening clatter of the demon-stration is an experience in itself. In the neighbouring Apprentice House you can see where a significant body of orphaned children lived and worked.

Lyme Park

A decent café provides refreshments and meals, setting you up for a walk around the Styal Country Estate on a route past the man-made lakes and tributaries that powered the mill.

Ten minutes' walk away is Styal village. Once an insignificant hamlet, it developed into a workers' colony when Greg established the mill, and today remains mostly unaltered from the mid 19th century – the shop, school, chapel and cottages are remnants of this sprawling monument to the Industrial Revolution.

Getting there: By car, take the B5167 out of the City Centre, then the B5166 to Quarry Bank Mill, a journey of about ten miles. Styal has a railway station but services (from Manchester Piccadilly) are infrequent.

Ramsbottom

This agreeable Victorian mill town in the moorlands of north Manchester was established in the early 19th century by Daniel and William Grant – who live on in fiction as Dickens' Cheeryble brothers in *Nicholas Nickleby*. The town nestles in the Irwell Valley below the looming Holcombe Hill and, while unremarkable for shopping (aside from the farmers' market on the second Sunday of every month), makes a good base for other activities. A good way to get there is on the East Lancs Steam railway (0161 764 7790, www.east-lancs-rly.co.uk), which chugs its way between Heywood, Bury and Rawtenstall at weekends.

Following Bridge Street up the hill brings you to the *Tilted Vase* sculpture in the marketplace, which is part of the 40-mile Irwell Sculpture Trail (www.irwellsculpturetrail.co.uk). A less ambitious hike is Holcombe Hill itself. Follow Carr Street and head uphill bearing to the left, past the Shoulder of Mutton pub (a decent stop for refreshment; 01706 822001, www.theshoulderofmutton.net) and take the path of your choice. Once you've ascended – a straightforward

hour's walk for all levels (or there's a road for cheats with cars) – you'll see the Peel Tower, a landmark for miles around. Built in 1852 in tribute to Sir Robert Peel, the 19th-century prime minister (born in nearby Bury) and founder of the modern police force, the tower is sometimes open at weekends (you'll know because the flag is raised; or you can call 0161 253 5899), its 148-step ascent offering an even more striking view than that from its base.

Getting there: By road, take the M66 then the A676. On public transport, take the Metrolink to Bury, then the 472 or 474 bus (except Sunday).

Ashton-under-Lyne

Ashton is one of the less glamorous satellites orbiting the M60 ring road (to the east); but despite its lack of pizzazz, it contains a pair of undersung but quietly excellent museums that should ensure a gently memorable day out.

In the town centre, the Museum of the Manchester Regiment (Ashton Town Hall, OL6 6DL, 0161 342 2254, closed Sun) commemorates the experiences and sacrifices of the Manchester Regiment, which was established in 1881 and associated with the town for many years. The Regiment is best known for the World War I poets who served with it, including Wilfred Owen. Among the regimental memorabilia, a recreation of a trench is a suitably sobering experience.

A mile away across the town centre, following first Stamford Street and then, after the roundabout, Park Parade, the Portland Basin Museum (Portland Place, OL7 0QA, 0161 343 2878, closed Mon) nudges up alongside the Ashton Canal, from where occasional barge trips run (call the Huddersfield Canal Society for details, 01457 871800). The old warehouse is crammed full of artefacts from a century or so ago, and also has a lovingly recreated 1920s street.

Getting there: Take bus 216 or 219 from Manchester city centre, or drive there on the A635.

Essentials

Abode

Hotels

Manchester's hotel scene has undergone a radical overhaul in recent years. The arrival in 2006 of the landmark **Hilton** on Deansgate set a new precedent. Located on the lower half of the 47-storey **Beetham Tower** (p128), the Hilton dominates the city's skyline.

Other hotels may not have been able to match the Hilton's size, but what they lack in square footage they've made up for in other ways. A rash of high-spec hotels have sprung up, while the city's older establishments have been treated to makeovers. The Eclectic Hotel Collection, for example, is a trio of the city's best 'boutique' hotels: **Great John Street**, **Didsbury House** and **Eleven Didsbury Park** each combine luxurious style with highly personal service. The Grade II-listed **Midland Hotel**, meanwhile, is still on form after its £15 million refit in 2005.

Business and budget chains have also smartened up their looks (and their acts), meaning that standards across the city are generally high. Despite the recession, few hotels have closed without swiftly reopening under new management. This – coupled with the number of new properties on the block – means that there's never been a better choice of places to stay in Manchester.

City Centre

Abode
107 Piccadilly, M1 2DB (247 7744, www.abodehotels.co.uk). Metrolink Piccadilly Gardens, or City Centre buses, or Piccadilly rail. **£££**.
The Abode chain has successfully made its modern mark on this Grade II-listed warehouse while retaining many original features, including the walnut and wrought-iron staircase. Its 61 rooms (rated from 'comfortable' to

'fabulous'; we know which we would pick) all feature luxury toiletries, monsoon showers and flatscreen TVs. The basement Champagne & Cocktail Bar serves Michael Caines' coveted tapas dishes, while discerning diners flock to his adjoining restaurant (p108).

Arora International

18-24 Princess Street, M1 4LY (236 8999, www.arorainternational.com). Metrolink St Peter's Square, or City Centre buses, or Piccadilly rail. **£££**.
Cliff Richard isn't a name you'd normally associate with cutting-edge design. Yet the holy rock 'n' roller is part-owner of one of the hippest hotels in the city. The Arora is a vision of contemporary cool, with sleek, modern rooms and funky furniture. (Five Cliff-themed rooms feature artworks and objects from the singer's personal collection.) A visit to the hotel bar and fine dining restaurant, Obsidian (p72), is a must.

Britannia Manchester

35 Portland Street, M1 3LA (0871 222 0017, www.britanniahotels.com). Metrolink Piccadilly Gardens, or City Centre buses, or Piccadilly rail. **££**.
The Britannia's main selling points are its location – on Piccadilly Gardens – and its very reasonable rates. The ostentatious decor will not be to everyone's taste, but it's perfect for those who like a bit of faded grandeur, with a sweeping gold staircase and huge chandeliers. A 2007 refurbishment smartened it up without sacrificing the traditional looks.

Great John Street Hotel

Great John Street, M3 4FD (831 3211, www.greatjohnstreet.co.uk). City Centre buses, or Salford Central rail. **££££**.
Great John Street, one of three Eclectic Hotels in the city, pulls out all the stops to deliver a luxurious boutique experience. Housed in an old Victorian schoolhouse, it offers uniquely designed duplex suites. Hand-carved furniture, roll-top baths and super-sexy fabrics lend the place a modern-vintage feel.

SHORTLIST

Best new
- Light Aparthotel (see box p182)
- Velvet (p179)

Best for hipsters
- Great John Street Hotel (p173)
- Lowry (p180)
- Velvet (p179)

Hotels with heritage
- Midland Hotel (p175)
- Palace Hotel (p176)
- Radisson Edwardian (p176)

Cheap as chips
- Hatters (p176)
- Islington Mill (p180)

Budget style
- Hilton Chambers (p176)
- Ox (p179)

Best breakfast
- Malmaison (p175)
- Lowry (p180)

Stellar restaurants
- Michael Caines Restaurant at Abode (p108)
- Obsidian at Arora (p72)
- River Restaurant at the Lowry (p139)

Best suites
- Didsbury House Hotel (p183)
- Midland Hotel (p175)

Best spa
- Lowry (p180)
- Radisson Blu (p180)

Location, location, location
- Britannia Manchester (p173)
- New Union Hotel (p179)

Best traditional
- Abbey Lodge (p180)
- Etrop Grange (p180)

ESSENTIALS

Although the hotel doesn't have guest parking or a restaurant (though there is informal dining in the lounge), the chichi bar and rooftop hot tub make up for it.

Hilton

303 Deansgate, M3 4LQ (870 1600, www.hilton.co.uk). Metrolink Deansgate-Castlefield, or City Centre buses, or Deansgate rail. **£££**.
There may be a set of swanky apartments above, but for 23 impressive floors, the Beetham Tower belongs to the Hilton, as witnessed by the unmissable branding. Rooms are equipped with the latest technology (ergonomic work stations, laptop access). Cloud 23 bar (p133), halfway up the tower, is straight out of *Lost in Translation*. The ground-floor Podium restaurant-bar doesn't have the impressive views, but does deliver great food.

Jurys Inn

56 Great Bridgewater Street, M1 5LE (953 8888, www.bookajurysinn.com). Metrolink Deansgate-Castlefield, or City Centre buses, or Deansgate rail. **££**.
Well placed for the Bridgewater Hall (opposite), Manchester Central and Deansgate Locks, this purpose-built Jurys Inn offers fairly priced, good-standard accommodation. The bedrooms and communal areas have been refurbished according to the inoffensive, generically modern brand spec. There's a relaxed atmosphere in the on-site restaurant, coffee-shop and bar.

Macdonald Townhouse Hotel

101 Portland Street, M1 6DF (0844 855 9136, www.macdonaldhotels.co.uk). Metrolink Market Street, or City Centre buses, or Piccadilly rail. **££**.
Originally a cotton warehouse, this Grade II-listed property has been a hotel since 1982. On the exterior, it's all Victorian splendour, but a recent £3.5 million makeover has left the interior looking far more modern. Its 85 boutique-style rooms offer free Wi-Fi,

laptop safes and flatscreen TVs. Brasserie 101, on the ground floor, serves exotic dishes and contemporary British cuisine in stylish surroundings. A handy location for Canal Street, Chinatown and the City Centre.

Malmaison

Piccadilly, M1 1LZ (278 1000, www.malmaison.com). Metrolink Piccadilly, or City Centre buses, or Piccadilly rail. **£££**.
A favourite with visiting bands and celebs, the Mal is a first choice for those who like to think of themselves as possessors of style. The old Joshua Hoyle textile mill's recent facelift introduced a dark-toned red, brown and black colour scheme to many of the suites. The star of the new line-up is the seriously sexy Moulin Rouge room; the freestanding bath in the lounge takes around 30 minutes to fill, such is its depth.

Manchester Marriott Victoria & Albert

Water Street, M3 4JQ (832 1188, www.marriott.com). City Centre buses, or Salford Central rail. **£££**.
Originally a textile warehouse, this Grade II-listed building now houses 129 hotel rooms, a conference centre and a bar and restaurant. The corporate feel is softened by exposed wooden beams, bare brickwork and quirkily shaped rooms, while photographic reminders of former occupier Granada TV line the mezzanine gallery of the reception.

Midland Hotel

Peter Street, M60 2DS (236 3333, www.qhotels.co.uk). Metrolink St Peter's Square, or City Centre buses, or Oxford Road rail. **££££**.
This grand old dame of Manchester hotels opened in 1905. It's had its fair share of high-profile visitors over the decades (Winston Churchill, Princess Anne) and goes down in history as the place where Charles Stewart Rolls and Frederick Henry Royce met. Owners Q Hotels lavished a multi-million pound makeover on the interior in 2005. The

ESSENTIALS

feel is modern classic throughout, from the marble-floored reception to richly furnished rooms.

Mint Hotel

One Piccadilly Place, Auburn Street, M1 3DG (242 1000, www.minthotel. com). Metrolink Piccadilly, or City Centre buses, or Piccadilly rail. **£££**.
Plush but unpretentious, the oddly named Mint Hotel (previously known as City Inn) has possibly the best location for commuters: it's just a short walk across a pedestrian bridge from Piccadilly Station. All 285 rooms come with iMacs, power showers and flexible check-in/out, while a decent terrace restaurant, cocktail menu and occasional art exhibitions also help to make it one of the city's better new hotels.

Novotel Manchester Centre

21 Dickinson Street, M1 4LX (235 2200, www.novotel.com). Metrolink St Peter's Square, or City Centre buses, or Oxford Road rail. **£££**.
Describing itself as a 'new generation Novotel', this hotel does have more to offer than similarly branded accommodation in the city. The rooms may be a set size, but effort has gone into funking up the decor, and a good spa and gym add to the appeal. There are busy bars in the vicinity, but if an evening in a Wetherspoons isn't your bag, then head to nearby Chinatown.

Palace Hotel

Oxford Street, M60 7HA (288 1111, www.palace-hotel-manchester.co.uk). Metrolink St Peter's Square, or City Centre buses, or Oxford Road rail. **£££**.
This well-loved, historic hotel is housed in the old Refuge Assurance Building (p120) and is owned by the Principal Hayley group, who gave it a £7 million facelift in 2005. The restored glass dome over the vast reception makes for an impressive entrance, while the Tempus bar mixes original Victorian flooring and tiles with cool

design. While many rooms have been completely refitted, some have yet to be revamped and perhaps don't reach the four-star standards of those that have. All, however, are charmingly traditional and have majestic ceilings.

Radisson Edwardian

Free Trade Hall, Peter Street, M2 5GP (835 9929, www.radissonedwardian. com). Metrolink St Peter's Square, or City Centre buses, or Oxford Road rail. **££££**.
Some may say that turning the Free Trade Hall into a hotel is criminal, but the Radisson has made real efforts to do so sympathetically, retaining many of the building's original features. A new extension houses 263 deluxe bedrooms, each with a king-size bed, lots of sleek technology and a marble bathroom. Suites are named after those who have performed or spoken at the hall, with Dylan and Fitzgerald making penthouse appearances, and Gladstone and Dickens patronising the meeting rooms.

Northern Quarter

Hatters

50 Newton Street, M1 2EA (236 9500, www.hattersgroup.com). Metrolink Piccadilly Gardens, or City Centre buses, or Piccadilly rail. **£**.
A short walk from Piccadilly station, Hatters offers hostel accommodation for backpackers and budget travellers. Rooms and facilities are basic, but added extras such as complimentary tea, coffee and toast, and quality mattresses on the bunk beds, make the stay more comfortable. An open kitchen and canteen area gives guests somewhere sociable to warm up their soup. Friendly and lively staff lead regular pub crawls and tours around the area.

Hilton Chambers

15 Hilton Street, M1 1JJ (236 4414, www.hattersgroup.com). Metrolink Piccadilly Gardens, or City Centre buses, or Piccadilly rail. **£**.

Great John Street Hotel p173

Whatever your carbon footprint, we can reduce it

For over a decade we've been leading the way in carbon offsetting and carbon management.

In that time we've purchased carbon credits from over 200 projects spread across 6 continents. We work with over 300 major commercial clients and thousands of small and medium sized businesses, which rely upon our market-leading quality assurance programme, our experience and absolute commitment to deliver the right solution for each client.

Why not give us a call?

T: London (020) 7833 6000

The Northern Quarter has little in the way of decent rooms, so hurray for Hilton Chambers. Part of the Hatters group, the accommodation falls somewhere between hostel and small hotel, with a mix of private en suite double rooms and dorms. It retains an informal atmosphere, with barbecues on the decked courtyard in summer, 24-hour reception and helpful staff.

Lowry p180

Gay Village

New Union Hotel

111 Princess Street, M1 6JB (228 1492, www.newunionhotel.com). Metrolink St Peter's Square, or City Centre buses, or Oxford Road rail. **£.**
Pink, but not exclusively so, the New Union has a great position on the corner of Canal and Princess streets. It's ideal for travellers who prefer to spend money on having a good time while saving on accommodation. Groups are well catered for with triple and quad rooms. Karaoke takes place in the venue below.

Velvet

2 Canal Street, M1 3HE (236 9003, www.velvetmanchester.com). Metrolink Mosley Street, or City Centre buses, or Piccadilly rail. **££££.**
This new boutique hotel offers 19 unique rooms, including a penthouse suite and three 'King Balcony Rooms', which overlook the throngs on Canal Street. REN toiletries, bathrobes and slippers and iPod docking stations are included in each high-spec room. Huge, ornately carved beds and opulent soft furnishings contrast against exposed brick walls. Downstairs, there's a Moulin Rouge-style bar and restaurant with canalside terrace.

Castlefield

Ox

71 Liverpool Road, M3 4NQ (839 7760, www.theox.co.uk). Metrolink Deansgate-Castlefield, or City Centre buses, or Deansgate rail. **£.**

ESSENTIALS

It's well known locally that this award-winning gastropub (p134) is the place for *Coronation Street* star-watching. What's less well known is that it has nine comfortable rooms, each with its own funky style; the overall feel is retro-cool meets vintage chic. And within easy walking distance of the City Centre, the hotel is great value for money. All bedrooms are en suite and although breakfast isn't available, there are plenty of places nearby to grab a cappuccino.

Salford

Islington Mill

James Street, M3 5HW (07917 714369, www.islingtonmill.com). Bus 36, 37, or Salford Central rail. **£**.
Not content with housing artists' studios, a live-music venue, an art academy and a gallery, the edgy Islington Mill has branched out into hospitality. An outbuilding facing the mill has been converted into a B&B, and offers a six-bed dorm and two double en suite rooms. Expect noise if there's an event on (reduced-price tickets can be included in the cost of your stay, so if you can't beat 'em…), although the decent breakfast and courtyard garden, an oasis of calm in this less than leafy part of town, make up for it.

Lowry

50 Dearmans Place, Chapel Wharf, M3 5LH (827 4000, www.thelowry hotel.com). City Centre buses, or Salford Central rail. **££££**.
The hotel of choice for visiting actors, politicians and Premiership footballers, the Lowry is Manchester's original five-star hotel. The address may be Salford, but it's located right on the City Centre's edge, on the banks of the murky River Irwell. Everything is as it should be – huge, achingly hip rooms with super-sized beds, original modern art, discreet service and clued-up staff. A swanky spa and the serene River Restaurant (p139) are further draws.

Manchester Airport

Etrop Grange

Thornley Lane, M90 4EG (499 0500, www.etrophotel.co.uk). Bus 18, 18a, 19, 20, 43, 199, 200, 369, 379, TS18, TS21, or Manchester Airport rail. **££**.
At the other end of the airport accommodation scale to Radisson Blu, Etrop Grange is a traditional English hotel of the pot-pourri variety. Built in 1780, the country house offers 64 bedrooms with flowery or tartan designs. Choose from huge oak four-posters or polished iron bedsteads with layers of bedding. The hotel's restaurant maintains the atmosphere of traditional elegance with candelabra and big white tablecloths.

Radisson Blu

Chicago Avenue, Manchester Airport, M90 3RA (490 5000, www.radisson blu.com). Bus 18, 18a, 19, 20, 43, 199, 200, 369, 379, TS18, TS21, or Manchester Airport rail. **£££**.
The most convenient airport hotel is directly linked with the three terminals via a futuristic walkway, and is also connected to the rail station. Shiny floors and low-flying spotlighting make it feel very 21st-century, if rather airport-like. Rooms are comfy and facilities good; there's a relaxing health club, beauty salon and pool, and for those in a rush, an express laundry service and checkout, plus a 'grab and run' breakfast.

Out of the city

Abbey Lodge

501 Wilbraham Road, Chorlton, M21 0UJ (862 9266, www.abbey-lodge.co.uk). Metrolink Chorlton, or bus 16, 46, 47, 85, 85c, 86, 86c, 168, 276. **£**.
A converted Victorian family home in the heart of Bohemian Chorlton, the Abbey exemplifies the perfect English B&B. Pristinely kept and expertly run, it's decorated in a classical but unfussy way. Bedrooms are of a good size and all are en suite. One pleasant innovation here is that, rather than breakfasting

Radisson Edwardian p176

Serviced apartments

Place Apartment Hotel

If you're keen to experience the city at your own pace, Manchester's wide choice of serviced apartments could fit the bill, providing space to live, work and play as you choose. A good option for families or groups, apartments often offer better value than hotels. Most come with the kind of appliances you'd find (or dream of having) in your own home, and while breakfast isn't made for you, there is also no room service knock on your door at 7am. And with spaces available in new, central residential developments, visitors have the chance to make themselves at home in some of the most fashionable addresses in town.

The **Staying Cool Apartments** (Clowes Street, M3 5NF, 0121 285 1250, www.stayingcool.com), in the Edge development, off Blackfriars (with further options in Castlefield and Deansgate), show that self-catering accommodation doesn't have to mean toning down on luxury. The boutique apartments have Apple Mac entertainment centres, free Wi-Fi, fresh fruit (and a juicer to squish it in) and good coffee in the cupboards.

Well located close to the Northern Quarter is the **Place Apartment Hotel** (Ducie Street, M1 2TP, 778 7500, www.theplace hotel.com). The spacious four-star accommodation has DVD, satellite TV and CD players as standard. As it's a converted Grade II-listed warehouse, there's plenty of exposed brickwork and original features. Elsewhere in the Northern Quarter, the swanky **Light Aparthotel** (20 Church Street, M4 1PN, 839 4848, www.thelight. co.uk) includes an on-site spa, and the penthouse suites have rooftop jacuzzis.

Perfect for groups, the **City Stop Apartments** (6-16 Dantzic Street, M4 2AD, 834 2963, www. citystop.co.uk), directly opposite the Printworks, sleep up to eight. Every apartment has a dishwasher, and some have pool tables in the living rooms. **Roomzzz Aparthotel** (36 Princess Street, M1 4JY, 0844 499 4888, www.roomzzz.co.uk) offers 48 luxury apartments in a Grade II-listed building. There's also a 24-hour concierge, free Wi-Fi and complimentary 'grab and go' breakfast.

in a morning room, guests are invited to take a tray from a continental buffet to the comfort of their own rooms, all of which are furnished with generously sized dining tables.

Best Western Willowbank

Wilmslow Road, Fallowfield, M14 6AF (224 0461, www.bestwestern.co.uk). Bus 41-44, 46-48, 142, 143, 145, 147, 157, 158. **££**.
First, a warning. If you like modern and minimal design, this isn't for you. The Willowbank is from the more-is-more school of style, with bedrooms busy enough to make you cross-eyed. If you can get past this, you'll find a pretty reliable hotel. It's also the only half-decent place that serves the student area of Fallowfield, otherwise dominated by rundown B&Bs and tatty hotels.

Didsbury House Hotel

Didsbury Park, Didsbury, M20 5LJ (448 2200, www.didsburyhouse.co.uk). Bus 23, 42, or East Didsbury rail. **£££**.
The second great townhouse in Eamon and Sally O'Laughlin's Eclectic Hotels collection, just up the road from Eleven (see below), Didsbury House has the attractive look and style of its older sibling, with a few added extras, including a small but perfectly formed bar. There are more rooms here, with 27 en suites, including two stunning loft rooms complete with vaulted, beamed ceilings.

Eleven Didsbury Park

Didsbury Park, Didsbury, M20 5LH (448 7711, www.elevendidsburypark.com). Bus 23, 42, or East Didsbury rail. **£££**.
Eleven Didsbury Park was the first suburban townhouse hotel to open in Manchester. It remains one of the city's best-loved destinations, and offers great rooms and calm, quiet surroundings in the trendy 'burbs. Interior design credit goes to Sally O'Laughlin, who has created an undeniably hip but welcoming hotel. The garden has a lovely decked area with white parasols and linen chairs, leading on to a manicured lawn.

Lennox Lea

Irlam Road, Sale, M33 2BH (973 1764, www.lennoxlea.co.uk). Metrolink Sale, or bus 99, 266, 267, 268. **£**.
This ivy-clad, red-brick house is family run and prides itself on its friendly welcome and its peaceful Sale location. Accommodation options are flexible, ranging from budget en suites to superior business rooms, family rooms sleeping up to seven, and an apartment with kitchen. Dine in the popular Alexander's Bar & Bistro, eat in your room, or take breakfast with you. Trams from nearby Sale station will whisk you efficiently into the centre of town.

Whitehouse Manor

New Road, Prestbury, Macclesfield, SK10 4HP (01625 829376, www.the whitehousemanor.co.uk). Bus 19, 19x, or Macclesfield rail. **£££**.
Leafy land of footballers' wives and long gravel drives, Prestbury is 20 miles from Manchester, but worth the journey if your destination is the Whitehouse. The lovingly restored Georgian townhouse has 11 individually themed bedrooms, all with stunning bathrooms. These range from rooms with traditional four-posters swathed in fabric, to more contemporary alternatives such as the (literally) sparkling Crystal suite. Owner Ryland Wakeham is a trained chef, so breakfasts are really something special.

Worsley Park Marriott Hotel & Country Club

Worsley Park, Salford, M28 2QT (975 2000, www.marriott.co.uk). Bus 26, 33, or Walkden rail. **£££**
Arriving at the Worsley Park Marriott, it's difficult to believe you're officially in urban Salford. This lush, green part of the city is ideal if you want fresh air and space without venturing too far from town. Just over ten miles from Manchester City Centre, the hotel offers plush parkside rooms, two bars, a restaurant, a golf course, leisure facilities and an indulgent spa.

ESSENTIALS

Getting Around

Arriving & leaving

By air

Manchester Airport

0871 271 0711, www.manchesterairport.
co.uk. About 10 miles south of
Manchester, junction 5 off M56.
The airport's three terminals are
all accessible by train, bus and
coach. All transport runs into one
interchange, which is open 24 hours
a day, with links to the terminals
via Skylink walkways.

Airport trains

Up to nine direct trains an hour run
to the airport from Piccadilly, taking
about 20 minutes and costing £4.10
at peak times and £3.50 off-peak.
Direct trains also run hourly from
Stockport, at £4.60/£3.50 for
peak/off-peak. Tickets must be
purchased before you board. Visit
www.nationalrail.co.uk or call 08457
484950 for departure times.

Airport buses

Buses leave the City Centre
every 30 minutes, 24 hours a day.
Stagecoach operates the 43 service
to the airport (around an hour),
while the 199 is the fastest service
from Stockport (around 20 minutes).
To check timetables, visit www.
gmpte.com. A shuttle bus also runs
between the airport and the Premier
Inn, Holiday Inn and Marriott hotels
(City Centre), three times an hour –
check www.manchesterairport.
co.uk for times.

Airport parking

All three terminals have ample car
parking. The cheapest option is the
Shuttle carpark, 15 minutes from
the airport and accessible by a free
bus. Discounted prices on the
web start from £2.99 per day
(for eight days plus). Visit
www.manchesterairport.co.uk.
Long Stay carparks, **Premier**
carparks and **Terminal** carparks
charge more accordingly.

By rail

Manchester Piccadilly is the
main rail station in the City Centre
and most trains stop here. **Victoria**,
Oxford Road and **Deansgate**
stations also serve the centre.
Smaller stations link the Greater
Manchester suburbs with the centre.
For timetables and ticket prices call
National Rail Enquiries on 08457
484950, or visit www.national
rail.co.uk. **Metrolink** trams (p185)
connect with trains at Piccadilly,
Victoria and Deansgate stations.

By coach

National Express

Manchester Central (formerly Chorlton
Street Coach Station), Chorlton Street,
M1 3JF (08717 818181, www.national
express.com).
Services to destinations around the UK.

Public transport

GMPTE (www.gmpte.com)
oversees all public transport.
Most bus stations have a GMPTE
Travelshop that provides general
travel and timetable information, as
well as selling multi-journey tickets.
In the City Centre, there are GMPTE
Travelshops at Piccadilly Gardens
and at Shudehill interchange.
On trains and trams fares cost less
off-peak (after 9.30am on weekdays
and all day on Saturday, Sunday
and public holidays). You can get
service and timetable information

by visiting www.gmpte.com
or by phoning 0871 200 2233.

System One Travelcards

DaySaver tickets are available
across the train, tram and bus
networks. There are Day Saver
tickets for each specific service but
if you plan to do a lot of travelling,
then the System One off-peak Day
Saver is the best option. This allows
you to travel on any bus, train and
Metrolink tram between 9.30am
and midnight any day of the week.
The day ticket costs £7 and can
be bought from bus drivers, at
rail stations and from Metrolink
ticket machines. For children's fares,
see www.gmpte.com.

Buses

Tickets can be bought from the
driver on all buses, but they only
take cash, so it's advisable to have
the correct change. **Stagecoach**
and **First Manchester** are the
main operators in the centre. Fares
vary depending on journey length.
The best-value fares are offered by
Stagecoach's Dayrider (£3.50) or the
First Day Saver (£4.10), which allow
unlimited travel for a whole day,
although travel is limited to the bus
company you bought the ticket on.
Alternatively, a System One Day
Saver can be bought from the driver
for £4.90 (£4.50 off-peak) and applies
to any bus for the whole day.

Metroshuttle

This brilliant free City Centre
bus service runs from Manchester
Piccadilly and visitors can hop on
and off at stops all around the city.
There are three circular lines, with
routes covering Deansgate, King
Street, Quay Street and Castlefield.

Night buses

Night buses offer a cheap and safe
alternative to getting a taxi home.

Late services run from Piccadilly
Gardens and other City Centre
stops, but most operate only on
Fridays and Saturdays. Night buses
run regularly until around 3.30am
(check www.gmpte.com for
timetables) and travel to many
destinations in Greater Manchester.
Fares are £3 or less.

Trams

Metrolink is a modern tram
system running through the centre
of Manchester and out to the
suburbs, replacing many of the
smaller local train stations and
services. It runs seven days a week
and is one of the most convenient
and quickest ways to travel into
the City Centre. Lines run from
the centre out as far as Altrincham,
Bury and Eccles, and plans to
extend the service to Rochdale,
Ashton-under-Lyne and Manchester
Airport are well underway. New
lines to Chorlton and Oldham
open in spring and autumn 2011,
respectively. The network also
provides links to some of the city's
main leisure and tourist attractions.

Fares

Single, return and Saver tickets are
available. Buy from the machines
on the platform before you travel, as
you cannot buy a ticket on the tram
itself. Prices vary depending on
journey length; for a fare calculator,
visit www.metrolink.co.uk.

Timetable

Services run every six minutes
between Bury and Altrincham
via the City Centre, and every
12 minutes between Eccles and
Piccadilly. Trams operate from
around 6am until roughly 11pm
Monday to Thursday, and until
midnight on Saturdays and 10pm
on Sundays, although these times
vary depending on the station.

ESSENTIALS

'Off-peak' applies to trams running from 9.30am onwards Monday to Friday and all day Saturday, Sunday and bank holidays.

Taxis

Hackney cabs ('black cabs') are licensed by the local council and can be hailed on the street or picked up at a taxi rank. Look out for cabs with their 'taxi' logo illuminated to show that they are free. There are many ranks around the City Centre, including Piccadilly Gardens, Piccadilly station, St Peter's Square and Albert Square. You can also book a black cab (for example Mantax, 230 3333); some accept credit cards, but it is best to confirm this before you start your journey. Taxi fares increase after midnight.

Minicabs

Private-hire cabs are usually saloon vehicles and are generally cheaper than black cabs. They cannot be hailed on the street and it is illegal for them to pick up customers on the road. Drivers touting for business on the street are often unlicensed, expensive and potentially dangerous. Book minicabs in advance over the phone; find taxi numbers on 118 500. Legitimate drivers should display their licence in the car and a licence plate on the back of the vehicle.

Driving

Manchester City Centre has more than its fair share of one-way systems, although its outlying districts are relatively easy to navigate and tourist attractions are well signposted.

Parking

Always read the signs. The City Centre traffic wardens aren't shy of slapping on tickets or wheel-clamps, and even of towing offending vehicles away. As a general guide, you cannot park on a single yellow line between 8am and 6pm Monday to Saturday. Never park on a double yellow line, in a loading bay or on a space marked for residents or the disabled unless you have the appropriate permit.

There is both on-street and off-street parking in the City Centre. On-street parking is often restricted to one, two or three hours maximum, depending on where in town you are. A ticket must be purchased from the machine on the pavement, with tariffs starting at 55p for 15 minutes. Parking on the road is free after 6pm and on Sundays and bank holidays. There are numerous **NCP** car parks (0845 050 7080, www.ncp.co.uk) around Manchester, many of which are 24-hour. These offer secure parking and charge around £2.90 for two hours.

Towed vehicles

Vehicles that are towed away are taken to the pound in Ardwick, which must be contacted to get your car back (234 4144). Proof of ownership and identity is needed – usually car keys and two other forms of ID. The basic charge is £135, plus £12 for each day the car remains in the pound. After 14 days, the basic fee increases to £175.

Vehicle hire

There are a number of companies around the city. **EasyCar** has an office by Piccadilly rail station (www.easycar.com), while **City Car Club** offers short-term hires via parking bays across the City Centre (hires from as little as 30 minutes, www.citycarclub.co.uk). Otherwise, try **Avis** (www.avis. co.uk) or **Enterprise Rent-A-Car** (www.enterprise.com).

Resources A-Z

Accident & emergency

The most central Manchester hospitals with 24-hour Accident & Emergency departments are listed below. The UK number for police, fire and ambulance is **999**.

Manchester Royal Infirmary
*Oxford Road, M13 9WL (276 1234).
Bus 15, 16, 41-44, 46, 47, 50, 53,
111, 130, 140-143, 145, 147, 157,
191, 197, or Oxford Road rail.*
**North Manchester General
Hospital** *Delauneys Road, Crumpsall,
M8 5RB (795 4567). Bus 51, 52, 88,
89, 115, 118, 149, 151, 156, 294,
or Crumpsall rail.*
Salford Royal Stott Lane, Salford,
M6 8HD (789 7373). *Metrolink Ladywell,
or bus 10, 33, 55, 63, 67, 70, 71, 100,
484, or Eccles rail.*

Credit card loss

American Express 01273 696933
Diners Club 01252 513500
MasterCard/Eurocard 0800 964767
Visa/Connect 0800 895082

Customs

For allowances, see
www.hmrc.gov.uk.

Dental emergency

University Dental Hospital
*Higher Cambridge Street, M15 6FH
(275 6666, 0845 601 8529 out of
hours). Bus 15, 16, 41-44, 46-48,
53, 85, 86, 99, 101, 104, 108,
109, 111, 140-143, 145, 147, 157,
191, 197, 250, 253, 263, 290, 291,
or Oxford Road rail.* **Open** 8.30am-
4.30pm Mon-Fri.
A limited number of patients can be
seen (on a first-come, first-served basis).

Disabled travellers

The majority of buses and trains
have disabled access. Metrolink
stations are equipped with ramps,
lifts or escalators and most platforms
have modified edges to help
visually impaired travellers. The
www.manchester.gov.uk website
lists hotels, restaurants, attractions
and shops in the city that comply
with most access requirements.
Shopmobility (839 4060), at the
Arndale Centre, provides mobility
aids and information for people
with physical disabilities.

Electricity

The UK uses the standard European
220-240V, 50 cycle AC voltage via
three-pin plugs.

Embassies & consulates

Contact the relevant embassy
or consulate in London:

Australian High Commission
020 7379 4334, www.uk.embassy.gov.au
American Embassy
020 7499 9000, www.usembassy.org.uk
Canadian High Commission
020 7258 6600, www.canada.org.uk
Irish Embassy
020 7235 2171, www.dfa.ie
New Zealand High Commission
020 7930 8422, www.nzembassy.com
South African High Commission
020 7451 7299,
www.southafricahouse.com

Internet

An explosion of free and paid-for
Wi-Fi access in cafés, bars and

hotels means that dedicated City Centre internet cafés are few and far between. Most public libraries do, however, have terminals. Free Wi-Fi is also available at:

Cornerhouse

70 Oxford Street, M1 5NH (200 1500, www.cornerhouse.org). Metrolink St Peter's Square, or City Centre buses, or Oxford Road rail. **Open** *Bar* 9.30am-11pm Mon-Thur; 9.30am-midnight Fri-Sat; 11am-10.30pm Sun.

Costa Coffee

Waterstone's, Arndale Centre, M4 3AQ (839 4732, www.costa.co.uk). Metrolink Market Street, or City Centre buses, or Victoria rail. **Open** 9am-8pm Mon-Fri; 11am-5pm Sat, Sun.

An Outlet

Carver's Warehouse, 77 Dale Street, M1 2HG (236 3043, www.anoutlet.net). Metrolink Piccadilly Station, or City Centre buses, or Piccadilly rail. **Open** 8am-5pm Mon-Fri; 11am-5am Sat.

Opening hours

Banks 9am-4.30pm (some close at 3.30pm, some 5.30pm) Mon-Fri; sometimes also Saturday mornings.
Offices Normally open from 9am to 5pm Mon-Fri.
Shops 10am-6pm Mon-Fri, but many stores now open until 8pm. Most shops in the City Centre are open on Sunday, either from 11am to 5pm or noon to 6pm.

Pharmacies

Britain's best-known pharmacy chain is **Boots**, with branches in the City Centre and most of the surrounding town centres. The main branch in Manchester is on Market Street, open until 8pm (5pm on Sun). There are no 24-hour pharmacies in Manchester, but a handful are open late. **A&A Pharmacy**

(58 Wilmslow Road, Rusholme, 224 8501) is open until 10.30pm (10pm on Sun) and is just a few minutes out of the City Centre on the 42 bus.

Police stations

Call **999** in an emergency and ask for the police, or call 872 5050 for non-emergencies. The main police station is on Bootle Street, but all suburbs are served by a local neighbourhood station. Call Directory Enquiries for details (118 118/500/888) or visit the Greater Manchester Police website at www.gmp.police.uk.

Bootle Street Police Station

Bootle Street, Manchester, M2 5GU (872 5050). Metrolink St Peter's Square, or City Centre buses, or Oxford Road rail.

Postal services

Post offices are usually open 9am to 5.30pm Monday to Friday and 9am to noon Saturday.

Manchester Post Office

26 Spring Gardens, M2 1BB (0845 722 3344). Metrolink Market Street, or City Centre buses, or Piccadilly rail.

Safety

Manchester is generally a safe city to visit. Visitors should remain vigilant in crowded areas – buses, busy streets, train stations – for petty criminals. Keep your valuables in your hotel room or safe and make sure the cash and cards you carry are tucked away in your bag.

Smoking

Smoking is prohibited in all enclosed public places, including bars, restaurants and stations.

Telephones

The dialling code for Manchester, Greater Manchester, Salford and Stockport is **0161**.

If you're dialling from outside the UK, dial your international access code, then the UK code (44), then the full number omitting the first 0 from the code. To dial abroad from the UK, first dial 00, then the country code.

US mobile phones will operate in the UK only if they are equipped with tri- or quad-band facility.

Public phones

Public payphones take coins or credit cards. The minimum cost is 20p. International calling cards offering bargain minutes via a freephone number are widely available from newsagents.

Tickets

The main venues in Manchester sell their tickets through third parties. (Note that there's normally a booking fee involved.)

Ticketmaster (www.ticket master.co.uk, 0844 844 0444) and **Ticketweb** (www.ticketweb.co.uk, 0844 477 1000) have tickets for the major theatres and venues in the centre. **Quay Tickets** (www.quaytickets.com, 0843 208 0500) also represents a good number of venues. Small, independent places generally sell tickets from their own box office or through promoters.

Time

Manchester operates on Greenwich Mean Time (GMT), which is five hours ahead of North American Eastern Standard Time.

In spring, the UK puts its clocks forward by one hour to British Summer Time. In autumn, clocks go back by one hour to GMT.

Tipping

You should tip in taxis, minicabs, restaurants, hotels, hairdressers and some bars (not pubs). Ten per cent is normal; note that some restaurants add on a service charge of up to 15 per cent.

Tourist information

Manchester's main tourist office is at Piccadilly Gardens, and offers a wide variety of information on accommodation and sights and more general details on Manchester and the surrounding suburbs. Stockport and Salford have their own centres.

Manchester Visitor Information Centre

Piccadilly Plaza, Portland Street, M1 4BT (0871 222 8223, www.visit manchester.com). Metrolink St Peter's Square, or City Centre buses, or Oxford Road rail.

Stockport Tourist Information

Staircase House, 30-31 Market Place, Stockport, SK1 1ES (474 4444, www.visit-stockport.com). Stockport Bus Station buses, or Stockport rail.

Salford Information Centre Lowry

Pier 8, Salford Quays, M50 3AZ (848 8601, www.visitsalford.info). Metrolink Media City, or bus 69, 290, 291.

Visas

EU citizens do not require a visa to visit the UK; citizens of the USA, Canada, Australia, South Africa and New Zealand need only a passport for tourist visits. Check current status on www.ukvisas.gov.uk well before you travel.

ESSENTIALS

Index

ESSENTIALS

ESSENTIALS

Manchester
Visitor Information Centre

Piccadilly Plaza, Portland Street, Manchester, M1 4AJ
Monday - Saturday: 9.30am - 5.30pm
Sunday: 10.30am - 4.30pm

Tel: 0871 222 8223
Email: touristinformation@visitmanchester.com

Buy Manchester merchandise online at
visitmanchester.com/giftshop

Also available at
The Manchester Store
The Trafford Centre, M17 8AA